MW01068456

SONS OF VIKINGS

HISTORY, LEGENDS, AND IMPACT OF THE VIKING AGE

By David Gray Rodgers and Kurt Noer

Sons of Vikings Books, 2018

Sons of Vikings

History, Legends, and Impact of the Viking Age

By David Gray Rodgers and Kurt Noer

Copyright 2018 David Rodgers. All rights reserved.

Cover design by Vlad MSLV. Raven shield design by Marsha CM Blasgen

Copyright 2018. All rights reserved.

Table of Contents

Introduction

On a cloudy morning in 793, the monastery of Lindisfarne (in what is now northern England) was attacked without warning by raiders from the sea. These "Vikings," as they would later be called, slew all who stood in their way, carried off the tremendous treasure Lindisfarne housed and disappeared back across the waves before any native force could mobilize against them. This attack left the people of western Europe horrified. In one fateful morning a new enemy had appeared – an enemy that had no fear of God or kings, that was fierce in battle and could move faster and escape more completely than any enemy they had ever known.

But what they did not yet realize was that the strike on Lindisfarne was only the beginning. The Vikings would raid again and again, with assaults that became exponentially larger and bolder. Soon raiders would become armies, and armies would become conquerors.

The period from the attack on Lindisfarne all the way until the Battle of Stamford Bridge, where the "last Viking" was killed in 1066, would come to be known as the Viking Age. As Sir Winston Churchill would write, the violence of the Vikings would "distract the weakened life of Europe for ten generations," redistributing wealth, interrupting cultural progress, and taking an inestimable number of lives.

But for all the harm that they did, the Vikings were not merely a force of destruction. These Norsemen, Danes, or "heathens" as they were called by their various enemies were a catalyzing force in world history. They helped re-draw the map of Europe and contributed to the transition from early medieval kingdoms to the nations of the modern world. The Vikings reestablished steady trade between east and west, creating a chain of communication and exchange that stretched from Greenland to Baghdad, and from Norway to Morocco. The intrepid exploits of the Vikings and the technological advances they made in shipbuilding and navigation laid the groundwork for later ages of exploration and founded the first European settlement in North America. Viking ideas of equality, fairness, and the rights of free persons have helped shape our laws and civic values.

The Vikings did not only tear down, they also built up; they adapted to the lands they were grafted into, but also conformed these lands unto themselves. It is these accomplishments, along with their proud spirit, boundless valor, and amazing tenacity that make the Vikings so worth learning about. The history and legends of the Vikings offer us great insight into both the darkness and the nobility of the human spirit.

How Do We Know What We Know About the Vikings?

History is the study of events, causes, and consequences. Today, the study of history is taken very soberly and seriously, with the attempt to shine light on the past in as impartial and scientific a way as possible. There are some exceptions, especially when nationalistic or racial biases worm their way into narratives in the guise of history; but, as a whole, the academic world works to guard against this. The aim of the historian is to be accurate and to present the truth as fully as possible.

This is not always an easy undertaking. Compare history to the news (which is easy, as today's news is tomorrow's history). Accounts vary substantially considering which witness one asks and who is doing the reporting, their bias, and their goals. It is the same with historical sources. Some sources – even primary sources (that is, sources that are written around the time of the events they describe) may be inaccurate, or even deliberately dishonest.

History is the study of what happened, but how that story is written is called *historiography*. Historiography has not always been as truthful, straight-forward, and accurate as it endeavors to be today. Sometimes the goal of the historian was to glorify his people, culture, or king. Sometimes the goal was to entertain the audience. Sometimes the primitive historian simply did not know that the many legendary elements of his stories (such as dragons, gods, giants, and elves) were not part of the actual events and should have been kept separate as fiction. So, it is one of the tasks of modern historians to sift through these accounts and to find what is useful and verifiable while allowing the rest of it to have its place in literature.

No study of the Vikings should be undertaken without first understanding where our knowledge of the Vikings comes from. The great civilizations of the world – the Greeks, Romans, Egyptians, Persians, Chinese, *et cetera* – made monuments of stone and wrote their stories down for anyone with the skill to now read. The Vikings did not. The Vikings made monuments and structures mostly of wood, which is largely perishable. While they had a form of writing, these runes were normally used for names, ceremonial epitaphs, or magic spells. The rest of the extensive Viking culture of stories, poems, laws, and knowledge were all passed down orally. Later, some of it would be written down – but only after a great deal of it had been lost and a great many things had changed in the world.

The people who wrote these stories down were men from Norway, Denmark, Sweden, and especially Iceland. They were descendants of the Vikings, and they lived in the High and Late Middle Ages when a lot of the values and ways of Viking life were still relevant. But these men were Christians, and in some cases (ironically) learned churchmen; and so, the accuracy of the writing is not only affected by the passage of time, but also by the cultural presuppositions of the later stewards of the stories.

What we have just briefly described refers to the Norse sagas and skaldic poetry (from *skald*, the Norse word for bard or poet). The Vikings loved poetry and took it very seriously, but by the very nature of oral tradition, events become embellished. The sheer passage of time between the composition of the poetry and their preservation in writing would be equal to someone today writing about the founding of Jamestown or Plymouth Rock purely from stories told by their string of grandparents. Therefore, we see things in Norse sources that we know for a fact are not accurate. This is true for both the more embellished sagas as well as those that are more serious histories, such as Saxo Grammaticus, the *Book of Settlements*, or the *Heimskringla.*

However, the Norse sagas and skaldic poetry are still very, very informative. While they cannot always be counted on for factual accuracy, they are still often thematically accurate. They also offer insight into the thought process, culture, and values of the Vikings that we simply would not have otherwise.

Another source of knowledge comes from the annals, records, and histories of the men (again, usually churchmen) who were the citizens of the Christian kingdoms of Europe, and thus usually the enemies of the Vikings. Unlike skaldic poetry, which intends to please a crowd with fantastic descriptions of battle and heroism, church sources are usually more straightforward and have far fewer dragons or giants. Nonetheless, they are still quite obviously prone to bias. By this we do not mean that the church writers were unjustified in their ill view of men who made a living killing their priests and stealing their relics. But as these sources also tend to be writen from a firm perspective, their statements must be evaluated critically. Another shortcoming of these annals and chronicles is that they tend to be distressingly brief and terse, leaving many more questions than answers in their dusty pages.

There are also the problems of accuracy and communications in pre-modern histories. There were no phones, no video footage, no radio transmissions – there were only eyewitnesses describing what they had seen and passing it on, until it could eventually be written down by a trained professional. Problems in pre-modern communication have literally led to the collapse of empires, and they now harry the historian, too.

Because of these challenges with our sources, it is probably true that there is not a single thing anyone can say about the Vikings that is not open for debate. We will keep that in mind as we go. The best approach is an open mind and a multi-disciplinary method of analyzing the available material.

Of course, the written word is not the only source of information. Though the Vikings' material world of wood, leather, and natural fibers may not have left many traces, there have been significant discoveries. Luckily, we are now on the cusp of a new golden age in archeology. Cutting edge techniques like ground-penetrating radar or satellite imagery can find fortress ruins or ship burials that have lain hidden in plain sight up until now. Emerging DNA research has begun to offer insight into the movements of ancient peoples and confirm or upturn historical assumptions. As archeology continues to advance, our picture of the Viking Age will undoubtedly develop and clarify.

What Does the Word "Viking" Mean?

The word "Viking" is one of those words that has been misused so often that it is almost not worth the trouble to correct it. Our word Viking in Old Norse came in two forms: the noun *víkingr* which meant an armed adventurer who leaves home by sea in search of gain; and the verb *víking,* which was the act of seeking gain by adventuring by sea. Norse sources often refer to individuals as "a great Viking." Etymologically, the word may have come from the word *vík* which meant 'bay'. As longships would shelter in and depart from bays, it is easy to see how this word would become associated with the Vikings. Therefore, being a Viking was what we would call a job or a role that someone assumed as needed. It was not an ethnic designation or the name of a people. In the kingdoms of England and France, the Vikings were called Norsemen, Northmen, Danes, or simply, Heathens. Though the term Viking was sometimes used in Ireland, the Irish more commonly called the Vikings "foreigners." They would sometimes go on to differentiate groups of Vikings as "fair [lighter] foreigners" or "dark foreigners." In eastern sources, such as Russian, Ukrainian, or Byzantine, the Vikings are usually called Varangians, meaning "sworn companion."

To our minds, problems of accuracy immediately assert themselves in most of these terms. It is important to remember that the concept of nationhood was not the same in the Early Middle Ages as it would later be. Norway, Denmark, and Sweden were regions with many kings and chiefs that would only later emerge as singular entities. England did not exist, but was a conglomerate of multiple kingdoms, as was France, Spain, etcetera. Viking armies may have come largely from one "country" or another, but larger armies tended to be mixed from many tribes and many areas. So, the invaders whom Saxon writers call Danes may be from Denmark, or they may be from anywhere else that Vikings tread. The problem gets bigger as the Viking Age wears on, and the men on longships may have been born in Ireland or the Shetland Islands (for example).

So, we are left with a problem of terminology. The term 'Heathen' is as inaccurate as it is unappealing. The term 'Northmen' has merit because it is the broadest. 'Norse' or 'Norsemen' are also good, provided that the words are not taken to mean people from Norway exclusively.

However, the term 'Viking' has stuck and has left an indelible impression on world consciousness. Despite its many disadvantages, the term 'Viking' has a very special connotation: Vikings *go out*. The Viking Age was a time when the vigor of Scandinavia was focused outward. There were important internal changes, too, but it is the outward push that made the biggest impact on world history. So, the men and women from Norway, Denmark, Sweden, and the many islands – as well as their immediate descendants who could have been born anywhere – who were part of this outward push are called Vikings.

Men and women who were involved in big or little ways with what happened in their native Scandinavian lands may be referred to by other terms (though people may inaccurately call them Vikings by association). Of course, many Vikings ultimately went home to Scandinavia and formed their future there.

For our purposes, the word 'Viking' will be used in this book to describe men and women of Scandinavian origin who raided and traded beyond their borders. Though there are many exciting stories to tell of change within Scandinavia, we will mostly be focused on the centrifugal effects of the Viking Age. We will still use other terms, such as Norsemen or Danes, to offer shades of meaning or to be consistent with our parent sources. Hopefully, this will offer clarity and not confusion. Ultimately, though, the word 'Viking' is the best term for the men and women of our story.

Sons of Vikings: History, Legends, and Impact of the Viking Age

The purpose of this book is to relate the story of the Viking Age, to help elucidate the meaning and consequences of the events, and to help the reader appreciate the heritage (both good and bad) to our times. But rather than just narrating a timeline of happenings, this book will look first to the stories of individuals who were the protagonists and antagonists of their day. We will do everything in our power to tell the stories accurately and thoroughly, making room for many conflicting viewpoints; but first and foremost, this is a book about people. It is our hope that by getting to know the people involved, the casual reader will easily acquire the heart of this history, while the more avid student of the past will find things that they may have previously overlooked.

SONS OF VIKINGS

PART ONE: THE VIKING IDENTITY

Chapter I: Odin and the Origins of the Vikings

In the beginning, there was no land, no sea, no sky – no anything. All was a formless void; a great abyss called *Ginnungagap*. To one extreme of this void lay a realm of eternal fire, and to the other extreme lay a realm of eternal ice. Over untold ages the fire and the ice grew towards each other until they came so close that the flames began to melt the edges of the ice. So great was the cold of the ice and the heat of the flame that the melted frost turned instantly to hissing steam, breaking the silence of the void with a great scream. From this scream a vast being formed – the giant, Ymir.

The fire continued to scorch, and the edges of the ice continued to melt. As the ice melted, it revealed a beast that was like a great cow. Ymir fed on the milk of this creature (who was called Auðhumla), and the giant grew even larger. When Ymir would sleep by the raging fire, he would sweat; and from his sweat more giants sprang. They were spirits of chaos, elementally negative anti-gods who transcended size. Meanwhile, Auðhumla would lick at the ice to find salt; and as it licked it gradually uncovered another being. Once freed, this being came fully to life. He was like the giants, but also not like them. He was called Búri, and he was destined to beget the Aesir gods.

While ice and fire still fought around the abyss, Búri had a son named Bor. The god Bor married the giantess Bestla. This union of god and anti-god gave birth to Odin, whose name means the Inspired, the Ecstatic, or the Furious.

Odin was unlike any of the giants or the primal gods who populated this universe of ice, fire, and void. He would not endure emptiness and chaos; for as his name relays, he had a mind of creativity and curiosity, and a character of action and passion.

With the help of his two brothers, Odin slew the great giant Ymir; and as they hacked his boundless body to bits, his blood became the great oceans. Ymir's flesh became the earth, and his bones became the stone beneath. Ymir's teeth and broken finger bones became the jutting rocks. His thick hair became the grasses, trees, and all plants. The dome of his immense skull became the sky, and the shreds of his brain became the dark, brooding clouds.

Odin and his brothers called this new realm Midgard, which means "Middle Earth", for it became the middle world in a universe of nine worlds, or nine dimensions.

Odin and his brothers built a fence around Midgard to protect it from the giants, but all manner of animals and spirits were allowed to live there. As they continued to shape their creation, the brothers encountered two pieces of driftwood; and they fashioned these into the first man, Ask (which is the word for an ash tree) and the first woman, Embla (which is the word for an elm tree, or a vessel for carrying water from wells). They not only gave these new creatures life, but also intellect, passion, and soul. From Ask and Embla came all the other men and women who would live. Humankind then made their home in Midgard, while the gods made their home in their realm of Asgard; but the fates of gods and humans were ever-more woven together.

Scandinavia

For the tellers of this creation story, the Midgard they knew was the region of Scandinavia in the extreme north of Europe, including what are now Norway, Sweden, and Denmark, along with many islands. This land stretched from the Arctic Circle to the Baltic Sea. While some of it (particularly in Denmark and Sweden) was flat and fertile, much of it was mountainous and forbidding. It is a land of startling cliffs, high ranges, and icy fjords; impenetrable forests and labyrinthine bogs; of glassy lakes and desolate glaciers; and, of course, miles and miles of coastline. The growing seasons are short, and the winters are hard. The coldest recorded temperature in Sweden was -56.6C; but there is evidence that the weather throughout Europe was significantly colder and wetter during the 7th through 9th centuries, while the Viking Age was beginning. Thus, the people who spoke of Odin and his battles with the ice giants lived with month after month of driving snows, and many were no strangers to the wonders of the northern lights and midnight sun.

The ancient Greek historian Herodotus wrote, "*Hard lands make hard men.*" He could have hoped for no better example of this than the people of Scandinavia in the 8th through 11th centuries. Forged by a landscape of stark beauty but grudging bounty, Vikings learned to place a high value on valor and detested weakness. Because of their often-harsh environment, hospitality was a cardinal virtue among Vikings, and a breach of this duty was considered equal to treachery. As a lack of arable land and short growing months led to more of a dietary reliance on pastoral farming and hunting for sustenance (i.e., a high-protein diet), Vikings tended to be bigger and brawnier than their southern counterparts. With only about half of their children surviving to the age of ten and an overall life expectancy of about fifty, the Vikings were well-acquainted with death, tragedy, and personal loss. These experiences contributed to one of their most distinct and powerful cultural and religious characteristics which we will explore soon: Norse heroic fatalism.

The Norse enjoyed passing their long, snowy nights with poetry and song; with drinking and telling tales; and with games of strategy, riddles, and tests of wit. Their religion (which is to say, their beliefs, values, and divine narratives – the Norse had no word for religion and were puzzled by faiths like Christianity and Islam when they encountered them) and literature were all oral, recited from memory by everyone from highly trained skalds to clever housewives.

While these mental activities were taken seriously, the Norse preferred to revel in their heightened physicality. They were avid runners, swimmers, skiers, skaters, climbers, hunters, and of course, sailors. They took extreme pride in their prowess at grappling arts or sparring with weapons. They practiced swimming with armor or weighted clothing. They were accustomed to long hours rowing the cold, rough seas. All this they enthusiastically engaged in when necessity did not require them to perform the hard, manual labor of building, plowing, or other tasks on their farms or homesteads.

A man or woman with this culture and upbringing who took their place on a Viking longship was therefore already extremely tough, agile, well-trained and formidable – long before they even gathered experience in war. The greenest Viking rookie was already formed by hardship, tested by adversity, honed by a lifetime of formal and informal training, intimate with tragedy, and inoculated against fear.

Odin the War God

The iron temper of the Norse spirit found its fullest expression in Viking warrior culture. Their songs and stories reveled in it, and their social structure demanded it. The Vikings believed that ordinary people who died ordinary deaths went on to a dim afterlife; but those who died gloriously in battle went on to Valhalla, where they would feast, love, and fight until the world itself ended. The pleasures of life might be a reward for valor but were not ends unto themselves; valor itself was the ultimate goal.

Because of these beliefs and attitudes, by the time a youth was old enough to take up the oar and the shield, he would have hardwired into him an "ecstatic joy of bloodshed;" and so, battles were undertaken many times "for the sheer delight of fighting" (Howarth, 1978). So, while their enemies huddled in their shield walls understandably shaking with fear, the Vikings had no fear – only excitement. If they won, they won glory; if they died, they were rewarded in Valhalla. For this reason, it was said that the Norsemen "*neither wept for their sins nor for the death of their friends.*" It was this extreme psychological advantage that was the Viking's greatest weapon.

Odin is best known today as a god of war for the Norse and other pre-Christian Germanic peoples. This is, however, a bit of a misunderstanding for two reasons. First, Norse gods were complex characters with overlapping attributes and realms of influence and were not so much "gods of this or that" the way other cultures may have conceived gods to be. Secondly, the Norse culture was so warlike before and during the Viking Age that almost every one of their gods was a war god. Even beautiful Freya, the Viking Aphrodite and fertility goddess, was also a goddess of war. Odin was the chief (usually) of the gods, and he was an astonishing, consummate warrior; and so, today many people simplify his role as the god of war. But to the Vikings he was more than that.

To the Vikings, Odin was not like the Greek Athena – the goddess of noble war – nor was he like Ares – the god of destructive war. Instead, Odin was the god of warlike inspiration; of lethal ecstasy.

In the sagas, we hear of him riding into battle and laying waste to his enemies with glorious joy. For this reason, the men closest to Odin (in this context) were the berserkers.

Berserkers

Berserkers were Viking heroes who would fight in a state of ecstatic frenzy. The word berserker (from which we get the English phrase, *to go berserk*, of course) means "bear shirt" or "bear skin." The etymology of this term is a bit complex with overlapping meanings. The berserker took on the essence and spirit of the great bears of the Scandinavian wilderness. He *became* the bear in battle, with all the creature's ferocity, bravery, strength, and indestructibility. Thus, he put on the bear's skin – which he may have also done literally, using bear hide for armor. Or, he wore no armor of any kind and had bare skin (the play on words is the same in English and Old Norse). In either case, the berserker was a warrior who entered battle insane with bloodlust.

There was also a similar type of Viking warrior called an *úlfheðnar,* which means "wolf skin" (or werewolf), but it is not entirely clear whether this was a synonym or a separate class of elite warrior. The *Hrafnsmol*, the earliest poetic reference we have of either berserkers or *úlfheðnar* mentions them together:

> *"The berserkers bellowed as the battle opened,*
> *the úlfheðnar shrieked loud and shook their weapons."*

Instead of fighting as a team, as other Vikings would, the berserker would "*dash into battle*" in advance of the line. The method to this madness was two-fold. His valor was meant to both inspire his comrades and to dishearten his foes. By single-handedly attacking the enemy lines (often with sweeping blows of the huge, powerful Dane axe) before his forces could make contact, he sought to disrupt the enemy's cohesion and exploit holes in their defenses that his brothers in arms could drive through.

The "berserkers' rage" that made these warriors so terrifying to their enemies and so held in awe by their peers has intrigued historians, writers, and even scientists. While berserkers are described as always being tough, aloof, and dangerous, sources agree that their fighting fury was the result of a ramping-up process, and that this explosion of violence was followed by a period of profound exhaustion. Some experts postulate that the berserker's rage was drug enhanced. The hallucinogenic red-cap mushroom (fly agaric) and the toxic leaf of a nightshade called henbane (possibly brewed into ale) are two possibilities. These are just theories, though, and the sources only describe the frightening transformation without being able to offer an explanation.

The skalds tell us that berserkers were impervious to iron or fire. Obviously, we should take this with a grain of salt. Unflinchingly offensive and heedless of his safety, most berserkers could not expect to live long lives. However, they were different (arguably) from other suicide soldiers in several ways. First, it was the valor of their actions and not their deaths that were of any importance to the berserker or his friends. He was not trying to die; it was that he was simply indifferent to life or death under Odin's inspiration. His actions were not of somber calculation, but rather out of the sense of the divine hand. Secondly, while the berserker certainly secured his position in Valhalla, he expected no special reward in the afterlife for his actions. Warriors behind him in their shield walls could expect the same reward if they fell bravely. But the berserker was not acting altruistically, either, for he would achieve great renown, regardless of whether he lived or died.

In other words, the berserker did not have the duty to his emperor that the World War II Kamikaze pilot had; nor did he have the terrorist's delusion of a special paradise. The berserker ran headlong into battle because his god inspired him to, and this act alone (independent of the act's results) was the point and purpose.

This is not to say that the berserker was entirely unique. Certainly, many examples of reckless, valiant behavior have been seen across all cultures and in many contexts. The phenomenon exists not only in war and other situations of extreme duress but also occasionally in sports. Celtic warriors before the Viking Age were sometimes touched by something called the *furor*, which was essentially the same as the berserker's rage.

However, one of the elements that did make the berserker special was that being a berserker was neither a fortuitous accident nor a mere matter of individual prowess, but rather a culturally-established feature of Viking armies. Berserkers were not an anomaly, but relatively common, and more importantly, these warriors seemed to have developed methods to consistently bring their heightened valor and abilities to the fore when needed. The sagas mention the berserker's rage being brought on at will, and post-pagan Icelandic law expressly forbade individuals from either going berserk or egging on one who was going berserk. Whether these methods were magic, as the Vikings considered them to be; advanced measures in performance psychology; or merely the result of the interplay between alcohol, drugs, and group dynamics, the results were advantageous to the Vikings and disastrous to their enemies.

The Viking Way of War

For the Vikings, war was fought face to face. The Vikings were marine infantry that used their revolutionary longships to achieve an extraordinary advantage in mobility over their enemies – but once it was time to fight, the battle was typically fought on foot. Horses were also used to achieve mobility, but the Vikings were not usually cavalrymen. Later they would learn this skill from those enemies who found it a useful tool against them, but for most of the Viking Age, the horse was only meant to take a warrior to the fight or away from the fight as quickly as possible. The Norse gods each had their own special chariot drawn by magical beasts, but by the time the Viking Age dawned, chariot warfare was rare in Europe, and we do not have many examples of the Vikings using it. No – for the Vikings, real fighting centered on an infantry formation known as a shield wall.

Shield walls involved warriors standing shoulder to shoulder with shields overlapping. They had been a mainstay of Germanic battles since the first contact with the Romans (700-1000 years before) demonstrated that individual prowess was no match for teamwork. The Germanic tribes quickly adapted the Roman fighting methods to their own purposes, and by the Viking era, tribes that had no clear idea of what Rome was could perform the maneuvers as well as Caesar's best legions had.

Viking ships were crewed by about fifty oarsmen – men who lived together and braved the seas together (and many of whom were already family or friends). These ship crews now formed the basis for the shield wall, with groups of fifty warriors now making a line of overlapping shields, reinforced with other lines of shields behind them. Shields could be raised as needed behind the first line to form cover for arrows, javelins, or other missiles.

According to Byzantine sources, the ideal density of a shield wall was five to ten lines. Too few lines could be knocked down by an enemy's shield wall; too many lines became an immobile and confused crowd. From this we can suppose that our average Viking ship would produce a section of shield wall about ten men wide and five men deep.

The round Viking shields were made of wood covered in hide (so that weapons would hopefully bounce off them rather than stick in them). They were held with a single, central grip rather than straps (for added maneuverability) and the hand had the added protection of a center-mounted iron boss (or bowl). They were about three feet in diameter, and so would cover most warriors from the groin to the eyes. If the warrior were lucky enough to have a helmet, he would then be reasonably protected from most attacks – provided that he and his fellow warriors maintained their shields overlapped.

An individual warrior would have little chance against a shield wall. They would be too exposed while having very few vulnerable points to aim their attacks and would probably be cut down very quickly regardless of how big or skilled they were. For this reason, most battles of Late Antiquity and the Early Middle Ages involved meeting shield walls with shield walls.

With both sides using the basic shield wall strategy, the fight became about which side could maintain their cohesion the longest. Though most warriors probably longed for the swift, flashy dances of death the skalds sang of, most battles started out as shoving matches with the frontlines of each opposing shield wall crushing against each other.

Death or debility would come as a blade under the shield rim or a spearhead over it. A simple slip could mean death.

When shield walls broke and gave way to melees, talent and prowess could again assert itself, but the Viking way of war was primarily organization, teamwork, patience, and courage in the face of blind chaos.

Recent Criticism of Shield Wall Theory

While the shield wall idea is widely taken for granted by historians, not everyone believes it happened that way. One particularly vocal critic is University of Copenhagen archeologist, Rolf Warming. Warming's research found – as countless other weapons tests had also found – that Viking shields cannot stand up to repeated determined blows of some battlefield weapons. Warming argues that the many references to shield walls in sagas are merely poetic descriptions and that Vikings instead charged in using a variety of formations, warding off attacks with their shields and overwhelming the enemy through shock and awe.

Most experts would agree with Warming that the Viking shield is better to ward away blows than to receive them flush, and that Vikings were known both for ferocity and creative battle strategies. Most would also agree that "hiding behind" a shield wall would be a bad strategy – but shield walls always move relentlessly (albeit slowly) forward. This forward motion removes the space necessary for an assailant's blows to have full power, like the crowding or clinching techniques used by boxers and MMA fighters today. By depriving the enemy room to swing, the Viking shield should have held up fairly well, though we do see throughout the sagas, poems, and histories that shields were routinely broken in battle. For example, the *Krákumál* (or, *The Dying Ode of Ragnar Lothbrok*) has no fewer than three such references in merely 29 verses, including this description of Viking battle, *"the whole ocean was one wound: the earth grew red with reeking gore: the sword grinned at the coats of mail: the sword cleft the shields asunder."* The fact that in ritualized, *holmgang* duels Norse law allowed each fighter three shields shows that broken shields were a risk Vikings accepted.

Warming's many valid points, as well as the arguments against them, are just one more example of how there is almost nothing one can say about the Vikings that is not open for debate.

Viking Weapons and Armor

As in most European and Asian cultures, the sword held a place of special honor in the Viking arsenal. The Viking sword was a natural evolution from the Germano-Roman *spatha*. It was about a meter long, straight, and double-edged (though some earlier examples of single-edged swords have been found). It was heavy enough to inflict damage through most armor, but it was light enough to be used deftly with a single hand (as it would normally be paired with a shield).

For much of the Viking Age, only the wealthier or luckier warriors would be armed with swords. Swords were expensive, requiring both a fair amount of hard-to-find iron and the time and skill to turn that iron into a worthy weapon of steel. Good swords – weapons that would not break under the strain of battle and would maintain their edge as they hacked into shields and armor – could take weeks of months to make and cost as much as a house, if we were to put it in today's terms. Archeology has recovered such weapons, including the famed Ulfberht swords, that were the inspiration for the magic swords of lore.

One weapon that no Viking would want to be without, however, was the seax. The seax was a single-handed, stout-bladed weapon that ranged in size from a big knife to a short sword. It was single edged. It was multi-purpose, both as a tool and as a weapon; and it was especially valued in the press of shield wall, where there was often not enough room to swing a longer blade. Every free Norse male would probably start carrying a seax even before reaching adulthood.

The Vikings had a variety of javelins and spears. Chief amongst these was the hewing spear – an approximately two-meter-long weapon with a long head that could slash as well as pierce. Vikings also used bows for hunting and for war, but combat archery was used opportunistically or for support and did not approach the levels of utilization seen with the Huns, Mongols, or English longbowmen of other periods. The Vikings are thought to have reintroduced the bow into Ireland, where it had fallen out of use in Neolithic times. So, perhaps Viking archery was yet another reason for their early successes on the Emerald Isle.

The most famous, and perhaps most common, Viking weapon was the axe. Viking axes ranged in size from hand axes (similar to tomahawks) to long-hafted battle axes. Unlike the axes usually depicted in fantasy illustrations, Viking axes were single-bitted (to make them faster and more maneuverable). Viking axes were sometimes "bearded," which is to say that the lower portion of the axe head was hook-shaped to facilitate catching and pulling shield rims or limbs. Others, instead of being bearded, featured axe heads that sloped up above the haft, allowing them to stab and pierce as well as hack.

The axe required far less iron, time, or skill to produce than a sword. Whether training for war or working in the forest or farm, the Norse would have had axes in hand since childhood. Though the battle axe has technical differences from the tool axe, the similarities in physical technique conveyed another serious advantage. The sagas describe Vikings killing with both battle axes and wood axes as the occasion dictates.

The Viking axe would make the Norsemen famous, and even after the Viking Age waned, the descendants of the Vikings (such as the Varangians of Byzantium or the Gallowglass of Ireland) would be sought after as bodyguards or elite mercenaries specifically for their axe skill.

The most prized armor in the Viking Age were heavy coats (or *hauberks,* or *byrnie*) of chain mail or lamellar scales. Made from riveted rings of steel or small pieces of steel mounted to an under-layer (respectively), these garments were hard to produce and therefore difficult to come by for your average Viking (especially early in the period).

Because the Franks and other neighboring cultures prudently had laws against selling the Norse weapons, any armor that could not be produced in resource-restricted Scandinavia had to be captured in battle. Remember, armies of the time were not typically uniformly outfitted as ours are today, and the Vikings were diverse gatherings of warriors and not enlisted forces as we think of them. Therefore, Vikings usually put together their own armor. This could be anything that a warrior thought might offer them some protection.

Unlike the wealthiest knights of the High Middle Ages, the armor of this time was never meant to make one impervious from all threats. Instead, it was meant to reduce the risk of injury (and the subsequent infection that could be even more dangerous) in the battlefield environment. In this way it was not that much different in concept than the PPE (personal protective equipment) used by firefighters or other hazardous environment workers today.

The Viking might assemble his armor from a variety of materials – fur, boiled leather, even padded linen. A great number of Vikings had no armor at all. Many of these were berserkers, who prided themselves in fighting unprotected to demonstrate their bravery and devotion to Odin. Eyewitnesses describe Viking armies as "*bare-armed and bare-backed*" even as late as 885.

One article of armor a Viking would certainly desire to have was a helmet, without which he would be vulnerable in the shield wall. Viking helmets were fairly simple caps of steel that may have the added protection of nose guard bars or even protection around the eyes (sometimes referred to as "spectacled helmets"). Except for later versions that were fitted with chain mail veils, they did not protect the entire face.

While it would be natural to decorate or embellish helmets (or any armor) to look fiercer, the idea that Viking helmets had horns is a myth – because helmets are designed to guide forces away from the skull, horns and other such protrusions offer a disadvantage. The idea that Vikings had horned helmets comes from the fashions of nineteenth-century opera costume designers, who probably got the idea from the ceremonial Bronze Age helmets that were on display in museums at the time.

Odin, God of Wisdom, Discovery, and Contradictions

The ancient geographer-historians, Tacitus, did not equate Odin with Jupiter or Mars, but Mercury instead. Mercury was the Greco-Roman god of travelers, medicine, and insight. Mercury's serpent-entwined winged staff is still the symbol of physicians in our culture. At first, it would seem Tacitus had made quite a mistake (or that things had certainly changed between the first and eighth century), but when we get to know Odin as the Vikings did, this begins to make sense. Odin was not just a war god, like Ares. Nor was he just a stereotypical chief of the gods, like Zeus or Marduk, sitting on a celestial throne and waiting to chuck a lightning bolt at somebody. At one point, Odin was even exiled from Asgard and replaced as chief for an apparent lack of interest in the place (which raises interesting points not only about Odin but also about the nature of Norse politics).

Odin was a god who could take on a variety of different forms. So diverse were his attributes that he had over 200 names. He was not only imagined in his shining armor charging into battle on his eight-legged horse Sleipnir; but also as an old, bearded traveler in a cloak and hood or broad-brimmed hat. In the twentieth century, J.R.R. Tolkien would base his famous character, Gandalf, not on the Celtic wizard, Merlin (as is usually supposed) but on the Norse god, Odin.

Odin's sphere of influence was very broad, and in many cases very contradictory. He was the patron of both royalty and of outlaws; of healers as well as one of the gods of the dead; of warriors and poets. He was the god of manly-exploits but was not hesitant to deal in something that Viking men considered effeminate and beneath them – the arts of magic. The Vikings would devote the destruction that they doled out to

Odin's glory, but he was also the god of discovery. Odin was a one-eyed god not because he had lost that eye in battle, but because he had voluntarily given it to obtain the gift of prophecy (i.e., second sight). On another occasion, he hung himself on Yggdrasil, the World Tree, for nine days and nights to obtain wisdom. Another time, he narrowly escaped with his life to steal the mead of poetry from the giants that protected it. Odin understood the secrets of the cosmos better than anyone and would travel far and wide through the nine dimensions ever-hungry to learn more. If the worship of Odin were widespread today, he would doubtlessly be acknowledged as a god of the sciences, for in Odin we see an insatiable curiosity and thirst for knowledge.

The unifying principle in these apparently-contradictory features was one thing: inspiration. Odin's name means Inspired. This is not only because he created the world and man, but because he was the spirit of inspiration. Whether it was inspiration in battle, inspiration in art, or inspiration in invention, Odin was there. It is telling that the Vikings worshiped this god above all others (for the most part – as we shall see, many Vikings preferred Thor and considered him to be the best of the gods). Inspiration opens the world up and makes life worth living.

People who do not understand the Vikings consider them to be destructive brutes. While it is an unfortunate truth that they were incredibly destructive and were not always as quick as Odin in embracing understanding, this view misses the Viking ethos entirely.

The Vikings did not leave Scandinavia on missions of destruction. They left on missions of discovery. They did not just want to see what was out there, but to take it and hold it for themselves. They were incredibly adaptive every place that they went. Every country and every people they encountered left their mark on them, and the Vikings left their mark in return. As we shall see, the Vikings were a major catalyzing force in the formation of Europe. This hunger for inspiration was one of the major reasons why.

Chapter II: The Gods of Asgard and the Viking Culture

You can tell a lot about a people by what they worship. Religions and cultures usually reflect each other, and a peoples' hopes, fears, and deepest values come from, and are expressed by, their faith.

The Norse arranged their pantheon as a model of their society. This does not mean that Asgard (the home of the gods) is some Utopia. Rather, the Norse gods live in a community that was familiar to the people who told their stories, complete with complex relationships and both internal and external strife.

As we have mentioned, the Norse gods had overlapping qualities and spheres of influence, just as people do in real life. The skalds even went so far as to arrange them in two different tribes – the Aesir and the Vanir. These tribes often compete with each other, as tribes would in the real world.

Outside of these tribes are the giants (called *jötunn* or *jötnar*), dragons, and monsters – the forces of entropy and chaos. The gods sometimes find themselves in shifting relationships (ranging from all-out war to marriage) with the giants, just as the Vikings would experience shifting relationships with the other peoples of Europe.

Of course, the purpose of Norse belief was not just to make a map of society (though, like all religions, reinforcing constructive social norms was one of the functions). The purpose of myth was to help people understand cosmic forces and spiritual truths. Unfortunately, this essential aspect of Norse myth is a massive subject and is beyond the scope of this book. But by taking a brief look at Norse mythology, we can see how the Vikings thought of themselves, thought of others, and how their world was ordered.

Thor and Viking Character and Values

Odin was the chief of the gods, but Thor may have been the most popular. A few experts have postulated that this was because Odin demanded occasional human sacrifices (a fact that is well-documented) while Thor did not, but the real reason for Thor's popularity is fairly obvious. Odin was the chief of gods, but he was also the god of chiefs. While he was the All-father, it was no real secret who his favorite children were. The men to which he was patron were kings, jarls, poets, and outlaws – individuals (rather than members of a collective community) who could see themselves in Odin's often-egocentric activities.

Thor, by contrast, was the great protector of all that was good (as the Vikings defined it). Where Odin was wise, Thor was strong. Where Odin was cunning, Thor was straightforward and stalwart. While Odin was wandering the nine worlds seeking insight into the arcane, Thor was riding across the skies in his goat-drawn chariot smashing giants with his hammer. Thor was a merry warrior. He was indomitable, indefatigable, and steadfast. If Thor were a mortal, every Viking would have wanted to raise an ale horn with him. He was the paragon to which Vikings aspired.

Evidence of Thor's popularity and status as a role model can be seen clearly in Iceland, where more than a quarter of the founding population had some form of his name in theirs (i.e., Thorkill, Thorgest, Thorfin, etc.). Hundreds of Mjölnir ("Lightning," Thor's mighty hammer) amulets have been discovered in Viking graves and other Norse archeological sites. Norsemen continued to wear these hammer amulets even after converting to Christianity (as the Viking Age waned and long afterward), suggesting that Thor's role as a hero and protecting influence had not diminished. Of course, he is still in that role today in our cultural lore.

No god was stronger than Thor. Some of the giants were, but that only made the challenge of beating them more enjoyable for the red-bearded god. His hammer, Mjölnir, was able to destroy mountains, and he used it to smash the heads of the giants that threatened Asgard and Midgard (the world of humanity). When the Vikings saw the skies flashing and felt the rumble of the storm, they knew that Thor was fighting for them again. But Mjölnir was not just a weapon. Thor used Mjölnir to hallow (that is, to restore, make holy, or to bless). With Mjölnir, Thor could bring some things (such as the goats who drew his chariot) back to life. Thor was invoked at weddings, at births, and at special ceremonies for these abilities to sanctify and protect.

Thor is often called the God of Thunder. This is not wrong, as his name means "Thunder," but his role was much bigger than that. Thor was a sky god, like Zeus or Marduk, and the god of weather. Thor was the son of Odin and Fyorgyn (also called Jord, as well as other names). Fyorgyn is called a giantess in some narratives, but seems to be associated with the older Indo-European tradition of the Great Mother earth goddess. That Thor was the principal male deity celebrated at Yule (a winter solstice festival with very deep roots) reinforces this association.

They say men marry women who are like their mothers, so Thor married Sif (one of the only mellow, submissive goddesses one finds in Norse myth) who seems to also be an earth/agricultural goddess. Herein lies another reason for Thor's popularity and importance in the lives of ordinary Vikings. For the Vikings, favorable weather at sea could give them great advantages over enemies (and competitors) while bad weather could be deadly. When they returned to their homelands in Scandinavia or their colonies, many Vikings were farmers. The relationship between the weather and the fertility of the land (often seen as a conjugal union in Indo-European religion) is the basis of feast or famine. So, Thor did not just protect humankind from the giants – the destructive cosmic/natural forces – his efforts and his favor blessed them with safety at sea and bounty on land. It is no wonder that he was loved, idolized, and revered.

Though Thor was profoundly strong, he was never reluctant to go out of his depth. In the stories, we often see him going far into the giant's territory with nothing to protect him but a disguise. He rows a giant's boat out into the ocean, beyond where anyone else has ever been, all so that he can pick a fight with Jormugundr, the World-Coiling Serpent.

This story, or the inspirations behind it, may be one of the reasons old maps had "*here be dragons*" scrawled on the watery edges of the known world. It is unclear in the story whether Thor already knew that this same monster was fated to be the death of him, but the battle was so terrifying that the giant accompanying Thor cut the god's fishing line and the Jormugund slipped back into the deep. Thor was so angry that the giant intervened that he killed the luckless wretch and went home in disgust. Here we again see Viking values of bravery and exploration, as well as complete intolerance of what they considered weakness or cowardice.

Thor was undeniably an alpha male, but he was also a team player – another indispensable quality for Vikings whose success or failure relied on their ability to work together on the ship and in the shield wall. He had a strong sense of community with his fellow gods. He had a violent temper, and most of his stories end up with him cracking the skull of the giant who galled him, but he was usually cheerful and could be forgiving. While Thor's children out of wedlock were further testament to his hot-blooded, virile nature, he was fundamentally a "family man" and was fiercely protective of his wife. Thor was the god the other gods often turned to and counted on, and this was how any good Viking would want to be thought of by his peers.

Most of these characteristics are still valued today, and Thor's archetype is still visible in the action heroes of our books and movies. What is completely missing in Thor is the self-doubt or any of the "reluctant hero" aspects that are so popular (for whatever reasons) in our culture.

Thor's ethics of whom he killed and why are also those of a Viking god, and not something most modern people would be comfortable with from their heroes.

Norse men and women would probably know all the stories of Thor by heart and would see in these stories what they should be. This exaltation of taking action, of going beyond boundaries, and of finding glory in battle were contributing factors to both the proliferation and the success of the Vikings.

Of course, models are just models, and there were undoubtedly plenty of Vikings who were the antithesis of Thor. But in the stories of their most-beloved god, we can see how the Vikings saw themselves and what they wanted to be.

Loki and Viking Ethics

If Thor was what Vikings considered to be good, then what did Vikings consider evil? An old view of the Vikings, authored by their enemies and cultivated by a lack of historical depth, is that they were just dirty, vile barbarians that answered to nothing other than their own lusts. We have already begun to see (and most readers of this book probably already knew) that this is untrue. The Vikings originated from and carried with them an ordered society. It would have been impossible to achieve anything if they did not. This society and culture carried with it an ethical system.

At the heart of this ethical system is was Norse honor culture – the idea that a man or woman must demonstrate the strength and qualities that advance their family's interests and add to their good name. This ethical system can be difficult to understand, because it is different from our modern ethical system and because it leads to behaviors that are highly contextual. An action might be deemed worthy or abhorant depending solely on the circumstances in which it was committed. In Norse literature, we sometimes see identical negative activities praised or condemned almost side by side, depending on who did them, where, and why.

There is no Devil in Norse mythology. The giants, dragons, and monsters are spirits/creatures of negativity and the destructive phase of the creation-destruction cycle. They are fearsome and terrifying to humankind, but they also serve a purpose in the cosmic order. Giants are not just enemies, but were sometimes the mothers, lovers, or friends of the gods. Even the fearsome wolf Fenrir – fated to someday devour the sun and the moon – was once the gods' pet.

As for the Vikings themselves, contemporary historians are very quick to point out that the Vikings did not *just* raid, pillage, murder, rape, and enslave – however, this does not change the fact that they did often do all these things. In the sagas, there are words translated as "evil" or "wicked" but the people these words describe do not seem expressly different from everybody else. Unlike contemporary fiction and film, which spend a lot of time demonstrating how evil the bad guys are, the skalds seemed to have no such artistic requirement. The "evil" king or the "wicked" jarl in these sagas turn out to be simply a powerful adversary, while the protagonist might also commit any number of crimes.

For example, in the *Volsunga Saga* (one of the most esteemed of all Norse epics), the hero, Sigmund, murders his nephews because they are too weak to help him take revenge on the villain – the man who murdered his father and brothers.

So, if the Vikings considered raiding, feuding, slave trading, and unprovoked war to all be good ethics, and if the lethal games of Odin and the violent temper of Thor were admirable, then what did the

Vikings consider to be wrong? The answer to this question begins with the character Loki.

Loki's name means "Tangle." He is known as the God of Mischief or the Trickster god. Others say that he is not a god at all, but a giant that was adopted into the family of the Aesir gods. Some Eddic poems refer to him being Odin's blood-brother.[1] There is no historical or archeological evidence of Loki ever being worshipped. But whether Loki was a god, *per se*, or not, he was a member of the Aesir, a resident of Asgard, and frequent companion of both Odin and Thor.

Loki was said to be very handsome and well-spoken, but he was a completely self-centered nihilist who was only interested in his own pleasure and his own amusement. Loki is constantly playing tricks or working elaborate schemes of mischief on the gods, but then sometimes also on the giants, depending on which side would give him the most enjoyment at the time. When called out for his misdeeds (and often threatened by Thor or the others) he usually finds a way to set things right through more trickery. We can speculate on his higher motivations but they are not expressed in the stories.

While Loki's tricks begin as fairly benign, they become increasingly cruel over time. The sequence in the tales of the gods is not

---

[1] Loki as a son of Odin, adopted or otherwise, is a modern contrivance, largely from comics and movies, and is not supported in Norse lore.

always clear, but in some stories, Loki is portrayed in a comic light, while in others he appears inexplicably spiteful.

Loki is the father of several beings, and he is the mother of several other beings. This accomplishment may have been achieved through shape-shifting, or is another reminder that the gods and giants represent cosmic forces and are not bound by the anthropomorphism used to describe them. In any case, Loki is the only god with this hermaphroditic distinction. With the exception of Sleipnir, Odin's eight-legged horse, all of Loki's offspring are horrible monsters or keepers of the underworld. This is a further indication of the true nature hidden behind his smile and smooth words.

Loki's mischief finally crossed the line into pure evil when he orchestrated the death of the god Baldur. Baldur was one of the most beloved and noble of the gods. Later, Christianized Norse writers would sometimes make into an allegorical Christ figure. His death devastated Asgard. Baldur's mother, Frigg, journeyed to the realm of the dead and pleaded with Hel[2] (Loki's daughter) to release her son from death. Hel agreed, but only if every living creature would weep for Baldur. Every

---

[2] Though a concept of an afterlife of punishment appears in several world religions, the Norse goddess Hel was only the queen of the most-populous afterworld. Her role in Ragnarok makes it clear that she is evil, but she is not really a Norse "Satan figure" or a tormentor of lost souls. Medieval European Christians would borrow her name (because she was so well-known) to refer to their Hell, which was called Sheol, Hades, or sometimes Gahenna in their scriptures. The pagan idea that those unfit for Valhalla went to live *with* Hel turned into the Christian idea that those unfit for Heaven went to live *in* Hell.

creature did – except one. Loki, disguised as a female giant, refused to weep; and so, Hel kept Baldur.

Loki's dark nature was finally revealed beyond question. The gods bound him in a cave, using cords made from the guts of his own son, and placed a serpent over his head. Loki's faithful wife stood by him, using a bowl to catch the poison that drips from the serpent's fangs. But whenever she empties the bowl, the poison strikes Loki in the face and burns him. At these times, his torment and the thrashings of his agony give rise to earthquakes.

Even as he lies bound, Loki plans his escape and his revenge. He is destined to break free at Ragnarok and lead the giants on their assault on Asgard and all gods and humankind.

We see in these stories that the Vikings did not fear and revile a devil that lived in some underworld or who waited to damn their souls. The Vikings reviled the traitor that hid in their midst. Duplicity, lying, scheming, cheating, and spite were what the Vikings most loathed. Along with cowardice, these things were the opposite of the characteristics of Thor. People with these behaviors and qualities undermine group effort, whether that be on the farmstead, in the longship, or on the battlefield. Individuals who use lies and subterfuge to preserve their interests at the expense of those whom they pretend to hold as friends could be far deadlier than an armed foe. This is what the

Vikings considered to be evil. As the Eddic poem, *Sigdrifumal* (v. 23) reads,

> "*The grim rope of a hangman waits for the oath-breaker,*
>
> *The fate of the liar is agony.*"

Heimdal and Norse Social Order

Heimdal is the watchman of the gods, an ever-vigilant being who is far-seeing and can hear everything. He is sometimes called "Heimdal the White" because of his unimpeachable honor. He stands guard over Asgard, watching the Bifrost bridge (the rainbow that links the home of the gods to the other worlds) from his high hall. He carries the great horn, Gjallarhorn, which he will sound when the giants attack at Ragnarok. Interestingly, it is he who is fated to fight and kill Loki on that horrible day, and not Thor or Odin.

Heimdal has a special place in his heart for humans and "gifted" them with the social classes. Viking society was divided into three classes. These classes were both a simple, practical reality in the early medieval world the Vikings occupied. They also were seen as a desirable structure (at least by those not at the bottom) to give order and stability to society. Modern people usually hate the idea of rigid social classes (though it exists in our society much more than we would like to admit) but ancient peoples tended to accept and perpetuate it.

The classes of the Norse world were not just about money. They were about status and function. Some of the people in the upper class could be quite poor, while some of those in the middle class could be very rich. Movement between classes was possible for individuals of special ability and tenacity, but it was difficult. In many ways, the Viking Age created a tempest in the social order, as individuals in the middle class tried to fight their way to a better spot, while many in the upper and middle classes of the losing sides were cast down.

Those in the Norse upper class were called jarls (usually pronounced 'yarls'), which is where we get the term 'earl.' A jarl could be a king or a chief. Poets (skalds), bards, and perhaps some artists were also considered to be of the jarl class because of the importance Norse society placed on their learning and abilities. Jarls had a special reverence for Odin and were expected to demonstrate wisdom, shrewdness, learning, valor, and generosity.

Being a Viking jarl was not a position where you could just kick back and enjoy the good life. A jarl was expected to be a "gold-giver" that is, to make decisions that would help his people thrive and advance their personal wealth. If a jarl made poor decisions or was unlucky, he may find his power undermined, his followers deserting him, and his position threatened.

The middle (and largest) class were the karls. Karls were men and women who were property owners, and thus considered accountable, vested members of society. Their holdings could be large or small. They could be very rich or rather poor. They could be merchants, farmers, or craftsmen. Karls are also referred to as "freemen" (not to be confused with "freedmen") though this term is a bit broader. The overwhelming majority of Vikings were karls. Unlike the unhappy image of people attached to land in feudal Europe (serfs), karls had a lot of legal standing and legal protections. Karls became the essence of Icelandic democracy during the 10th century, and in many ways set the example for citizens of developed nations today.

The lowest class were called thralls. Thralls included slaves, bondsmen (what was later called an "indentured servant," a free person who was reduced to slavery for a set term to satisfy some financial or legal obligation), and vagrants. Of these, vagrants had the least legal protection and were the most reviled because they were considered to have no investiture in society, while the slave and the bondsman still belonged and contributed to society's order.

Slavery was an unfortunate reality in the pre-industrial world, and remains so today in places where law and enlightenment do not reach. Human trafficking and slavery even exist in various underworlds within our society. There have always been people who knew slavery was wrong. Aristotle mentions ancient Greek abolitionists (and why he feels they are fools) in his 4th century B.C. treatise, *Politics*. The Romans – whose western empire had ended 317 years before the dawn of the

Viking Age, but who still formed the theoretical foundation that kings of Europe aspired to – had slaves comprising about a quarter of their population. During the Viking Age the proportion was lower than that, but still quite significant.

Viking slaves had more legal protections than Roman slaves, such as the ability to marry and to form families (Roman slaves almost certainly formed families, as this is human nature, but these families had no legal status or protection). Common sense dictated that slaves were not treated to extreme brutality, as this damages one's "property" and pushes the slave towards the invisible line where he or she will potentially kill the master in their sleep (which plenty of the Vikings' slaves did). No matter what face of normalcy one puts on it, though, slavery is one of the cruelest things one human can do to another. The Vikings' heavy involvement in the medieval slave trade is a stain that cannot be erased.

Tyr and Norse Law

Tyr is a Norse god of war and strongly associated with law and order. The minor god, Forseti, also shares this role, but we have far less information on him. Tyr is best known as the god who was brave enough to bind Fenrir the wolf and lost one of his hands for his troubles. Tyr was the only god who could bind Fenrir because Tyr was the only god that Fenrir trusted. Of the many things one can extrapolate from the metaphors and allegories in this story, some lessons may be that the Law only work when it is fair, and that justice comes with a price to both the griever and the aggrieved.

Many experts suspect that Tyr's role used to be much larger and that he was even at one point the king of the gods before his position was usurped by Odin. This hypothesis is based on the relationship of Tyr's name and character to older Indo-European god-forms and is too complicated to go into here. Tyr is the only god with his own (explicit) rune. This rune resembles a spear, or perhaps suggests a sword blade. Though Odin was wise, and Thor was strong, sages and heroes were referred to as "Tyr-wise" or "Tyr-strong". Tuesday is named in honor of Tyr, further suggesting the forgotten heights of his status.

It is important to point out that Odin supplanting Tyr is a matter of ethnographical/anthropological activity and not part of the narrative of the Gods of Asgard as the Vikings knew it.

The Vikings were from an ordered society that placed a high value on the law. As our picture of them is men jumping off a ship to slaughter people and break things, this may seem paradoxical. However, it is the very order of Norse society that allowed these Vikings the ability to go adventuring abroad. If Norse society had been lawless, the efforts of the Vikings would have been concentrated on defending their homes. If there were no laws (or if these laws were under-developed), then the Vikings would have found no markets for their captured treasures when they returned. If there were no law and order, there would have been no craftsmen to build ships, make weapons, and outfit further expeditions. So, the Vikings did have a strong sense of law and order, and they took these ideas of law and order with them wherever they went.

Like Viking ethics, however, Norse law has some paradoxical elements that we will need to examine more closely. Viking ethics and laws depend largely on context. For example, stealing was considered one of the lowest things a person could do, but stealing was okay – even something to brag about – if the items were taken as part of a raid. The rationale was that the raid was an act of war, and the other party had the chance to defend themselves but failed to do so. Therefore, the loss of their possessions was the result of their weakness and not the Vikings' theft. The Vikings who plundered the items deserved them more than those who had lost them, because of their strength, skill, and superior strategy.

There is a scene in the famous Icelandic *Egil's Saga* that shed light on this thought process. Egil Skallagrimson and his Vikings were captured during their raid but managed to escape with some of their loot. On their way back to their ships, Egil is suddenly overcome with guilt because the items they were taking – while originally taken in battle – were now being taken by stealth. This was stealing, which was unacceptable. The Vikings decide to go back and attack their captors again, this time killing all of them. They were then free to take their plunder and leave with clean consciences.

The same line of thinking applied to other crimes. It was considered morally wrong and even illegal to sleep with another man's wife (and as people married quite young then, most women would be other men's wives), but rape was commonplace in Viking raids and sexual abuse of slaves by some Vikings is attested to in both Arabic sources and even Norse sources like *Grettir's Saga*. Murder was wrong - except in war, where non-combatants and combatants alike could be killed with impunity.

Some experts state that the killing of non-combatants only applied when the Vikings were abroad, not when they were raiding at home, however, this is open to debate. Some sagas mention feuding Vikings letting women and even slaves leave the hall that they are about to attack and burn, but this may have been to lessen their legal liability in Icelandic law as much as it was proto-chivalry or fairplay. Saxo Grammaticus's *Gesta Danorum*, the *Heimskringla*, and other primary sources describes many examples of what we now call war crimes performed within home territory. Certainly, practices varied. This way of thinking seems hypocritical and even abhorrent to us, but this was how the Norse viewed their ethical and legal responsibilities.

As the Vikings were traders even more often than they were raiders, laws ensuring fair trade were especially important. Other Norse laws shine light on aspects of their society. For example, it was illegal (and highly insulting) to throw dirt onto someone or to push them in such a way that they fell into the mud, suggesting the degree to which the Norse valued cleanliness and good personal presentation. Bullying activities like knocking off someone's hat could be considered assault, opening opportunities for revenge. Love poems (offered to someone other than one's wife) were also outlawed as a form of seductive witchcraft, demonstrating how the Norse revered the power of poetry.

Aside from the warriors sworn to the kings or chiefs, there was no police to enforce laws. Therefore, one always had to be ready to defend oneself and one's family (another testament to the importance of strength). As the revered eddic poem, the *Havamal* puts it,

> *Let a man never stir on his road a step*
> *without his weapons of war,*
> *for unsure is the knowing when need shall arise,*
> *of a spear on the way without.*

Law enforcement often came after the fact, when anyone (whether they were affected by the crime or not) could accuse a man or woman, forcing them to appear for judgment. The accused would then be tried by a jury of 36, where at least a 30-vote majority would be required in the rendered decision.

There were no real prisons in Norse society. The courts could impose the seizure of property to be granted to victims. The greatest punishment was outlawry. Outlawry meant that a person was banished from society and that others (such as victims or bounty hunters) could take their own revenge on the outlaw with impunity if they could catch him. The sentence of "lesser outlawry" made the guilty party an outcast for three years, as opposed to the usual lifetime on the run that regular outlawry carried.

Unlike modern times, where a criminal is seen as someone who has transgressed the state, the Vikings saw legal matters as being fundamentally between the perpetrator and the victim. At the center of this legal system was the concept of *"weregeld"* (literally, "man-gold," the price of a life demanded in recompense in Germanic law) or compensation. The aggrieved party was not only entitled to compensation (a set amount of wealth determined by the severity of the crime and the social status of the victim) – they were absolutely honor bound to demand it. If the victim or the victim's family failed to extract compensation from the perpetrator they were essentially victimized twice. In the sagas, it is more common to see men and women angry and grieved that they are being denied compensation (and therefore losing honor) than they are over the crime itself. This should not be interpreted as a lack of feeling on the part of our ancestors. It was simply thought that the only good response to grief was to take action.

If appealing to courts was unavailable or unsatisfactory, disputes could be settled through dueling. Dueling in Norse culture did not have the same expectations of the divine hand that Trial by Battle had in other places and other times in the Middle Ages but was a simple fight between aggrieved parties. Originally, duels were called *einvigi* and were one-on-one fights with whatever weapons or means combatants had on hand. If one or both men died, their families could take revenge or demand *weregeld.*

Later, *einvigi* duels began to give way to *holmgang* duels. *Holmgang* literally meant "going to the island," though this became just an expression and the duel could take place in any defined area at a specified time with agreed-upon weapons. *Holmgang* duels were undertaken through mutual agreement and so, families of those who were killed in *holmgang* duels were not entitled to revenge or recompense. This institutionalized sense of fair play did not always thwart the strategy of the cunning or the abuses of the strong. The sagas are full of episodes were villains (often berserkers) challenge weaker men to *holmgang* simply for material gain. There are also many incidents of shrewd men using concealed weapons at moments of opportunity – especially if they believe that their enemy might be using magic spells against them.

Holmgang duels eventually became highly-ritualized in an effort to make them less lethal and have less impact on the community. The aggrieved parties were given a specific sword (with one backup weapon allowed) and three shields. They stood on cloaks and attacked each other with one blow at a time, starting with the accusing party. Witnesses kept things fair, and the fight was over when all the shields were broken or one man's blood touched his cloak. Fleeing from the cloak also forfeited the match. These changes were designed to save lives, as it would be a difficult thing to cut through a shield and the man behind it while he was expecting the single blow.

When courts or duels did not solve problems, the Norse resorted to feuds. Feuds could be undertaken for any reason, and just like gang wars today they could escalate egregiously. One of the most frightening acts in a feud was a "hall burning." The Norse tended to live in longhouses or halls, where sets of families, any sworn men they may have, and slaves might live together. In a serious feud, sometimes the opposing party would set fire to these structures while their enemies were inside, then kill them as they tried to escape.

Feuds were considered miniature wars, and so violence was for the most part considered legal. Anyone might get involved with the feud (if they were reckless of the consequences) but no one (except for perhaps a king, if it suited him) was going to step in and put a stop to it. In the *Greenlander's Saga*, we see a local democratic body – the *Thing* – intervene in one of Eric the Red's feuds, but only after it had become a public nuisance.

While duels and feuds were realities, they were the exceptions to the norm. Respect for law and the very real fear of reprisal kept most people out of trouble – at least while they were at home. Testimony to the natural lawfulness of the Vikings can be seen in the founding of

Iceland in the late 9th century. Iceland was founded as a democratic republic. There was no king. Rule came from assemblies of landed men (karls as well as jarls) in local assemblies called the *Thing* and national assemblies called the *Althing*. Essential to these gatherings was the Law Speaker, a man who would memorize and recite the people's laws. Law Speakers were elected and served for three years at a time, ensuring that no one acquired too much power.

Both *Things* and *Althings* have well-established roots in Germanic tribal law, but the Vikings of Iceland were the first people in a long time who had instituted them on such a broad level. Because of its roots and unbroken line to the *Althing,* the parliament of Iceland is still considered to be the oldest parliament in the world.

Frey and Freya: Norse Sexuality, Gender, and the Family

Frey and Freya were brother and sister fertility gods of the Vanir who came to live with the Aesir as part of the peace treaty that ended the war between the two tribes (another common Viking tradition).

Freya (which simply means "the Lady") is considered by some experts to originally have been the same goddess as Frigg (or Frigga), Odin's wife and Baldur's mother, as they have almost identical characteristics. But by the time the works of the skalds was written down Frigg and Freya are treated distinctly and can be in the same place at the same time. One could speculate that Freya is more of the maiden aspect of the Indo-European Triple Goddess, while Frigga is the mother aspect – though it is dangerous to interpret the beliefs of one culture through the lens of another. Whatever the case may be, the recorders of the skaldic tradition and probably the Vikings themselves regarded the two goddesses as distinct individuals.

Frey (which means "the Lord" and who is also called Yvngi or Frodi) is often characterized in period idols with a massive erection. He is sometimes accompanied by a further symbol of his virility, a great boar named "Golden Bristles." Frey is the god the Vikings associated with male fertility, prosperity, abundance and peace. Along with Freya, he aptly lends his name to Friday.

Freya is a great deal more complicated than Frey. Freya is hands-down the most venerated of all the Nordic-Germanic goddesses (and may actually be the conglomerated archetype of many local fertility goddesses). Her essential role is bringing grain from the fields, lambs and calves from the flocks and herds, and children to the household. But Freya is not just another incarnation of the Great Mother, nor is she just a Viking version of Aphrodite/Venus. Though she can sometimes be seen weeping for her missing husband (who, as we've said, may just be Odin out on one of his walkabouts), Freya is a fierce and independent feminine divinity with a broad, layered sphere of influence. She fights in battle, accompanied by her own boar "War Pig." She is a seeress and the model of volva sorcery (a type of magic that involves discerning and manipulating the threads of fate that the Norns are weaving). She taught

Odin much of what he knows about magic, pointing him in the right direction to be able to glean the deeper secrets of the cosmos as he did at the Well of Urd and in finding the runes. Her chariot is drawn by cats (chief animals amongst her familiars, and the possible origin of the association between cats and witches in later cultures).

Some see Freya's ability to get cats to go together in the same direction as representing the strength and subtlety of feminine influence. Assuming Freya and Frigga once overlapped, she was not afraid to use this influence. Frigga once organized the gods to kick Odin out of Asgard for neglecting his duties as chief. Odin made a comeback, won his wife back, and forgave her for sleeping with his brothers while he was gone.

That was the other element of Freya's character – she had a rampant sexuality. In the *Lokasenna*, (*"Loki's Wrangling"*), a strange skaldic poem from the *Poetic Edda*, Loki crashes a *symbl* (a ritualized Norse drinking party) and insults all the gods one by one with what we infer are their deepest, darkest secrets. It may have just been vitriol on Loki's part, but he publicly accuses Freya of sleeping with all the gods (even Frey) and some of the giants and elves, too. Though Freya becomes as angry with Loki as the other gods do, her denial is insubstantial. The events of the *Lokasenna* seem to take place just before or amidst the drama of Loki's assassination of Baldur and permanent falling-out with the gods. We would not just take Loki's word for it – the Eddic poem *Voluspa en Skamma* makes similar assertions and there are many other indications of Freya's sensual nature throughout Norse mythology.

Now, before we extrapolate too much from this, we must remember, Freya is a goddess and represents cosmic forces, and therefore her actions should not be taken as representative of her entire society. But in proudly acknowledging the feminine sexuality of their most important goddess – not just for procreation, but for its own sake – the Norse did what their Christian neighbors (with their preoccupation with saintly chastity) had no interest in doing and went further even than the Greeks and Romans.

Like almost all Indo-European peoples throughout recorded history, the Norse were a patriarchal society. Gender roles were well-defined and based on the concept of division of labor that was proven to be advantageous for survival under the circumstances of climate and technology. As we look back from a modern perspective, it is important to remember that people of the past did not necessarily have our views or values. What we see as bleak, they probably just saw as mundane. The average person then probably found as much joy in their existence as the average person now does. In the farmsteads of Norway, Sweden, Denmark, and Iceland, both men's work and women's work were hard, dreary, often-thankless, and at times dangerous. Both men's work and women's work were respected, however, and a person's social standing (regarding respect, not affluence) was determined by how well they met those roles and expectations.

In pre-industrialized societies, the maternal death rate during labor and delivery could approach 30 percent, and with only folk medicine for birth control, most women would become pregnant repeatedly. In Christian Europe, many women became nuns to escape a life of toiling on a farm while constantly pregnant until one day dying during childbirth.

So, did women escape childbirth and agrarian toil by becoming Vikings? This is a topic of some debate, and it will receive its own chapter in this book. We have records in the sagas and histories (most notably Saxo Grammaticus, but others as well) of "shield maidens" – women warriors. We also have some archeological finds that might support the idea. But we also have considerable evidence to the contrary. Among this counter-evidence, we have laws in Iceland (from the *Gragas* book) prohibiting women from cutting their hair short, dressing as men, carrying weapons, or assuming masculine roles. But would there be such laws if there was not first the inclination against them? We will delve into this topic in chapter seven.

While we do not really know to what extent women were free to pursue alternative paths, what we do know is that women were more liberated in Norse culture than anywhere else in Europe. Marriages were arranged, occurred at a young age, and adultery was illegal (with impunity given to the husband under that circumstance should he kill both the woman and her lover), but women had to agree to the marriage and could choose to leave it at any time. Divorce was easier (for both parties) in Norse culture than it is in ours. Reasons for divorce included the husband not satisfying his wife or otherwise neglecting his husbandly duties. In cases of divorce, if the husband were considered at fault, the wife would be entitled to her dowry and bride-price back, and if she had been in the marriage for 20 years (which she may have been by age 32 or 33), she was entitled to half of their joint property. Such terms should have ensured that most husbands did whatever they could to make their wives happy.

At the same time, we must not be naïve and believe that this made everything rosy for everyone – certainly there were considerable social and psychological pressures working against individual happiness, just as there are today. The Norse woman was, however, freer than her other European counterparts.

Women had considerable status in the home. They usually controlled the finances. Norse poems mention a ring of keys being part of the traditional bridal costume, as a symbol of this importance. Women managed the household while men were away. Women could inherit property at the death of their husbands, and some became wealthy property owners. Women could become reigning queens and chiefs (in some places but not in others), as we will see in future chapters;

however, women were prevented from speaking or voting at the *Thing* or the *Althing*, and so did not receive the more common political power of the day.

Women compensated for this lack of political power by influencing things behind the scenes. Almost all the women in Norse mythology or the sagas are very strong characters – even driving forces. A quote from the *Brennu-Njals Saga* sums up the Viking respect for feminine wisdom and influence, "*Cold are the counsels of women.*"

Everything we have said so far applies to free women, and not slaves. While free women even had legal protections against any unwanted sexual attention, the same could not be said of slaves. Any domestic violence brought great shame on a man, though it is not clear how much this carried over to the treatment of slaves. Even if it did, the power-differential of slavery created unending potential for coercive predatory behavior in unprincipled men. As is usually the case in history, this occurred behind closed doors. We do know that Viking slavers targeted women and this is incompatible with any amount of evidence of "gentlemen Vikings" we may gather. Of course, it is likely that there were considerable individual differences on this matter, and that not everyone could be bad any more than not everyone could be good. In the Viking Age – as in all other ages – slaves are generally ignored by chroniclers, and so the course of their lives can only be guessed at.

The Norse lived together in extended families. It was expedient for work, warmth, and protection to live in big structures called longhouses. As mentioned, a longhouse may be home to several generations of a family, possibly some friends or what we would consider employees, and possibly some slaves if there were any. A longhouse would usually have barns, boat sheds, or perhaps other houses (i.e., slave quarters, or lodgings added on to accommodate a growing family) around it, and this may or may not be fenced in or have some other defensive structures, depending on the environment.

This arrangement made up the farmsteads of the Viking diaspora as their way of life spread beyond Scandinavia. It was perfect for farming and the division of labor. It was also perfect for defense against raids or feuds, for one's family and friends would always be close at hand. It is easy to see how this living arrangement gave rise to Viking cohesion in battle, for ship crews may be the men of just a few farmsteads (who knew each other well) and these ship crews may naturally stay together as semi-formal units in war.

There were exceptions to the farmstead as a living arrangement. There are written and archeological records of hovels that might house just a few persons. There were also much, much larger settlements. Viking fortified ports – called *longphorts* – gave rise to many of the towns and cities of Europe.

Chapter Two Conclusion

Norse culture is reflected and subtly codified in their mythology and beliefs. This mythology created a form that served to perpetuate that culture as the Vikings proliferated and spread to new regions. Encoded in that culture are some of the very things that made the Vikings so successful, and so difficult for their enemies to deal with. Their culture, as much or even more so than any technological or physical advantage that they had, held the secret to their tenacity and their effectiveness. The next chapter will look at the aspect of Viking culture that was to serve as their ultimate weapon: the Norse philosophy of heroic fatalism

.

Chapter III: Ragnarok and Viking Heroic Fatalism

The Vikings believed all things – even the gods themselves – were bound to fate. The concept was so important that there were six different words for fate in the Old Scandinavian tongues. As Daniel McCoy (2016) writes,

> *"Fate occupied roughly the same position in the Norse worldview that the laws of science do in the modern world; it provided an unseen guiding principle that determined how events in the world would unfold, and could explain them after they occurred"*.

It was in large part this deep conviction that *"fate is inexorable"* that gave the Vikings their legendary stoicism. Because the outcome was determined, it was not for a man or a woman to try to escape their fate – no matter how grim it might be. The essential thing was in *how* one met the trials and tragedies that befell them.

We see this in the Viking idea of Valhalla – the heavenly realm where the souls of those who have died valiantly feast and fight beside the gods. But this submission to fate is even stronger and starker when we consider the purpose of Valhalla. The gods were not simply drawing the souls of the worthy and the brave to reward them – they were calling for heroes because *they needed them.*

The reason they needed them was because Ragnarok, the inevitable cataclysmic destruction of everything and the end of the world, would one day come.

Like the Apocalypse of Christianity and the Qayamat of Islam, Ragnarok is the culmination of a series of prophesied events. No one knew when it was supposed to happen. They could only look for the signs. Just as some Christians throughout history have believed they were living in "the end times", as the Viking Age waned, some Norse believed they were living through the tribulations of Ragnarok.

Ragnarok's great doom was set into motion with the murder of the beloved god, Baldur, by the hand of Loki. Loki was bound for this crime, in a deep cave where he was tormented by the burning poison of a magical serpent. But Loki swore revenge and will one day throw in his lot with the giants and Hel, goddess of the underworld and keeper of the ignoble dead. Furthering his treachery, Loki will lead the giants in a massive assault on Asgard, the home of the gods.

People will know that Ragnarok is beginning when a great winter takes hold of the earth. The sun and the moon shall be devoured by the wolves, Fenrir, Skoll, and Hati. Humankind will abandon faith, loyalty, and honor. Great wars will break out, and the world will be battered by floods, winds, and famines. Yggdrasil itself will shake. But all of that is just the preamble to the destruction that awaits.

Hel's ship, Nalgfar – a longship made from the fingernails of all the forgotten dead – will rise from the bottom of the cold ocean. It will be oared by giants – ancient enemies of the gods who are each supernatural beings of chaos. The ship will be helmed by Loki, who will lead it to Bifrost, the rainbow bridge that is the entrance into Asgard. They will not come alone, for all the horrible monsters that the gods had fought so bravely to bind will break free and will join the attack. This army of abomination will crush Bifrost under their weight and will lay waste to Asgard.

But the gods are not so easily undone. Odin, Thor, Heimdall, Frey and Freya, and all the others will lead the heroes of Valhalla onto the "field of surging battle," a place called Vigrid. There the last battle will rage. Odin will don his eagle helmet and ride his eight-legged charger straight at the great wolf, Fenrir; but before the Allfather can level his spear at the beast's heart, he will be devoured. Odin's son Vidar will slay Fenrir, but also die in turn.

Thor will battle the world-coiling serpent, Jormungand; and though he finally slays his ancient nemesis with his hammer, he will collapse dead from the snake's venom.

Heimdall and Loki will die on each other's blades.

One by one, the gods and heroes will fall; and as they do, there will be nothing to save the world from the giant's fire. The fire will consume every one of the nine worlds. The giants and creatures of darkness, too, will die by the fire and destruction they have created. All shall perish and fall into the sea, and everything will be as it was before creation ever happened.

Many of the older accounts leave it at that. Other versions (particularly the ones written down many years after the worship of Odin had faded) go on to describe a rebirth. There will be a new creation of the world(s) these writings say, and a few descendants of both gods and humankind will survive Ragnarok and the coming darkness. These descendants will repopulate the earth, and life and light will return.

Many experts find in this epilogue evidence that the Norse view of time was cyclical, a circle of creation and destruction. Others see in the story attempts by later writers to introduce some of their Christian ideas into the tale, a way to exonerate the abandoned beliefs of their people as being precursors to the faith they went on to hold. At least one of these poems, *The Song of the Seeress,* is less than subtle in that regard when it talks about one great god who would then rule over all in this new creation (though some experts argue this stanza may have been tacked on later).

As we consider these different versions of the story and their different interpretations, it is important to remember that Viking religion was not a structured, codified faith with scriptures and dogmas the way most religions we are acquainted with today are. Rather, it was a flexible, fluid, adaptive culture that lived through stories and songs from many voices. Hence there is no correct or incorrect view of Ragnarok.

Ragnarok is a hard story. It is a grim tale of doom, where those of us who have listened to the many wonderful tales of gods and heroes must now watch them die. It would have been many times more distressing for the Norse people, who wore the symbols of these gods, and put their faith in them. Whether this doom led to rebirth or not did not change the horror of the events the Norse fully expected to come true.

Again, this is where we see a clear view of the Viking heart. Just as Odin, Thor, and the gods of Asgard were not afraid to stand shoulder to shoulder with worthy souls and fight unimaginable, invincible foes, so also the Viking knew that he or she was to face adversity, fear, tragedy, and loss the very same way. With a sword in hand and a shout on their lips, the Viking would never ask for any lighter fate or any lesser doom – only to be given the chance to live and die well, as the gods do.

Aspects of Viking Heroic Fatalism, and its Effects on the Viking Age

Because all events were fated and ordered, there was no point in being afraid of them, or desperately trying to escape them. To the Viking, he or she had no power over what happened – but had every power over how he or she responded to it. This does not mean that Vikings were eager to die or that when things went poorly they simply accepted them. Viking military strategy is not one of suicidal charges, but rather a masterclass in feints, using strength against weak points, well-timed retreats, subterfuge, ambushes, and other tactics that would have greatly pleased Sun Tzu. Seldom was it the Viking's goal to die, however valiantly.

This carried over to every aspect of life – if the Vikings would have been simple fatalists, as we think of it, they probably never would have left Scandinavia and we would not be talking about any of this now. So then, what does heroic fatalism mean? Heroic fatalism (which we should mention, is a phrase we are using to describe natural Viking attitudes, and could just as easily be called by other terms) means that the Viking would respond to their circumstances in as bold a way as possible. They would act without worrying about negative outcomes because there simply was no such thing. We are told by Christian chroniclers of the period that Vikings neither wept for their sins (i.e. felt no regret) nor for the death of their friends. If all was in the hands of fate, then a man or woman had nothing to lose. They could only win by responding to events in a way that would bring them honor.

Viking heroic fatalism has much in common with Greco-Roman Stoicism. Obviously, the two schools of thought evolved separately and had negligible contact with each other. Stoicism is a form of philosophy, while heroic fatalism comes from the Vikings' religion and the environment in which they lived (though philosophy and religion overlap significantly, and so this distinction may be arbitrary). The mechanisms of the two may be quite different, but the exterior is similar in the bottom-line distillation of "it is not what happens that matters, it is how one responds to it that matters." Heroic fatalism is a more radical in its approach than Stoicism, perhaps. Other Greco-Roman virtues (from bona-fide Stoics or not) would have resonated with the Vikings, such as Tacitus's "*If you must go, go boldly*," and "*In valor there is hope.*"

Heroic fatalism gave Vikings a serious edge over many of their enemies. Psychological elements are some of most powerful factors in combat. As mentioned in chapter one, Vikings armed with a sense of heroic fatalism would have nothing to lose and everything to gain in battle, while the defenders would almost certainly struggle with the natural human emotions of fear. We now know that the biochemistry of fear and excitement are really no different – it is only how these chemical signals are interpreted by the mind that separates terror and arousal. So, as the Vikings would become more excited as their shield wall advanced, while many among the native defenders (especially the citizen-soldiers of the part-time *fyrds*) would become increasingly fearful. There are few things more intimidating than someone who is not the least bit intimidated, and this is what the defenders would have seen as the Vikings drew nearer.

Battles are made up of many, many factors. The Vikings did not always win. Some of the Vikings' enemies were very capable, and sometimes the desperate passion of these defenders proved more powerful than heroic fatalism. There were also times as well that Viking heroic fatalism seems to have back-fired in terms of results, such as in the Battle of Stamford Bridge, where some of the Viking relief force even cast-off their armor in order to rush at their enemies faster. The appalling casualties at the Battle of Clontarf, as well, suggest a losing side that happily chose death over dishonor. In both these battles, the Vikings are believed to have suffered casualties of 80-90 percent.

Ultimately, belief in the gods, the intractability of fate, and the existence of an afterlife for the worthy, combined with a familiarity with death and hardship and a social structure that rewarded bravery while punishing weakness made the Vikings one of the most feared and respected warrior cultures that have ever lived.

Most of us do not live lives that require us to be this comfortable with the inevitability of our own destruction; and we also know now that it is not only strength that deserves respect. Most of us also do not think about fate as much, or believe that the divine makes the same requirements of us that Odin did for his followers. But the Viking mindset, as much as their exploits, is still something that we can learn from and hold up as an ideal. We may find that the world is actually a less-frightening place when we focus less on our problems and more on how we face them.

Chapter IV: Odoacer, Cuthbert, and Charles Martell – 3 Glances at Europe Before the Vikings

Odoacer, the Fall of Rome, and the Migration Era

On September 4th, 476 – about 317 years before the dawn of the Viking Age – Romulus Augustus, emperor of the Western Roman Empire came face to face with Odoacer, the "barbarian" general who had killed his father, defeated his army, and pursued him to his last stronghold of Ravenna. Romulus was only 14 years old and had been placed on the throne by his father, Orestes (another Romanized Germanic general) only ten months before. Romulus was the fourth emperor in five years, and that, along with his age and the dubious way in which he was elevated to the throne, made him so unpopular that people called him Romulus Augustulus ("Little Emperor Romulus"), or more cruelly, "Momyllus" ("Little Disgrace").

Despite Romulus's lack of popularity with his people, it was the Germanic *foederati* (foreign tribes who served Roman interests as mercenaries) who rebelled against him first. Odoacer was the leader of this band of Heruli, Sciri, and Turcilingi. His complete victory over the accomplished general Orestes and the taking of the stalwart city of Ravenna showed him to be an officer of great talent.

Luckily for Romulus, Odoacer was also a merciful man. He stated that the "little emperor" was too young to die, as so many others had. In an equally unexpected move, he took the crown jewels and the Tyrion Purple vestments (only emperors of Rome were allowed to wear this color made from oyster shells from the bay of Tyre), folded them neatly, and sent them to the Eastern Roman Emperor. These articles of authority over all the lands of Italy, Gaul (France), Spain, and Britain (theoretically) were accompanied by a politely-worded letter asking the East to not appoint any more Western Emperors, as they had undeniably become an unnecessary distraction.

So, Romulus was exiled to live in comfortable obscurity, Odoacer was named King of Italy, and in this anticlimactic way, the Roman Empire ended in the west.

The Roman Empire was one of humankind's greatest accomplishments. Rome went from an aggressive city-state republic in Italy around 700 B.C. to an empire that spread from the windswept moors of Britain to the palm oases of Iraq, and from the forests of Germany to the Nile in Egypt. Those lands and peoples that were not controlled by Rome were still affected by it, becoming trading partners, or serving Rome as mercenaries (as Odoacer's people did). Rome was more than a political superpower, it was a unifying identity, with all citizens of this vast dominion thinking of themselves as Romans.

The Romans could be alarmingly cruel, but their primary method of controlling so much territory was not through fear, but through inclusivity. The basic model Rome used was to take over an area through shock and awe, but then to offer the people there a place in the Roman collective through trade and by building cities. While country people in the far-reaches of the empire might not notice a big difference, but would go on speaking their languages, keeping their customs, and worshiping their gods; men and women in cities all over the world saw these cultures and religions syncretize, and could speak a common language. The rule of law and the security brought through Rome's armies (which grew with every people they conquered) became the *Pax Romana* – the Peace of Rome.

The *Pax Romana* and the prosperity caused by all this collective effort ensured that human culture and civilization moved forward. Under Rome, Europe, Africa, and Western Asia reached levels of peace, plenty, population growth, cultural achievement, life expectancy, and other markers of human optimization that have not been reached again until recently. As a republic, Rome lasted 500 years, and then as an empire Rome lasted an additional 500 years in the west. It was divided not in terms of boundaries but in terms of leadership, for the sake of efficiency in the 4th century. The Eastern Roman Empire (called the Byzantine Empire by historians, for clarity sake, though these Eastern Romans made no such distinction) lasted an additional thousand years until Constantinople finally fell in 1453.

The great historian Edward Gibbon said, "The question is not 'why did Rome fall?' but 'why did it last so long?'." Experts have hypothesized more than 200 reasons for Rome's collapse. Which combination of these many factors it may have been is the perennial topic of academic debate, but the mechanism by which the Western Roman Empire fell was set into motion by a tremendous crisis at the beginning of the 5th century, a few decades before Odoacer was born.

Rome had been united under a very effective emperor known as Theodosius the Great. But when Theodosius died in 395, he left the Empire again divided between east and west, with each half led by one of his sons. While his son Arcadius, the Eastern Emperor, was weak and sickly, Theodosius's son Honorius was indolent, incompetent, and grossly negligent at almost every turn. Unfortunately for the people of Rome, it was at this moment that a triple-threat of fantastic proportions was unleashed upon them.

The first arm of this triple-threat to Rome was a great, warlike host of people called the Goths. The Goths were originally from Scandinavia and showed distinctly Viking-like characteristics whenever they came in contact with water. For about two hundred years, they had been occupying lands just outside of the northeastern edge of the empire, in what are today Hungary, Bulgaria, and Romania. In the late 4th century, the Goths were put completely on the run by an even fiercer confederation of tribes – the Huns. To escape the Huns, the Goths made a treaty with Rome to allow them to cross the Danube and come inside the Eastern Empire.

If the Romans had known just how much damage the Huns would someday cause them, they might have treated the Goths better, but petty Roman bureaucrats mismanaged the Gothic migration so badly that the Goths rebelled, ravaged the countryside, crushed the Eastern Roman Army, and even killed the Emperor.

Peace was eventually made, and the Goths began serving Rome again as mercenary armies. But when Theodosius the Great came to the throne he sought to solve his Gothic problem by using these allies (Gothic *foederati*) as suicide soldiers.

Though at first happy to fight, the Goths quickly came to resent the duplicitous treatment by their Roman "allies." New rebellion was not long in coming. Around the time Theodosius died, a man named Alaric became king of the Goths and led this great host (their ranks swollen by other "barbarians" and escaped slaves) on a rampage throughout Italy, Greece, and Thrace.

To make matters worse, the only Roman general who could match Alaric in combat – Honorius's father-in-law, Stilicho – was killed at Honorius's command on trumped-up charges of treason. Alaric's Goths were then unstoppable – and yet, all they wanted was a favorable treaty, which Honorius refused to give them. In 408, Alaric besieged Rome and was bought-off with a humiliating tribute from the Eternal City. Honorius's situation worsened when the Goths raised up a Roman senator as a puppet emperor. Still, Honorius was in Italy, hiding in

Ravenna (as Romulus later would) just a few days' march away from a winning Gothic army and their replacement for him.

But that was only one of his problems.

On New Years' Eve, 406, primary sources say, it was so cold that the great river, Rhine, that separated Roman Gaul from the lands of the Germanic tribes, completely froze over. It was in the dead of this miserable winter – a time that no one would wander far from home, much less raid – that whole tribes of Sueves, Vandals, and Alans walked across the ice into what is now France and Belgium.

We do not know what motivations would drive such desperate action (though the "butterfly effect" of the Huns is again suspected), but the results were devastating for Rome. The Germanic forces overwhelmed the Roman garrisons on the border and drove into the snowy countryside, taking food and shelter at the expense of the Roman civilians. *"All of Gaul,"* says our primary source, Zosimus, *"burned as on a single pyre."*

The Alps were snowed over, and so no one could come to save the defenseless Romans. The Germanic Frankish tribes who helped Rome defend its border claimed to hold to their treaties but were unable to stop the flow of migration into the fertile fields, rich cities, and comfortable villas that were the jewel of one of Rome's oldest territories.

When spring finally came, however, Honorius took no action. Distracted by his Goth problem, his dying brother, Arcadius, in the East, and his palace intrigues, Honorius let the Romans of Gaul and Spain fend for themselves.

Finally, around the summer of 407, an army did come to help the people of Gaul and Spain against the Germanic invaders – and this was Honorius's third problem.

Also suffering from perceived imperial neglect and repeated incursions by the Germanic Saxons, the Romans of Britain had spent 406 and 407 in revolt. They went through two usurpers quite quickly, but the third was a battle-hardened soldier named Constantine. When Constantine (who is known to history as Constantine III and should not be confused with Constantine the Great of the previous century) became "emperor" in Britain, he immediately crossed with an army of perhaps 6,000 Roman soldiers to land in Gaul.

Though vastly outnumbered, Constantine won victories against the Germanic invaders (who were scattered after months of rampaging). As he won, Constantine applied the time-honored Roman strategy of turning beaten enemies into *foederati* allies and using these now-friendly Germanic tribes to fight the other Germanic tribes. His strategy bore fruit, and soon Constantine's small army was backed by numerous Frankish, Sueve, Alani, and eventually even Burgundian peoples. Thankful to finally have help, the people of Gaul and Spain supported this usurper, and Constantine became the ruler of everything west of the Alps.

Such was the chaos of the age.

The Goths finally got angry enough at Honorius to sack Rome in 410 – a brutal blow to the Roman (and indeed, the European) psyche. This event was not the fall of Rome as an empire but seemed to herald the End Times in every way.

Meanwhile, Constantine's luck ran out. He lost Britain (which finally chose to give up on Rome altogether) and was betrayed by many whom he trusted. When Honorius finally did send armies into Gaul, it was not to attack the Germanic tribes that increasingly dominated the landscape, but instead to defeat Constantine. In 411 they succeeded.

But the aristocracy of Gaul and Spain who had supported Constantine expected both brutal retributions to themselves coupled with more negligence towards their domains should Honorius regain control, and so they raised up more usurpers. The Roman government in Italy responded by finally making peace with the Goths – and offering them land in Gaul and Spain to crush these new rebels. So, the chaos intensified, along with staggering loss of life, and shifting alliances that the most ardent student of history struggles to follow.

As this was happening, the Vandals who had crossed the Rhine had now moved into Spain, and from there they took ship to northern

Africa. The Vandals were also originally a Scandinavian people, and as they swept across Roman Africa, they acquired more strength, more confidence, and more ships. They unleashed their natural talent for naval warfare into terrorizing the rich Roman cities along the Mediterranean and even destroyed the massive Roman navy sent to check their meteoric rise. In 455 they, too, sacked the city of Rome, furthering the humiliation of the once-great ruler of the west, and making it undeniable that the world had changed irrecoverably. This sack was more brutal and sustained than the Gothic sack had been, and so the Vandals have passed their name on to the English language for one who destroys for the sake of destruction.

It was at this same time that the full fury of the Huns was unleashed as Attila and his hordes swept relentlessly west from the grasslands of Asia. The Huns were different from the Germanic invaders that had been devouring the Roman world. As damaging as the Goths, Alans, Sueves, and others were, it was never their intention to destroy Rome. Rather, the Germanic tribes were seeking a prosperous place for themselves within the paradigm of the Empire. They wanted to share in this wealth and security, as they repeatedly demonstrated not only by their easily-shifted allegiances but also by their eager assimilation of Roman culture. Conversely, the Huns seemed to want to destroy Rome and anyone else who opposed them. Under Attila, they very nearly succeeded.

But Attila, his Huns, and their Germanic and non-Germanic allies were stopped in Gaul by an alliance of Romans, Goths, and Franks. The Huns were beaten back, and Attila died under mysterious circumstances not long afterward. The descendants of the Huns can be found all through Eastern Europe today, but they never threatened the Roman empire the same way as they did under their great leader Attila.

The damage to Rome was already done, though. The defeat of the Huns did not bring about a return to Roman peace or prosperity. It was clear to all that western Rome was unraveling. It was into this theater of uncertainty that Odoacer entered with his Heruls, Scirians, and Turcilings in the mid-fifth century.

Odoacer was about 43-years old when he deposed Romulus and took control of Italy. He is thought to be the son of a man who was one of Attila's chief advisors (though this is sometimes debated). Odoacer's tribe, the Sciri, was a relatively minor people of whom not a great deal is known. His allies, the Heruls are more familiar, but aside from their valor in battle much of what Roman writers documented about them paints them as the most barbarous of the invaders. Odoacer did not present himself that way, though. Like many of the Germanic leadership of the day, he had an excellent knowledge of Latin, Roman warcraft, culture, and customs. Some state that Odoacer was an officer in the Roman army itself, and not just a member of the Sciri *foederati* (the two views are not necessarily mutually exclusive). In any case, Odoacer frequently referred to himself as a *patrician* (high-ranking Roman official) instead of the king and added the Roman name Flavius ("Blonde" or "Golden") to his Germanic name. That Odoacer chose this name, which is associated with many previous Roman emperors, was certainly no accident.

Like many of the other Germanic invaders, Odoacer had adopted the religion of the Romans, Christianity. Herein lies another problem, however. While Christianity spread over the Roman world in the first few centuries of the common era, the faith was not completely standardized. It was not until the Council of Nicea in 335 that it was finally determined what marked the official, universal Christian faith. The many, many forms of Christianity that contained doctrines that did not conform with the Catholic faith institutionalized at Nicea then became heresies. A church document from around Odoacer's time lists over 400 heretical forms of Christianity. The problem was made larger in that many of the Germanic tribes that had been in contact with Rome over the years had already converted to one of these pre-Nicean forms: Arian Christianity.

Arian Christianity rejects the doctrine of the Trinity and therefore was considered by the Catholic Church to be heretical. Meanwhile, Arians like the Vandals and the Goths considered the Catholics to be heretics. With increasing numbers of Germani in power within the former empire, religious strife (which could be violent) broke out anew.

Our word *bigot* (derived from Alaric's people, the Visigoths) comes from these conflicts.

King Odoacer set an example, however, and saw that religious tolerance was practiced in Italy. He tried to ensure that both Romans and Germani received justice and were treated fairly. His reign prospered, and in time he added to his kingdom the territory of Dalmatia (including modern-day Croatia) on the opposite bank of the Adriatic Sea. He did not, however, attempt to gain anywhere-near the amount of territory that a western emperor would have considered their due.

The fifth-century world was too turbulent a place for Odoacer's reign to last. His kingship had always been at least nominally endorsed by the Eastern Roman Emperor, Zeno, in Constantinople. But when Odoacer – now towards the end of his fifties – put down a rebellion of the Rugii tribe in the Balkans, Zeno began to feel that he had let this neighbor become too powerful. So, Zeno influenced the Gothic king Theoderic to attack Odoacer.

When the few years of pitched warfare ended in a draw, Theoderic found a chance to kill Odoacer by subterfuge. By his own hand, the Gothic king cut Odoacer down while they had dinner together. Theoderic would later admire his own martial technique, telling his friends that the sword went so deep, it was as if the old man had no bones. Apparently lamenting how such a treacherous end could have come to him after his life or mercy and tolerance, Odoacer's last words as he bled out were "Where is God?" But it was Theoderic who summed up the spirit of this wolf age when he answered, "This is what you have done to my people, so this is what I did to you." The next action of this king of the new Ostrogothic Italy was to have all of Odoacer's family murdered.

Odoacer came onto the world stage from obscurity, and after less than two decades (during which time he seems to have done his best to be just and fair) he and his line had vanished forever. This was how the 5th century was, a time when the greatest power in Western Europe so quickly and irrecoverably fell apart and were replaced by chaos. It was the end of Antiquity or the Classical Era and the beginning of what has long been called the Dark Ages. The term Dark Ages comes from the frightening view of life we get from those centuries, but more so from the scarcity of written sources we have from it. The conclusion of most traditional historians has been that the chaos and violence of the era made our sources "go dark."

Many contemporary historians have started to challenge this, though. Experts like Peter Brown state that while there may have been war, famine, and plague that by no means meant that civilization somehow ground to a halt or that every life was grim. Some go so far as to state that "Rome" never really ended at all, as there were always people somewhere carrying on those institutions and expectations that were the essence of the Roman world.

Other historians vigorously counter this, acknowledging that yes – things were not singularly bad – but that the evidence does point to significant collapse in economics, population, and expectations. Civilization, as we think of it, had certainly slowed down its development. One snippet of telling evidence: according to the study of human remains in Britain, a person was four times more likely to be stabbed to death after the end of the Roman Empire than they were before!

Whether it is right to call the time after 476 the Dark Ages, or whether it is right to consider it Late Antiquity – the continuation of what the Classical World, just under changed circumstances – the nature of government and other institutions was different after Odoacer deposed Romulus. One of the most unmistakable features of this period (i.e., 400-800) is the tremendous amount of movement of peoples. Historians, anthropologists, and ethnographers on both sides of the debate often refer to this time in the Early Middle Ages as the Migration Era. It was as if the map of the Roman world had suddenly become a high-stakes game of musical chairs. Peoples from Sweden could wind up in northern Africa, while peoples from the prairie lands of western Asia could be assimilated and forgotten amongst the peoples of Spain.

These extensive movements of peoples were difficult for these nomadic tribes but were probably even harder on the native population who endured one wave of foreigners after another. That these tribes usually came as warrior elites (either endorsed by or in opposition to the native governments) only made things worse.

These migrations formed the political landscape the Vikings would encounter 317 years after Romulus – Europe would no longer be one empire then, nor were there nations (as we think of them). The Vikings encountered a Europe that was shaped by the wanderings of other Germanic peoples and the struggles with the Roman populations they encountered, and the shape of this landscape was largely one of petty kings and small kingdoms.

Paradoxically, the mindset of the people in these kingdoms was not as insular as the kingdoms themselves. Rome was gone, but Roman ideals and culture had not been forgotten, as we shall see in our next glimpse of Europe before the Vikings.

Saint Cuthbert of Northumbria, the Monastic Movement, and the Medieval Church

In the mid-seventh century, in the Saxon kingdom of Northumbria, lived a young man named Cuthbert. Some legends say Cuthbert was the son of an Irish king, while most sources say that he was of the humble, Briton-Saxon origins of his home, Melrose, near what is now the English-Scottish border.

In any case, we first meet Cuthbert at the age of 16, while he is tending sheep. Saint Aiden, an Irish evangelist remembered as the

"Apostle to the Saxons", had just died; and the pious young Cuthbert saw a vision of the venerated old man being carried up to heaven by angels. At that moment, the young man knew that he wanted to become a monk, like those of the nearby abbey at Melrose that had so profoundly influenced him … or better yet, the monks of the famous monastery at Lindisfarne, about 45 miles away.[3]

His ambitions of becoming a priest and a scholar would have to wait, however. The kingdoms of the Isle of Britain – which include four major Anglo-Saxon kingdoms, three minor ones, the Celtic kingdoms now known as Wales and Cornwall, as well as the Scotts and the Picts to the north – are often at war with each other. At the time of Aiden's death and young Cuthbert's vision, King Pendra of Mercia was preparing to invade Northumbria with a large army. So, Cuthbert exchanged his shepherd's crook for a spear and went to war.

We next see Cuthbert about four years later, riding back into Melrose on a horse, carrying his spear on his shoulder. He had done well in the war, and the people of Northumbria preserved their kingdom; but Cuthbert was more than ready to leave the horrors of medieval tribal warfare behind to finally pursue his dream. He took his vows and joined the monastic community.

---

[3] There can be some confusion about the difference between an abbey and a monestary, and indeed historically there can be some overlap. It is not so much a distinction of size or gender. Both are religious communities were monks and/or nuns reside, work, and worship. Abbeys are ordered somewhat differently and are under the management of an abbot or abbess.

We are told that as a monk Cuthbert has a very serious but gentle nature, and that he was often moved to tears, especially during mass. He was hard-working and eager both in evangelism and in acts of charity to the poor. The medieval people of Europe fully believed in miracles, and many of these were ascribed to the young monk as well. By the time Cuthbert was about thirty, he became headmaster of a new monastery at Rippon.

By Cuthbert's time, monastic life already had a long history. The idea that those wanting to cultivate the spirit should try to separate themselves from the cares and distractions of the temporal world is one common to many cultures. During the early days of the Church, many Christians believed that the world had few years ahead of it anyway, and that the life of the spirit was the only one that mattered. They began to form communities in desolate areas, away from cares and persecutions. They had examples in their scriptures to inspire them, for Moses, many of the prophets, John the Baptist, and Jesus had all sought periods of fasting and seclusion. The very influential apostle, Paul, had written some of his best work while in prison and Saint John had written his apocalypse while in exile on the island of Patmos. There were non-Christian examples too, found in Egyptian and Greco-Roman mystical cults (many of whom were flourishing around the same time that the Church was growing).

As Christianity spread to northwestern Europe, monks and ascetics found that the wind-swept sea and the rocky shores were as close to God as any eastern desert could be, and so they began to form these communities there. In Ireland, the far-flung edge of the world, monasteries proliferated.

After the Saxons – who at the time of their invasions of Britain had more-or-less the same religion the Vikings did – pushed whatever degree of Christianity that had supplanted Roman or native paganism to the edges of the island, the Irish monks found that they had yet another missions field. Like Saint Aiden, they came to the Scottish, Pictish, and Saxon kingdoms, where they met with a great deal of success. By Cuthbert's day, probably the majority of Saxons were Christians, as they would be when the Vikings came almost 150 years later.

Now, we tend to think of abbeys and monasteries as places where austere monks sit in cold, dark rooms praying and painstakingly copying books by hand. There is some truth to that, and some monks lived lives that were very ascetic (including long hours of mental or physical toil, fasting and other privations of food, and various, creative ways to "mortify the flesh" or in other words, get their physical beings out of the way of their spiritual development). In the Middle Ages, rules were developed that gave these spiritual centers an almost military-level of order. In fact – their order was probably greater than many militaries of those days.

Abbeys and monasteries were much more than dreary scriptoriums, though. These places were the centers of learning and culture, intellectual discovery and discourse, music and the arts in the medieval world. While the European countryside and what dwindling cityscapes seem to have been fully preoccupied with simply avoiding famine, plague, and war, the collective culture of the Roman Empire continued within the stone walls of these monastic conservatories. While the monks and nuns were primarily concerned with Christian studies, and a great deal of secular knowledge of the Roman world was lost in favor of saints' lives and the like, most of what we have left from the Greco-Roman philosophers comes to us through the diligent efforts of these monastic scribes.

Monks also preserved (and even sometimes set into writing for the first time) material that was not only secular, but pagan; works like the *Iliad*, *Odyssey*, the *Táin Bó Cúalnge* of Ireland, the Anglo-Saxons' favorite, *Beowulf*, and – eventually – even the Norse sagas. It is not hyperbole to say that the monks and nuns of the middle ages saved civilization. If it were not for them, we would not have (as Isaac Newton put it) "the shoulders of giants" on which to stand.

Medieval monasteries, abbeys, and other spiritual centers were also, in many cases, very wealthy. The idea of material sacrifice for spiritual gain is heavily imbedded into the human psyche and can be found in almost all cultures. But Christianity did not require animal sacrifice, and so monetary sacrifice was seamlessly substituted in the minds of both the clergy and the congregation. Monasteries received regular offerings from the people who lived around them. This income could take on the aspect of taxation, something that the medieval Church has often been criticized for. The lion's share of Church wealth, however, was from another source: since the late Roman Empire, nobility had been making large (sometimes very, very large) donatives to the Church and to sacred centers as a way of not only securing their salvation but to demonstrate the grandeur of their wealth.

Because of the high social status of the Church, and the nobility's need to have enough children survive to adulthood to ensure an heir but then not have to divide their property amongst many heirs, noble families often sent their younger sons and daughters into monasteries and abbeys. Hence, most of these centers would have strong connections to the rich and powerful.

So, in the agrarian society with few cities, wealth would aggregate and accumulate either in the strongholds of the ruling class or in the monasteries.

While wherever there are people there can be corruption and abuse, the average monk or nun did not misuse this wealth in ways that we would normally think of financial misuse – their food was plain (or, when fasting, non-existent) their clothes uniform (except for ceremonial vestments for higher status individuals), and they had no retirement program. While some individuals may have been indolent or selfish, as a group, monks and nuns valued preaching to hostile audiences, helping the poor or sick, and even martyrdom. As the Vikings would later discover, the monks would eagerly part with chests of cash to ransom back an old man, or even the bones of a dead saint, so money to them was a means to an end. Rather, the wealth of medieval monasteries enabled monks and nuns to live the lives apart that they wanted to live, and to create all the gilded, jeweled ornaments that they thought showed the grandeur of their god.

They would soon find that their wealth could be a curse as well as a blessing.

Cuthbert's time at Ripon was limited. During the seventh century, there was a huge debate in the churches of Britain and Ireland. Looking back, we identify the two sides of this debate as the Celtic Rite versus the Roman Rite. The Roman Rite was that of the mainland Catholic Church; the Celtic were the customs that had evolved in the rich monastic traditions of Ireland, where so many missionaries originated.

To the non-Catholic mind, the differences of these two traditions seem very small: the day on which Easter should be celebrated, how monks should cut their hair, and obscure differences in baptisms. But these differences were big enough to the monks of Cuthbert's day to fight about.

This may have less to do with the differences themselves and more to do with history. There was tremendous theological diversity in the early Church, but when the doctrines were made official at the Council of Nicea in 335, as we have mentioned, there was a great deal of strife between "orthodox" and "heterodox" sects that exacerbated conflict between ethnic and political groups. It appears that after the smoke started to clear from the wars of the 5th and 6th centuries involving heterodox (Arian) Germanic tribes, the Medieval Catholic Church was intent on not letting any differences of doctrine get that bad again.

Unfortunately, this policy of homogeny became a feature of the Middle Ages in general, sometimes going well-beyond intellectual appeals into armed struggle and creating great loss of life and loss of liberty. It would go on to impact several crusades (not only those in the Holy Land, but also those against the Cathars, etcetera), lead to the Great Schism between the Roman and Greek churches, and later impact relations between native populations with Viking colonists.

Medieval intolerance would become an entrenched habit. The following ages would see religious ideals exploited for military power on many sides, and most states seeking to justify their aggression with appeals to divine right.

Cuthbert had no interest in pursuing any belligerent aspects of religious quarrels. He represented his school of Celtic Christianity well whenever he could, but when Ripon adopted the Roman Rite, Cuthbert retreated to the Celtic fold at Melrose. When the Synod of Whitby decided once and for all in favor of the Roman Rite, Cuthbert accepted the decision. It was this humble acquiescence that led to him finally being assigned to Lindisfarne, so that his even-keeled personality could help smooth things over with the strongly-Celtic adherents there.

Cuthbert would stay at Lindisfarne for only about two years before attempting to retire as a hermit. Though only in his late forties, his health had never recovered from war and a serious illness in his twenties, and – reading between the lines – maybe he just wanted to get away from all the politics so that he could concentrate on his actual spirit.

He was called out of retirement for his talents and status and sent to Lindisfarne once more, before again retiring and soon thereafter dying (age 52) at his hermitage with the monks of Lindisfarne standing somberly at his bedside.

Cuthbert became the patron saint of Northumbria. More miracles were attributed to Cuthbert's corpse (which allegedly remained "uncorrupted") than the holy man had instrumented in his life, and his shrines became the site of veneration for years to come. When forced to move to safety, to avoid Vikings or other political problems, the monks of Lindisfarne would carry Cuthbert with them, so that in many biographies the story of his weary remains takes up more lines than his life.

Charles Martel, the Islamic Invasions of Europe, and the Rebirth of European Empires

The Western Roman Empire had collapsed into a mosaic of petty kingdoms, but its ideals were still alive in the European imagination. Roman learning and organizational structure lived on in the Church, while secular Europe struggled against the myriad cares of the age. Some still believed that Roman-style power could again be brought into effect, if only a ruler and his people were capable enough to do it.

As is so often the case in history, it was only through greater crisis that the opportunity for this strengthening of centralized power became possible.

This crisis came from the east and the south. Towards the end of the 7th century, the wanderings of the Germanic peoples of the Migration Age were beginning to slow down, but elsewhere another migration was beginning. In Arabia, a prophet named Muhammed introduced a new religion, Islam. With its doctrines of submission unto God and its imperative to spread the faith throughout all lands, Islam was embraced by the Arabic Moors and the Turkish Seljuks and (much later) Ottomans. All three of these groups were tough, nomadic warrior cultures that fought on horseback. All three of these groups were growing and ready to expand their borders.

The combination of military acumen, population explosion, and religious fervor have ever been the charcoal, sulfur, and salt-peter of history, and now these Muslim forces were ready to conquer. In the late 7th century, they launched a series of offenses that put the Byzantine Empire on its heels. Meanwhile the Moors obliterated the Vandals of North Africa and then, in 711, crossed the Straits of Gibraltar to attack Spain.

The ancestors of the Goths of Spain had humiliated the Romans and even finally chased off the Huns years before. However, in the early 8th century, they were disorganized and consumed with internal quarrels. The Moors conquered most of Spain in just three years, leaving the Goth-Iberians just a few small kingdoms in Northern Spain and Portugal. The Moors would dominate Spain for more than 700 years, calling the land *al-Andalus*, from their name for the Goths and Vandals.

Once they had taken the rich fields of Spain it was not long before the Moors began looking across the Pyrenees into the lands formerly known as Roman Gaul. The Islamic military machine began devouring land in Aquitaine and Bordeaux, along with territory in Provence. In 732, they concerted their efforts into taking over the rest of Gaul, an action that would set them in a good position to conquer all Europe and set the former Roman world to be crushed in a pincer attack from west and east.

At this pivotal moment, a man named Charles Martel (Charles the Hammer), the bastard son of a petty ruler, intercepted the Moors with his mobile force of cavalry and light infantry composed of Franks and various allies. At the Battle of Tours (also called the Battle of Poirtier) Charles the Hammer destroyed the Moorish forces with a 10:1 casualty rate, killed their Emir, Abdul al-Rahman, and broke their momentum entirely.

It would take further efforts to drive the Moors back into Spain, but "Christendom" was saved. Moreover, the concept of Christendom was solidified, and violent rivalries between Christian kingdoms – while barely abating – began to be recognized as counter-productive.

Charles Martel was called a "mayor" of the Merovingian Dynasty (similar to the British or Scottish idea of a steward) and not a king due to his illegitimate birth. The Battle of Tours made him a great hero, and more territories and peoples accepted his rule. Still, he spent the next decade or more fighting to consolidate a kingdom and to defend it from further Moorish incursions. He passed this realm on to his son, Pepin the Short, who (through a usurpation supported by the Pope) took control from the last Merovingian king and thus became the first king of the Carolingian Dynasty.

Pepin's son was the famous Charlemagne – Charles the Great. After imposing his will on a wide stretch of Europe, Charlemagne revived the title of Roman Emperor in the west. Though his less-capable progeny could not continue in this ambition, he showed that unity and centralization were again possible.

Though mired in the here-and-now struggles of enmity and foreign threats, people's hope in something better (peace, stability, and prosperity) was rekindled.

Charlemagne's hands were red with blood by the time he was anointed Holy Roman Emperor, and his reign made him as many enemies as it did friends. His reign also brings us (finally) to the dawn of the Viking Age, and late in his life the Emperor would look out the windows of his grand tower and see dragon ships on the waves.

PART TWO: THE SAGA OF THE VIKING AGE

V: The Dragon Ships

In the latter days of Spring, 793, the monks of Lindisfarne knew that something horrible was about to happen. The previous harvest had been poor, and famine threatened parts of Northumbria, and now the weather on the exposed peninsula where the monastery was built was plagued by frequent tempests and violent storms. Great displays of lightning filled the sky and thunder interrupted prayers in the cloisters. Some monks had even seen dragons whirling through the air, circling high above the sacred church of Saint Cuthbert, the sacramental seat of the northern kingdom. Whether the chronicler's sparse words describe the monks' impassioned interpretation of cloud formations, or whether these dragons were visions, the portents could not have been more apt.

Every event in history is the result of a well-balanced equation of other events and occurrences. The dawn of the Viking Age was the result of several pressures – the overpopulation of a Scandinavia strained by cold, a culture that depended on war, solidifying political power pushing independent people out, and the irresistible lure of wealth. Valid as these factors may be, none of them could have created the crucible of the Viking Age without one thing: the quantum leap of technology that was the Viking longship.

Scandinavians have always been into their ships. Greco-Roman geographers in the first century immediately mention the ship in connection with the peoples of those northern territories. This is not surprising considering the thousands of miles of coastline and hundreds of islands of the region, or that the challenges of inland living kept population centers along these coasts. For the Scandinavians, there were livelihoods to be made in fishing, whaling, and the hunting of other aquatic mammals for food, fuel, and ivory. The ship was so important in Scandinavian culture that the most high-status people were buried or cremated in ships while people of lesser means were still interred in graves shaped like ships.

However, ships before the end of the 8th century were different. They were suitable for transporting goods or fighting men along the coasts, but there was a reason why the ancients took their pre-voyage sacrifices so seriously. These ships had no keel, and so could easily be capsized on the open seas. When the Anglo-Saxons invaded Roman and post-Roman Britain in the beginning of the Migration Era, most of their ships did not even have sails. Mediterranean ships, by contrast, were extravagant vehicles that had sails, oars, multiple decks, and various highly-refined design features. These ships were difficult and expensive to make, however, and were still best suited for island-hopping in the sunny, southern seas and not crossing long stretches of rough water (as the numerous wrecks discovered on the bottom of the Mediterranean, Aegean, and Black Seas attest).

During the 8th century, Scandinavian ships evolved from the clunky, slow, unstable ships of their Germanic neighbors. Norse ships began to feature a keel – the spine at the bottom of the ship that cuts the water, providing stability and speed.[4]

With the keel, masts (which could be as high as 40 feet in the largest ships) became more practical. While the keel increased stability, the large, single sail (some of which were 15 feet tall, and contained 950 square feet of tightly-woven, treated cloth) greatly increased the ships' range.

The steering oar (forerunner of the rudder) was also added to improve responsiveness and negate the need to steer by coordinated effort of oarsmen.

One of the greatest differences between a Viking craft and other ships of the time was that the longship had a very shallow draft, sitting in just a few feet of water.

All these innovations meant that, beginning in the late 8th century, Vikings could cross the ocean with confidence and speed, augmenting their sails with oars but still saving much of their strength, then maneuver into narrow inlets where they could then travel up rivers that were hitherto only navigable by ordinary fishing boats. Quite suddenly, the Vikings could go farther, strike deeper, and disappear faster than any other force before them ever had.

---

[4] Before the Viking Age and the invention of the keel, the word "keel" was used to simply mean "warship", and so this transfer of word meaning to this part of the Viking's ship suggests that the advantage of this feature was quickly appreciated. I.e., the keel "makes" the longship a war ship.

These long, sleek, fast ships were called *langskip* by the Norse (as opposed to the heavier, slower *knörr* trading ships), but have often been referred to as dragon ships. The sight of these ships in action would have immediately called to mind the dragons and sea serpents of Germanic mythology to Viking and non-Viking alike, and it was an association the Vikings wanted to reinforce. The prows of the *langskip* were often carved in elaborate dragon head designs, adding to their frightening appearance. Sagas also remark that the best warships were brightly painted above the water line and, of course, had the warrior's shields decking the gunwales. The sight of one or more of these vessels emerging from the fog must surely have had significant adverse psychological impact on any would-be defenders.

According to Icelandic law of the later Viking Age, the dragon heads were only to be displayed if the longship was raiding, and were to be veiled or removed (when removable) if the ship was trading, as not to distress the land spirits that inhabited each place. From this we can gather that the dragon features of the *langskip* was not merely for decoration or bravado, but were meant to terrify natural and supernatural forces alike as the Vikings came for war.

Dragon ships were built to flex with the forces of the water, rather than to resist them. They were built with overlapping pieces of oak, sometimes only about an inch thick. The boards were held into place by iron rivets. The dragon ship was built with green wood, so that as the wood cured the ship would tighten. Further water-tightness was achieved by stuffing the joints and empty spaces with moss or hair mixed with pitch. This water-tightness only went so far, and – along with the fact that the top of the ship was only a few feet above the water's surface – at least one Viking was probably on water-bailing duty at all times, even in good weather. This was normal in pre-modern ships. Still, the flexibility of the longship must have created a unique feel on the wild, North Atlantic waves, and – along with the ships' long, sleek designs and the fearsome carved heads on the prows – added to the fittingness of the term, dragon ship.

Exactly how fast a dragon ship could go depended on conditions. Sailing with a decent current on a river, the Vikings may have been able to do forty miles a day – about twice as fast as the best Roman armies before them and several times faster than local *fyrd* militia. Rowing, especially against current, was slower. Average Viking ships had around 12-16 oars per side, which would allow an average sized crew to work in shifts of two hours on and two hours off. According to modern interpretation of sagas, along with experiments on replica ships, each two-hour shift would row about four nautical miles. Modern experiments show that the rowed vessels could go twice as fast for short periods of time (about 15 minutes or so) if Vikings needed to make a fast get-away or catch a fleeing enemy.

Vikings would avoid travelling at night as not to get lost, so on a summer day a Viking may spend up to eight hours rowing – showing how tremendously fit these people were. Speed in travel at sea was also dependent on the accuracy (and luck) of the navigator. Navigation in the Viking Age was much more of an art than a science, and so the differences in voyage times could be considerable. We will discuss Viking navigation more in a later chapter.

How Much Did a Dragon Ship Cost?

Owning even a single dragon ship made an individual quite important; not only for the potential of raiding and trading, but because the ships required a sizeable subset of the economy to produce. Ship building demanded the specialized labor of four distinct types of craftsmen, in addition to other laborers. Each ship was made of several, select oak trees. Oak was ideal because of its strength, but also because of the resistance it offered to aquatic parasites. Straight oaks from the forest made the masts and the long planks of the sides, whereas old, big, sprawling oaks that stood where there was plenty of room to grow offered the best wood for the curved or specialized parts of the vessel. Only about 25 percent of the harvested wood was of use for the ship, and so the crews that cut the trees would then decide if the value of the rest of the wood (for furniture, houses, weapons, or fire) matched the hardship of lugging it out of the forests where they had found it.

Much of Scandinavia was forested, predominantly with pine. Nonetheless, the requirement for very specific wood may have been one of the many factors for the Viking quest for more and more land. By the height of the Viking Age, the proliferation of dragon ships had outstripped the oak available, and lesser woods (eventually even cheap pine) were substituted.

Each dragon ship also contained about 350 pounds of iron in the form of nails, rivets, and joiners – something that was not easy to come by. The ideal rigging for the dragon ship included ropes made from seal or walrus leather, which required specialized hunters and tanners.

Last but not least, the massive square sail of the dragon ship took an estimated four years-worth of loom hours to produce, as well as the wool from a very large number of sheep. In other words, if one wanted their ship to be ready for the raiding season in late spring, one would need 10 women to start working on the sail by November, and would need to provide them with rooms full of wool or flax. In ancient and medieval Europe, weaving was considered the paramount feminine skill, and (along with more nefarious purposes) was a driving force in the Viking slave trade. Women kidnapped from Ireland, Scotland, Britain, or France may have found themselves working hard, thankless hours to produce sails to equip more kidnappers.

Because of the great expense of building, outfitting, and maintaining a longship, we can see why Viking naval warfare was usually focused on capturing a ship rather than destroying them, and why Moorish, Anglo-Saxon, or Byzantine forces burning their precious ships would immediately put the Vikings on the run.

Military Applications of the Dragon Ship

The primary military application of the dragon ship was the rapid deployment and escape of troops. A dragon ship could land about 30-60 warriors anywhere adjacent to just a few feet of water. Hull and keel wear on archeologically-recovered longships confirm that these vessels were landed directly onto the shore, with no secondary landing craft needed. When the longship was beached, the Viking warrior could be confident that the water he was about to jump into was only knee-deep.

Local military leaders were repeatedly shocked and dismayed by the Vikings' ability to attack targets more than 100 kilometers inland (by going up rivers) and then disappear out of reach. It would take the powers of Europe many years to find ways to counter such a distinct advantage in mobility.

Dragon Ships in Sea to Land Battle

Centuries later, with the development of the cannon, naval forces would attack seaside fortifications and other land assets directly. This was not usually practical in the Viking Age. Vikings could of course launch arrows, javelins, and other projectiles while safely on the decks of their ships, but it would be easy for land forces to simply step out of range.

Despite the suggestions of some experts, Viking longships most likely did not use heavy weapons like catapults or Roman-style *ballista* (giant crossbows). This technology was known (even well-established) but we do not have evidence of Norse naval use, and these weapons could prove dangerous to the stability of their own ships.

There are a few accounts of Vikings and others using their ship masts as floating siege towers to send warriors or projectiles over enemy walls when attacking seaside fortifications. Although this is difficult to imagine as a reliable strategy, it was successfully repeated by Venetian forces during the notorious Sack of Constantinople during the Fourth Crusade (just 146 years after the Vikings).

A ninth century Arab source describes the Vikings as "excelling in ship-borne rather than horse-borne combat."

Dragon Ships in Naval Battles

Ancient Mediterranean naval battles involved ships trying to ram and sink each other. With their thin hulls and curved prows, the Vikings usually avoided ramming. Viking naval battles involved crews of ships trying to kill each other in much the same way as they would on land (only now with the added risk of unstable platforms and certain drowning if one were to go over the side). Sometimes friendly ships would lash themselves together in "floating islands" to achieve the advantage in these battles, while other times hostile ships would try to join together to board and capture each other.

Most Viking naval battles were against other Vikings. At the time, few other kingdoms had the naval forces to compete with them. The Franks, beginning with Charlemagne, has some success using patrol boats to hinder the Vikings, but it proved inadequate. Alfred the Great thought to develop an English navy to solve his Viking problem, but he was not very successful in either the building of it or its use. It was more effective to use existing Viking enmities (or their readiness to be mercenaries) to protect native interests at sea. So, while it is tempting to call Alfred the father of what would one day be history's greatest navy, it is probably more accurate to say that the Vikings themselves were the fathers of the English Navy.

The Moors and Byzantines had some success against the Vikings at sea by changing the rules (as the Vikings saw it) and so the Vikings tried to make sure that did not happen again in the future. We will tell those stories properly in chapters nine and fifteen.

The Viking Age Begins: The Sack of Lindisfarne

Because most of Europe did not have anything like the technology of the dragon ship, they did not know the danger they were in until it befell them. Certainly, there had been centuries of piracy and seaborne raiding between Ireland and Britain; Germania and Britain; and between Britain and Gaul/Francia, but most of this had been across relatively narrow bodies of water and did not involve ships penetrating upriver.

Monks and other civilians living by the expansive sea did not think that ships could reach them, and even if ships could, they would not be able to land warriors so quickly or escape so completely. Abbeys and monasteries were built along the sea for this very reason – the remoteness offered them peace and protection. In these refuges they took their safety for granted, for the few enemies that would be sacrilegious or brazen enough to attack a church would have to cross through the lands of the monasteries' patron nobles to do it.

On June 8, 793, the monks of Lindisfarne and indeed all the people of Europe would find that this assumption of safety had been a fatal mistake.

On that late-spring morning, an unknown number of dragon ships led by an unknown leader landed on the stony shores of the Lindisfarne peninsula. The warriors leapt over the sides and raced up towards the church and the outer buildings. They grabbed everything valuable they could find (which was a great fortune, for the miracles attributed to Cuthbert and his corpse had made Lindisfarne a place of prestige and pilgrimage) and they slaughtered any monks who dared to resist. We are told that some of these hapless men were dragged down to the sea and forcibly drowned, and that others were carried away as slaves. The attack was sudden, swift, brutal, and complete, and the marauders were gone before any armed resistance could even begin to assemble.

As the terrified survivors spread the word, the kingdoms of Europe were left to wonder what was happening. As we described in the previous chapter, monasteries were more than just religious institutions – they were the centers of learning, music, art, and culture. In the generations since Cuthbert, Lindisfarne had grown in size, wealth, and prominence and become world-famous as the epicenter of what some historians now call the Northumbrian Renaissance. To put it in modern terms, the sudden destruction of Lindisfarne by Vikings would be like biker gangs looting and burning Harvard University.

The Vikings did not see it that way, though. To the Vikings, sacking a monastery was like robbing a bank, and they could not believe their luck that anyone would be foolish enough to leave so much gold and jewels lying around virtually undefended.

The Vikings had an oral culture not a written one (runes were predominantly for magical or ceremonial uses), and theirs was not an organized religion the way Christianity was. While we may understand that the peaceful resistance of Lindisfarne's unarmed monks required great bravery, the Vikings probably interpreted it as weakness (which only made them more violent, as weakness is despised in Norse culture). So, while the targeting of monasteries that was about to intensify has sometimes been portrayed or interpreted as a religious war, for the

Vikings it was usually "just business." It is safe to say that there were no injured consciences on the ships that left Lindisfarne for Scandinavia.

There was many an injured conscience in Christendom, though. It must be remembered that Medieval people (and Medieval Christians in particular) were very literal and that they made little distinction between the natural and the supernatural world. It also must be remembered that the Christian scriptures (especially the Old Testament) were full of examples of God chastising his chosen people through military defeats and other calamities.

Thus, hardly had the bodies of the martyred monks been pulled from the surf before the churchmen of Europe began responding to the disaster with self-deprecation and victim-blaming. The relationship between church and state being what it was, the monks of Lindisfarne had accepted financial gifts and political promises to allow the recently-dead king of Northumbria – a man who had been a usurper and had died as a suicide (which was a nearly-unpardonable sin in Medieval Church teaching) – to be buried on the monastery's consecrated ground. This had occurred only about two weeks before the attack, around the time (proponents of the theory may have argued) that the Vikings would have set sail.

Were the Vikings God's punishment for this or other sins? Many of the Christians of Europe began to think so. This line of thinking would soon become much more prevalent and would prove to become one of Christendom's major disadvantages in dealing with the Vikings.

Meanwhile, the Vikings who had ravaged Lindisfarne made it home and showed off the riches they had won to their friends and families. We can imagine the celebrations in the mead halls as men tried to outdo each other in their boasts and stories. It had been an unprecedented success, for as far as we know the Vikings had not lost a single man.

In these songs and tales that spread across the area, the real star (explicitly or implicitly) was the dragon ship. People must have begun to realize – if they had not already – the advantage that their ships gave them. They must have realized, too, that there was little point using their advantages in shipcraft, daring, and arms to fight each other when they could be helping themselves to the riches of the south that had been conveniently gathered and stored for their taking.

It took very little time for the Vikings to repeat their Lindisfarne experiment. The great abbey of Iona (in the Scottish isles) was sacked the following year. It would be sacked again and again, and in 806 almost all its inhabitants would be massacred. Other monasteries followed. It was as if for every dragon ship that returned laden with treasure, several more went out the following season.

From an economic perspective, the Norse had found a new "cash cow" and were not hesitant to apply their efforts to exploiting these resources. Foreign expeditions dramatically increased, ship building increased, more slaves were taken to make more sails, and warlords arose and became fabulously rich.

Soon it was not just the remote abbeys and monasteries on the windswept coasts that were vulnerable. The Vikings followed their fortunes deep into the European heartland, braving Charlemagne's empire and other capable enemies. There was no reason not to – fate was on their side and the Christians could do little to stop them. The Viking Age dawned over Europe, and change rode the waves on dragon ships.

Chapter VI: Ragnar Lothbrok

Ragnar Lothbrok (or Lodbrok) is one of the most interesting, celebrated, and controversial characters of the early Viking Age. Many scholars over the years have considered Ragnar to be legendary or semi-fictional, perhaps the composite of many figures who together represented some Viking ideal. This opinion is understandable, especially since one of the legends that occur in almost all the major sources is that of Ragnar slaying a giant serpent that guards a golden horde and a beautiful princess.

Spurious nature of some of these stories notwithstanding, Ragnar was – at least in some part – a real historical figure, whose life and death are implicated in some of the best-documented events of the 9th century.

Before looking at what we know about his life, we will first look at his legend. Ragnar is mentioned many times throughout medieval Scandinavian sagas and histories, but the most detailed accounts (on the Scandinavian side) that have come down to us are Book IX of Saxo Grammaticus' *Danish History*, *Ragnars Saga Lodbrok* (*The Saga of Ragnar Lodbrok and his Sons)*, and the *Krákumál* (or *Song of Kraka*, also called the *Death Ode of Ragnar*).

Of these sources, Saxo Grammaticus attempts to be the most organized and to present a dispassionate, reliable history. However, even he cannot resist the dragon slaying and other hyperbolic achievements of this incredible hero.

Ragnars Saga Lodbrok is a source we will come back to over and over again in the next few chapters because it portrays Viking culture and mindset so well, but the story itself is less reliable.

The *Krákumál* is a song reveling in the glory and gore of Ragnar's exploits, and it relays the Viking soul and sensibility as truly as any poem could, but all it offers to our tale is another list of Ragnar's wars to piece together. With less reliance on details (conflicting or otherwise) and more emphasis on the thrust of the tale and the personal clues that come with it, Ragnar and the other Vikings of his time begin to come to life.

Ragnar Lothbrok, According to Scandinavian Sources

According to Saxo, Ragnar was born in Zealand – one of the islands of Denmark, where Copenhagen stands today – as the son of the king, Siward. Ragnar's extended family, including his grandfather (also a king named Siward), were jarls in Norway (illustrating, once again, that the kingdoms and territories of this time were much different from the nations we have today). Ragnar's father, King Siward, had many enemies, and was a brave king who preferred to take his fight to other lands rather than invite invasion at home. It was at such a time when Siward and the strength of Zealand were engaged in raiding and tribal warfare elsewhere that a traitor by the name of Ring (or Hring) usurped his throne.

Other sagas reverse these roles, saying Ring was Ragnar's father and Siward his enemy, illustrating the many contradictions in the sources and difficulties in aligning our knowledge of this shadowy age.

To resist Ring, the loyal followers of Siward raised his son Ragnar up as king – though Ragnar was just a boy.

Even at this young age, Ragnar showed great charisma, wisdom, and courage and had that quality which made people want to follow him. Nonetheless, fearing for his safety his subjects sent him to his family in Norway to finish his training, while they fought for his family's throne.

Siward returned (we are not sure when) to save his brave subjects from Ring, and in a great battle he slew the usurper. Siward received a horrible wound through, and when Ragnar returned to Zealand he found that his father was dead.

Peace was indeed a fleeting thing in Scandinavia at this time, for though Ragnar now reigned in Zealand, a king of Sweden named Fro attacked his grandfather in Norway and killed him. Proving his wickedness, the Swedish King forced the women of the royal family into sex slavery for him and his men.

When Ragnar heard of these outrages, he and his followers took dragon ships to Norway to confront Fro and avenge his family. Ragnar's small army was not only joined by men loyal to his grandfather. Along the way they were met by women escaping King Fro's exploitation, who begged Ragnar to be allowed to fight back against this monster who had done them so much evil. Ragnar agreed, and so as his forces arrayed to fight the Swedish Vikings, he was accompanied by a young woman named Lagertha – a girl who "*though a maiden possessed the courage of a man, and fought in front among the bravest with her hair loose over her shoulders.*" With Lagertha's help, Ragnar slew Fro and drove the Swedes back across their borders.

Lagertha certainly merits her own chapter in this book, and so we will examine her part of the story more closely soon. Ragnar was quite taken with Lagertha, and she became his first wife (according to Saxo). Though their love lasted, their marriage did not, however, and though the two remained allies, they went their separate ways. It was at this juncture that Ragnar, who was still a young man (20 years-old, according to the *Krákumál*) with a small but valiant following, earned the name "Lothbrok."

Ragnar and Thora

There was a king in Denmark who had a lovely young daughter named Thora. One day when the king was hunting he found an especially beautiful serpent, whose scales glinted green and gold. The king knew his daughter loved animals, and the creature was too small to be much harm, and so he took it home as a gift for her. Thora was ecstatic, and immediately gave the serpent a shiny gold coin to roost on.

The next day there were two gold coins where there had been one, and the snake was twice as large.

The day after, the same thing happened, and so on … until the serpent coiled around and around the house, amidst a great horde of gold, and Thora was his prisoner.

After a few disasterous attempts to assault the lair and save his daughter, the distraught king offered Thora's hand in marriage, along with all the gold the serpent guarded, to anyone who could kill the beast. Some found the courage to try, and each of them lasted mere moments – for not only was the serpent massive, there was also highly-potent venom in his long fangs.

When Ragnar, who by now was divorced and more than a little restless, heard of this wonder, he had an idea. According to the saga, he took a pair of thick, leather chaps and boiled them in pitch. He then rolled them in sand before the pitch had hardened. The result was a flexible garment of great strength. Saxo's version of the story says that Ragnar's chaps were of fur-covered hide that he deliberately soaked in water and then allowed to freeze solid in the chill Scandinavian morning air. Ragnar was confident that this armor would protect him from the poison of the serpent, and so he took his spear and his shield and went to rescue Thora.

Ragnar knew armor, weapons, and skill were important in battle, but nothing was as essential as strategy, and so he ambushed the serpent.

His luck held, and his innovative armor served, and he killed the serpent with a spear thrust through the heart.

The king was as good as his word, and married his beautiful daughter to the impetuous youth he called Ragnar Lothbrok – or, literally, Ragnar Shaggy Pants. The name stuck.

Thora was a beautiful girl inside and out, and Ragnar was very happy with her. They had two children together (Ragnar had two daughters and one son in his brief marriage to Lagertha). Unfortunately, Thora became very sick and died, leaving Ragnar alone.

Now Ragnar, born to lead and gifted in battle, had suffered the death of his father and many members of his family, the demise of his first marriage, and the tragic death of the love of his life. He soon found a way to try to fill the void.

Ragnar Versus the World

In the years that followed, Ragnar flew his raven banner in raids not only throughout Scandinavia, but also far to the west, east, and south. An ever-increasing number of Vikings added to the ship crews under his command, and he went from being a petty king of an unimportant Danish territory to a true "sea king" – that is, a Viking with a virtual empire not of land but of water. This sea king ideal was perhaps one of the loftiest and most defining goals for a Viking, for it combined the bravery, lust for life, rejection of boundaries, and contempt of fear that formed the spine of the Viking character.

According to Saxo's history and the *Krákumál*, Ragnar led daring, successful raids into Sweden, Gotland, Livonia, Elsinore, Norway, Bornholm, Flemming, Belgium, Kent and Northumbria (both now part of England), Orkney, the Hebrides, the Isle of Sky, and Perth (Scotland), Ireland, Anglesey, and throughout Russia, Finland, Estonia, and the Baltic – even all the way down to the Hellespont in modern Turkey.

Of all these places, we are told that it was the Finns and other Baltic peoples that gave Ragnar the most trouble, because they could fight on skis and were highly adept at the use of "wind magic" to turn the weather against the Vikings.

Dragons and wind magic aside, such an explosion of bellicose activity led by one man is difficult to accept uncritically. What we do know is true is that during Ragnar's time the Vikings did in fact expand their activities in such an exponential and vigorous way. Even if the authors of our Scandinavian sources are describing the activities of many Viking leaders rather than one, the sudden tempest blast of Viking raids took Europe completely by surprise, with shock and awe.

Two passages are of particular interest to forming our historical image of Ragnar. Saxo mentions the Finns giving Ragnar more trouble than the Romans "*at the height of their power.*" This would certainly be impossible without time travelling 700 years before his era[5]; but what it may be referring to is the first Viking Siege of Paris in 845. Oddly, Saxo does not mention the Franks, who would have been well-known to him. But at the turn of the 8th century, the Frankish emperor, Charlemagne had been crowned Roman Emperor of the West by the Pope, and he and his successors were attempting to resurrect the Roman Empire in their image. Charlemagne's empire would be known as the Holy Roman Empire after that. Saxo's use of the term "Romans" for Charlemagne's empire is confirmed towards the end of Book VIII of his Danish History, where he writes about the Emperor Karl (i.e., Charles – Charlemagne) and his struggles with Denmark.

Another curiosity is the mention of the "island of Lindis" in verse 20 of the *Krákumál*. At first glance, this seems a referrence to Lindisfarne (which is built on a peninsula), and seems to suggest that Ragnar was in fact the leader of the notorious expedition that began the Viking Age. Most historians reject this, citing the line in the same verse: *"The blood of the Irish fell plentifully into the ocean, during the time of that slaughter,"* leading them to conclude that the verse may refer to Ragnar's raiding in Leinster or some other part of Ireland. While the truth is impossible to know with certainty, it is worth noting that many of the monks of Lindisfarne would have been Irish, or at least seemed Irish to the Vikings, due to the vigorous activity of Irish missionaries in

---

[5] See Chapter 4. The height of Roman power would certainly be in the first two centuries C.E.

Northumbria and the territories of what are now Scotland; and many of these monks were – we are told in church chronicles – martyred in the waves. However, as Lindisfarne was sacked about 52 years before the siege of Paris, it would be unlikely that one Viking leader could have done both.

Modern research, as well as common sense, has repeatedly reminded us that the Norse of the Viking Age were not the stock character barbarians of fantasy movies, but were pragmatic traders and settlers who enjoyed peace, kept their laws, and loved their families. While this is true, we see in the tales of Ragnar what made the Vikings so terrifying to their enemies. The Krákumál reads:

We fought with swords, before Boring-holmi. We held bloody shields: we stained our spears. Showers of arrows brake the shield in pieces. The bow sent forth the glittering steel. Volnir fell in the conflict, than whom there was not a greater king. Wide on the shores lay the scattered dead: the wolves rejoiced over their prey.... The blue steel all reeking with blood fell at length upon the golden mail. Many a virgin bewailed the laughter of that morning. The beasts of prey had ample spoil.

But Ragnar's life was not all war. He was a beloved and competent ruler. He found love again, with an exiled princess named Aslaug, who was beautiful, wise, brave, and cunning (we will discuss her more in the next chapter, also). Though Thora's two sons (Eric and Agnar) died in battle, Aslaug gave Ragnar Ivar, Bjorn, Sigurd Snake in the Eye, Halfdan, and Hvitserk (though Halfdan and Hvitserk might be the same person, literally "Halfdan Whiteshirt"). Through an affair, Ragnar also had a son named Ubba (also written Ubbe or Hubba). Ragnar accepted Ubba as a legitimate son, though Saxo tells us Ubba would always resent his father.

These sons all grew up to be extraordinary heroes, and to each make history in their own right. Indeed, the sagas tell us that as Ragnar aged, he began to worry that his sons might eclipse him in accomplishments and renown. This fear was so real to Ragnar that it drove him to actions that ultimately led to his final demise – but we will defer this part of the story for a moment, in order to look at Ragnar's tale from the view of his enemies.

The Viking Siege of Paris, 845

There were two Norse sieges of Paris. The first was in 845; and though a fairly minor affair in terms of battle, it had great symbolic significance. The second was roughly two generations later, in 885-886; was much larger (and deadlier); and had greater direct ramifications. Before the first siege, Viking raids were a new and growing problem for the peoples of Western Europe; but hitherto raids had been made by relatively small war bands bent on plunder. The Scandinavian adventurers might sack monasteries or villages, but would usually shun larger, better defended targets. However, success was making the Norsemen bolder.

Aware of this growing threat, the aging emperor, Charlemagne, built a series of maritime defenses to protect his coasts and rivers from these new dragon ships. For the first few decades, the defenses worked; but the Vikings were growing in number, ability, and ambition and a new breed of leaders was coming to the fore. One of these leaders was a man the Frankish chroniclers call Reginheri; but who has since been widely equated with Ragnar Lothbrok.

As in the Scandinavian legends, Ragnar was a jarl in Denmark with ties to Norway; though he was a vassal of the leading power in that land – King Horik. Perhaps Horik was jealous of Ragnar's raiding success and strategic acumen from the beginning; and perhaps he was galled by the young warlord's use of the raven banner and his other claims that he was descended from Odin (an insinuation of parity if not superiority to Horik himself) – we cannot know. What we do know is that under Ragnar, Vikings were ready to step foot on the world stage. They were ready to capture the jewel of Western Europe, the city of Paris.

So, in Spring of 845, while Horik slept at home, Ragnar led 120 dragon ships carrying about 5000-6000 Vikings into the heart of the late Charlemagne's empire. They broke through Frankish defenses and surrounded the walled city of Paris.

In the 9th century, Paris was already more than a thousand years old. It was wealthy from its position as a trading center and was the seat of one of Charlemagne's three competing heirs, Charles the Bald. At this time, the heart of the city was confined to the islands in the center of the Seine, the Île de la Cité where the cathedral of Notre Dame stands today. This position made Paris eminently defensible in the eyes of the Frankish elite that ruled there; but it made it easily surrounded by the ship-borne Vikings.

Not a very good tactician at this time, Charles the Bald (Charlemagne's grandson, who in all fairness, was only about 22 and new to his position as king) split his forces between the two banks of the Seine to better defend the nearby Abbey of Saint Denis. Ragnar's Vikings concentrated their attack on the forces on one bank of the Seine and easily defeated the Franks.

The Vikings took 111 Frankish prisoners in the battle. This relatively small number further emphasizes the Frank's level of surprise and unpreparedness, for either Charles's force was assembled so quickly that it was undersized, or the defeat had been so utter that they had almost all been wiped out.

In full view of the city and the army on the opposite riverbank, the Vikings further terrified their foes by hanging all 111 prisoners as a sacrifice to Odin. The Vikings then moved on Paris and captured it with equal efficiency.

Faced with these appalling developments, Charles took a course of action that was as practical as it was controversial (both at that time and ever after). He offered Ragnar 7000 *livres* (more than 5600 pounds) in gold and silver to take his men and leave. This cash pay-out became the first of many, many *danegelds* (roughly translated, "money to the Danes") that the princes of Europe would offer Viking armies to leave them alone.

To pay such a tremendous sum to "heathen savages" must have been a brutal humiliation for the grandson of the man who united most of Western Europe under his implacable will; but Charles was already facing rebellion in Aquitaine and Brittany, and had no wish to risk his troops, the citizens of Paris, or the religious and cultural treasures of the several nearby abbeys in a prolonged battle he would likely lose. His hands were tied, and so he paid.

Over the next 273 years, many would follow his example. Historians (as well as many medieval critics) have called this policy foolish or worse, because it would likely only encourage the offenders to return for more and more cash. However, while it is true that the Vikings in general did raid perennially, and did demand larger and larger *danegelds*, in a testimony to the peculiarities of the Viking ethical system, no Viking leader is known to have reneged on a *danegeld's* specific demands.

For Ragnar, the offer could not have come at a better time. The Vikings held Paris, but now they were suddenly under attack from the greatest bane of all armies – disease. Ragnar and his Danes were consummate fighters, but up to this time the Viking way of war was not usually one of siege craft. In their haste to defeat their foes they may have overlooked critical elements of sanitation in their encampments; or they had been tardy in burying the dead; or it could be that they entered a Paris that had already been festering from the Vikings' blockade. Or perhaps it was, as the 9th century clerics contend, that the Norsemen were smitten by the wrath of Saint Germain and the other spiritual protectors of the ancient city of Paris. In any case, by the time King Charles was making his offer, Earl Ragnar's mighty army was doubled-over with dysentery.

The Vikings took their fortune in gold and silver and the sailed back to Denmark, feeling healthy enough to attack a few more places along the way.

It is here that the reliable part of the narrative ends. Medieval Church writers, still reeling from the abomination of the defeat and the ignobility in which the situation was resolved, were quick to add an epilogue. They assert that when the Viking army returned to their King, Horik, it was as broken men; and that the King – in great fear of this Christian curse – executed all the survivors to extirpate it. Ragnar (or Regniheri) also allegedly died of illness, weeping of his sins.

Several details of this epilogue are openly ludicrous. First, even if the disease contracted by the raiders was especially virulent, it is unlikely that more than 50-60% could have died (and probably more like 10% based on established data of armies under similar conditions); which means that we are expected to believe that Horik (the king of one of the most warlike cultures the world has ever known) executed 2500-4500 heroes who had just pulled off the greatest heist in Scandinavian history. Many of these men would have been jarls, and so even if Horik had wanted them dead, it is unlikely that any king in this time of unstable rule could have that kind of power. It is also unlikely that churchmen in West Francia would know reliably what occurred 770 miles away in pagan Denmark.

Finally, if Regniheri had been *the* Ragnar, his death under these circumstances would not have launched one of the most well-documented of all 9th century events, the invasion of England by the sons of Lothbrok (about 20 years later). *The Anglo-Saxon Chronicle* specifically mentions Ragnar's raven banner, and several of his sons by name.

Despite these issues and the obvious propagandist quality of the tale, the story survives to this day and is taken for granted by a number of modern writers.

The Aftermath, as Interpreted by the Historian, Lars Brownworth

One analysis of the aftermath does help reconcile the facts and chronicles. According to historian Lars Brownworth (in 2014's *The Sea Wolves*), it was not fear of a dead saint that drove Horik to redress the injuries done to Paris – it was fear of Charles's brother and co-emperor, Louis the German. Denmark bordered Louis's lands, and this powerful heir of Charlemagne had military might and strategic acumen that Horik had neither the means nor the appetite to deal with. Horik's upstart competitor, Ragnar, had thus made a great deal of political trouble for the King, both in his own court (through Ragnar's greatly-bolstered popularity) and abroad. By making a show of retribution, Horik could assuage Louis the German and remove his competitor, Ragnar, as well.

Carolingians and Sea-Kings

In terms of foreign policy, Horik may have been worrying needlessly, though, as Louis the German saw his brother Charles as a competitor more than a kinsman. Louis may have seen West Francia's loss as East Francia's gain. Indeed, conflict between the various Carolingian rulers left many openings for Viking incursions throughout the 9th century, and the preference of the Carolingians to fight each other rather than the foreign raiders would severely discredit their dynasty.

As for Rangar's exile, the various medieval chronicles are full of "sightings" and clues. For example, the *Fragmentary Annals of Ireland* tells of a sea-king they call "Ragnall" having a base of operations in the Orkneys at the time in question (circa 846-860). The Irish Ragnall has several parallels with Ragnar, including two sons (perhaps Bjorn and Hvitserk) who raid the Mediterranean.[6]

History as well as legend strongly suggests that Ragnar (and most others) escaped Horik's politically-motivated cleansing, and left Denmark in exile. Such an exile (whether imposed by self-preservation or royal decree) further explains Ragnar's prolific career as a raider and sea king – he literally had no home to return. Horik died in a battle against rebels a few years later in 854. He was replaced by son, Horik II, who was still a child. But rather than becoming enmeshed with the chaos that was taking hold in Denmark during the late 9th century, Ragnar's gaze was turned outward.

The Legacy of Ragnar's Siege of Paris

Whether the men who took Paris lived on as wealthy heroes or died as accursed pirates, the first Viking siege of Paris was a tremendous event symbolically. It made the statement to all the peoples of Europe that the Norsemen were no longer just a menace, a disparate and uncoordinated group of thugs who threatened settlements but made no political impact. With the first siege of Paris, the Norse people saw what they could accomplish; and so did their enemies. It is no coincidence that the next few generations witnessed major Viking armies seize large territories in Britain, France, Ireland, Russia, and elsewhere. It is no

---

[6] See Chapter 9. The reader is also cautioned, there are several different Ragnalls in Irish sources, just as there are multiple Imars/Ivars.

coincidence that Viking influence could soon be felt as far away as Constantinople and the Eastern Mediterranean.

Norse forces were organizing, consolidating, and spreading after the 845 siege of Paris, and the tributes they claimed were ever-growing. Yet, it was not just the Vikings that were learning, but the defenders too. After his humiliation at Paris, Charles the Bald spent the rest of his career preparing to fight the Vikings again. He built fortified bridges and ordered many other ingenious defenses and reinvigorated what would become the most recognizable symbol of the Middle Ages – armored, mounted cavalry. Charles was not going to be unprepared again, because he knew that sooner or later the Vikings would be coming back to Paris.

As for Ragnar, his story continues – but first we will look at the legends and evidence of some of the fantastic figures surrounding him.

Chapter VII: Lagertha and the Shield Maidens

Near Birka, Sweden in 1880, the burial mound of a Viking leader was discovered, complete with a magnificent array of weapons and the remains of two sacrificed horses. In 2017, the remains of the "Birka Warrior" were reexamined; and the suspicions of astute researchers were confirmed through DNA evidence – the remains are of a female.

This find certainly seems to lend credence to stories the Norse skalds have long told – that it was not only Norse men who could become Viking warriors, but also Norse women. In the sagas, these female warriors are often referred to as "shield maidens."

The discovery raises the question of how many other times archeologists have made this mistake. There are three ways the sex of human remains could be determined – DNA (the most expensive and least common), osteological examination (which can be tricky) or through the gender associated with their grave goods (items buried with a person, presumably to follow them into the afterlife). But the Birka Warrior has proven that the grave goods method of engendering archeological remains can have significant flaws, including circular reasoning.

While the Birka Warrior is the most sensational grave of a Viking warrior woman, it is not the only one. There are not many, and the weapons in these women's graves have been fewer and usually less extravegant.[7] But more may be out there, misidentified, or undiscovered.

---

[7] One exception to this is the Sountaka Sword – arguably one of the most exquisite

Female skeletons have been identified in Viking warrior group graves (like the burial mound at Repton, England); but these may have been the women who accompanied their Viking husbands as colonists, or they could be local captives. The archeological uncertainty is further complicated because Vikings did not always inter their dead, but practiced a range of burial rituals including cremation, exposure to the elements, and burial at sea.

So, archeology has not been able to confirm or refute the legend of the shield maiden, but new DNA/genome techniques soon may.

Traditionally-minded or otherwise cautious experts were quick to point out that just because the individual at Birka was buried with the tools of war did not make her a warrior. However, it would be highly unusual to bury her so if she were not. In ancient societies, someone would be buried for what they were known for, and what they might need in the afterlife. A man would not need a distaff and a loom if he were a warrior, so why would a woman need weapons if she were a homemaker? Not only was the Birka warrior interred with a sword, spear, bow, axe, two shields, 12 armor-piercing arrows, two war horses with riding gear, and a gaming board (denoting strategy), but she was not buried with anything else – nothing exclusively feminine. Before science proved her to be female, the Birka Warrior was looked to as one

---

swords from the Viking Age. It was found, along with another sword in a woman's grave in Finland. The artistry definitely appears Norse, but the ethnicity of the warrior is the subject of nationalistic debate.

of the best examples of a warrior's grave. Only now, after the DNA finds, are some archeologists back-pedaling on this.

Perhaps (the argument goes) that it was because the woman was royalty, and so she was a leader; and a leader rules through force of arms. This may well be. Perhaps being buried with weapons does not make you a warrior much more than owning them in life does. Better answers could be gleaned if archeology could study whether these female remains and others like them had any of the injuries – acute and chronic – that are associated with warriors, and by re-examining the wider sample of warrior skeletons to better determine gender instead of simply assuming masculinity.

One female skeleton buried with warrior grave goods was found near Solør, Norway. This woman (who died before she was 20) did indeed seem to have a battle injury – a wound to her forehead consistent with a sword strike. But she was apparently both tough and lucky, and this wound showed some signs of healing. In 2019, archeologists at the University of Dundee, Scotland used facial reconstruction technology to re-create what she looked like. The Solør Warrior is thought to be from around the year 900.

A more intensive study of other Viking remains would require a lot of money and time – two rare commodities in current archeology. So, since archeology has said all it can say for now on this issue, we must turn to historical records and literature for more clues.

Women in Norse Culture

There is no question that Norse society was a patriarchal one; however, women had more freedom, self-determination, and rights than they did in most other societies of the time. Noble and free-born women (that is, everyone except the many slaves) in 8th-11th century Scandinavia and the Viking colonies could own and inherit land; they could choose to divorce their husbands; oaths to them were as binding as to a man; and they had many other legal protections.

In the Norse sagas, we see women portrayed as being just as courageous, wise, cunning, well-spoken, and respected as men. An example of this would be Aslaug, from the *Saga of Ragnar Lothbrok*. In the story, when Ragnar meets Aslaug, she is disguised as a poor but free-born woman. Despite these ordinary circumstances, Aslaug can decide if she will marry Ragnar; and if so, when. She can come and go as she pleases. Later, after she becomes Ragnar's queen and the mother of some of the most celebrated heroes in Viking lore, her voice holds great sway, and she even leads an army against the king of Sweden. The fictionalized Aslaug has a number of historical counterparts, including Olga of Kiev and Freydís Eiríksdóttir – Norse women who used cunning, influence, tenacity, and ability to accomplish their ambitions and become powerful rulers. However, though Aslaug leads an army, there is no overt mention of her physically joining the battle.

Lagertha

Another woman associated with the legendary Ragnar is described fighting alongside men in the shield wall – a woman named

Lagertha (or Lagerda). According to Saxo Grammaticus, Lagertha was a member of a royal household of Norway. When a Swedish King defeated this Norwegian king, he captured his kinswomen as slaves. When Ragnar heard of these outrages, he came to Norway with his followers to avenge the king's death and to set things right. Women who had either escaped or fled the invaders came to Ragnar and begged to join him in the fight against their oppressor.

Among these women was one named Lagertha, described as having "*a matchless spirit though a delicate frame.*" She showed such skill and fury in the subsequent battle that Ragnar "*declared that he had gained the victory by the might of one woman.*"

Smitten, Ragnar wooed Lagertha. She initially played hard-to-get in a very Viking fashion. She even loosed her pet bear on Ragnar at one point.[8] But Lagertha eventually married Ragnar. They had a son named Fridleif (who did not achieve the same fame as his later brothers). They also had two daughters, whose names are unknown but may be the daughters who wove Ragnar's famous Raven Banner, as mentioned in Old English source, the *Annals of Saint Neot.*

The happiness of the marriage was short-lived, and the two divorced after only about three years.

---

[8] Viking jarls treasured bears (especially polar bears) as "pets" and status symbols, hence this part of the story may seem unlikely but is not impossible. These animals represented Odin and power, and they made an impressive statement. Bears can be trained, but certainly not dependably domesticated.

Some years later, Lagertha would again come to Ragnar's aid. When Ragnar was attacked and nearly-overwhelmed by Jutes and Skanians (Germanic/Nordic tribes also inhabiting Denmark), Lagertha led the warriors of 120 ships into battle. Again, Lagertha's great skill and valor saved the day and saved her ex-husband's fortunes.

Lagertha was not only a skilled warrior but brilliant tactician, and she managed to outmaneuver Ragnar's enemies and attack them from behind – and of course, only the best-trained warriors were able to flip their shield walls around seamlessly. The enemy was slaughtered.

Returning from this victory, Lagertha slew her new husband for unknown reasons and seized control of their kingdom for herself alone.

Saxo chalks this assassination and usurpation (which are Lagertha's last recorded actions) to mere ambition. Lagertha seems more complicated than that, and so the reader is left to ponder the mystery. We do see signs of a recurring theme in Lagertha's story that can be found in the majority of tales of female warriors from Artemesia of Cara to Joan of Arc: whether the female warrior is successful or unsuccessful, her story usually ends unhappily.

Some experts (including feminist and non-feminist historians) see in this an attempt by chroniclers to guide condemnation of women who reject the roles placed on them by society. Others take this motif as evidence that the stories are fictional after all. It should be remembered, though, that the lives of many rulers and heroes in the ancient world ended with being on one side or the other of a bloody blade, and so the lonely fate of Lagertha and others should not be surprising.

Other Shield Maidens

Saxo mentions other shieldmaidens throughout his long and bloody *History of the Danes*. In Book VIII alone we meet no less than four of them. These include Hetha (or Heid) and Wisna, who lead warrior into battle. Wisna was a standard bearer for her king, Harald, and was said to be "*a woman filled with sternness and a skilled warrior.*" Saxo leaves no room for mistake as to her role as a shieldmaiden (and not merely some tactician who gave orders from safe positions), stating that she along with her male and female companions "*exposed their bodies to every peril, and entered battle with drawn swords.*"

In the same great war between King Harald and King Ring (called the Bravic War, believed to be in the mid-8th century), Saxo tells us of a shield maiden named Weigbiorg (or Webiorg) who slew Sloth the champion and would have killed many more champions had she not been shot through with arrows.

Hetha survived the great slaughter of Bravic, and though her king died, she was appointed to rule the Zealanders (who would someday become Ragnar's people). The Zealanders did not want to follow a woman, though and chose another king (named Ole) who forced Hetha through political means to give up all her territory except Jutland. Ole and his son Omund were tyrants, and Saxo tells us that those who had forsaken Hetha lived to regret their decision and greatly missed her leadership.

Saxo goes on to describe in Book VIII how Omund's rise to power was thwarted by another warrior queen – a Norwegian Viking named Rusla. Writing in Latin, Saxo describes Rusla as an *"Amazon… whose prowess in battle exceeded that of a woman."* Fighting on both land and sea, Rusla defeats all the Danes Omund can send against her. She is killed by her brother, Thrond, whom she had also been warring with – an event that sets off even more blood feuds in the turbulent Scandinavian territories.

Other shieldmaidens also populate the rich world of Norse lore. They include the woman Hervor, who led a Viking lifestyle while disguised as a man, but also her granddaughter, also named Hervor, who led her Goths (i.e., the Swedes of Gotland) against the Huns. The story of the two Hervors is related in the *Hervarar Saga* (also known as the *Saga of King Heidrek the Wise*). Like other *fornaldarsögur*, (that is, a classification of sagas about distant ancestors, usually set in the murky Migration Era) the story is so full of legend as to make its place in any historical construct difficult.

The *Vǫlsunga Saga*, which has been called "the *Iliad* of the North," features several shield maidens. The most conspicuous of these is Brynhild, who is not only a warrior but a cunning tactician. Brynhild is fiercely independent, and only wants to submit to a man who is better than herself. She finds such a man in Sigurd Fafnir's-bane, a dragon slayer and the best of all men (though perhaps not the smartest).

Incidently, Brynhild and Sigurd have a love child, who is Aslaug, wife of Ragnar and mother of Ivar and most of his children. The timetable on this is impossible, though, and it just goes to show how the Vikings loved to attach their realities to legends until the truth could not be (and perhaps did not need to be) disentangled.

Brynhild loses Sigurd to the more conventional leading lady, Gudrun. Towards the end of the saga, even Gudrun enters battle as a shieldmaiden during a time of great distress. These legends are backed up in the more-continental version of the story, the *Nibelungenlied*, which inspired Wagner's famous *Ring Cycle*. Through Wagner's enduring operas, the shield maiden became one of those cultural images that everyone recognizes though few understand.

Throughout Norse lore and mythology, we find the idea that the brave warriors who died in battle were carried from the field by armor-wearing, horse-riding female spirits known as Valkyries. Some Eddic poetry call shield maidens like Brynhild Valkyries, and this conflation of natural and supernatural designations may further blur the lines between fact and fiction. Eddic poetry also describes how many of the Norse goddesses – including Freya, the goddess of love, sex, and fertility – were also goddesses of war. Some of these poems and myths say that of all the worthy warriors the Valkyries carry from the battlefield, half go to Odin and the other half join Freya's army. It is clear from all these stories that the Vikings did not see war in strictly masculine terms.

However, throughout Saxo's history and the body of Norse lore every time we meet a shield maiden, she is presented as an exceptional character. For all her prowess and worthiness, Lagertha is initially driven to her martial exploits through dire circumstances and later through ambition. Wisna, Hetha, Rusla and the others are compared to men, not presented as some standard for women. While Norse sources have plenty of female heroes, many of whom do battle as shield maidens, they never really portray the shield maiden as an everyday occurrence or as something normative. So, the questions of shield maidens continue to be not only "did they exist?" but "how common were they?"

The next place to turn to answer these questions is non-Norse period sources. Here we find the same vague answers. Byzantine sources occasionally mention female Vikings as warriors. Most notable among these sources is John Skylitzes's 13th-century account of a 10th century battle between the Kievan Rus under Sviatoslav and the Byzantines in Bulgaria.

In western sources, though, we do not find much mentioned about female Vikings in combat. As the Saxons, Franks, and others did not have women warriors in their armies, one would think that if the Vikings did it would have made it into the chronicles.

As mentioned in Chapter 2, there is also the matter of recorded law from the Norse world, particularly that of Iceland, banning women from dressing as men or handling weapons (and significantly limiting their political power). Once more, though, people do not tend to make laws against what no one is doing. The presence of the law at least suggests that there was such a tendency for women to assume masculine, martial roles (however occasionally).

As we study the question of shield maidens, one hypothesis that begins to emerge is that shield maidens were perhaps a feature of the past that Norse cultures – moving as they were towards becoming more lawful and established (and eventually, more Christian) – left behind. If accounts of war in the mid-8th century includes several shield maidens, but by the time we come to our more well-documented periods we have few mentions of them, then either the original accounts are legendary, the later accounts are censorious, or times had simply changed.

Women Warriors in Other Cultures

To further consider the plausibility of shield maidens, we can also look to cultures that were neighboring or analogous to the Vikings.

Going many centuries before the Vikings, to Celtic Britain at the time of the Roman conquest and occupation; we see women joining the men in battle (though these women are described in very witch-like terms, and may have been female druids). Roman occupying forces complained that while trying to arrest men, they would often be ferociously attacked by their wives. Unease and underestimation culminated when Boudicca, queen of the Icenii, avenged the war crimes of certain Romans by unleashing one of the greatest massacres ever to occur on British soil.

The Romans, for their part, had female gladiators (called gladiatrix). Roman armies, however, were all male. Still, the question arises that since most gladiators were foreign-born warriors turned slaves, were the gladiatrix also warriors for some of Rome's many enemies before stepping onto the sun-scorched sands of the arena.

In the Ulster Cycle of 7th-8th century Irish literature (i.e., just before the Viking Age), the young Achilles figure, Cu Chulainn, is told that his martial training will not be complete until he travels to Alba (Scotland) and studies under a famous female warrior named Scathach.

Interestingly, when Cu Chulainn first faces Scathach, he apparently takes her by surprise and overpowers her, but still demands to be her pupil. His continued desire to train under her despite his victory suggests that Scathach's real merit was as a technical fighter, and it was this superior level of technique that Cu Chulainn needed to turn his raw power and talent into true greatness.

Another interesting detail about the Scathach story is that she has sons and a daughter, demonstrating that becoming a warrior was not necessarily seen as a complete alternative to other gender roles.

Scathach's enemy is another female warrior and leader named Aoife, who later becomes Cu Chulainn's lover and the mother of his ill-fated son. One of the most important characters in the Ulster Cycle is the famous Maeve (or Medb), who was a cunning and formidable warrior queen. One would be hard-pressed to find a more feminist character than Maeve, even if one looked in modern literature.

The legacy of female warriors would continue throughout history. In the mid-sixteenth century, Grace O'Malley became one of the most successful pirates of the golden age of piracy, following in the footsteps of Viking shield maidens.

In our own time, some of the most dangerous fighting in the War on Terror is being undertaken by Kurdish and Yazidi women, and militaries around the world are increasingly opening combat roles to women.

Shield Maidens – Literary Convention or Relic of the Past?

The shield maidens of the Viking Age have left us with many clues and many questions, but few firm answers. We do not definitively know if they existed; or – if so – how common they might have been. We do not know if they would have been used reactively to defend hearth and home, or if they might have also been involved in Viking raids and expeditions.

In the opinion of your authors, there is not really enough evidence to suggest that female warriors constituted a constant and significant portion of Viking raiding parties or other armies. At the same time, it is our opinion that experts who proclaim that shield maidens are merely a literary convention and were not real are discounting a large body of written, cultural, and archeological evidence.

It seems reasonable, based on the evidence, that some women occasionally became shield maidens, especially during the centuries that the Norse were most tribal and their lands most chaotic. These character traits expressed themselves in Norse women throughout the Viking Age (and beyond) in other ways, but would again manifest when the group was threatened – as described in the Byzantine sources or in the accounts of the Vikings in North America, which we shall examine soon. Lagertha may be shrouded in legend, but her spirit lived on.

What we can see from the evidence is that Norse women may have been far less constrained by their society than they have been constrained by historians. Norse women were more than nurturers who stayed at home tending the children and the animals. They were respected voices in their communities and brave colonists ready to start lives from scratch in hostile lands. They could be able rulers, and may also perhaps have sometimes tested their bravery as warriors.

Chapter VIII: Saint Patrick and the Devil, the First Raiding Period in Ireland

The success of the Viking sack of Lindisfarne in 793 made the Viking invasion of Ireland a certainty. Ireland was the heart of the monastic world in the Early Middle Ages, and this lure would prove irresistible to the dragon ships.

Hundreds of years before, the Romans – even at the height of their power – conquered Britain but balked at invading Ireland. Hibernia, as they called it, was like Caledonia (Scotland). It was a dark land of savage men with savage customs, a land where the brave legions of Rome would chase shadows into the wilderness until ambush and plague made campaign unsustainable. There was too much to lose and too little to gain, and so Ireland was left alone.

But Ireland would not leave the Roman world alone. The Irish invaded Roman Britain several times – most notably as part of the "Barbarian Conspiracy" of 365, and they raided the coasts of Britain regularly for slaves and other portable wealth.

One of the slaves they took (in the early 5th century) was a Briton youth named Patrick. Patrick's strong Christian faith sustained him through his days of slavery, and gave him the courage to escape back home to post-Roman Britain. Patrick became a priest and then did what was almost unthinkable – he returned as a missionary to the place where he had been a slave.

Contrary to legend, Patrick probably did not find Ireland wholly Pagan, nor leave it wholly Christian. Ireland had taken many Briton slaves over the years, and even though Christianity was probably still a minority religion so far away from the Roman cities of Eboracum (York), Londinium (London) and Camulodunum (Colchester) there must have been many Britons who carried the faith with them. Histories and legends mention other contemporaries of Patrick, like Saint Declan, who made an early impact in the secluded land. Some modern scholarship and research also suggests that the transition from the Druidic to the Christian faith may not have been finalized until the 6th century, when "Justinian's Plague" (probably an early strike of bubonic plague) ravaged the population, leading people to doubt their old ways and seek something new, even as the Black Plague of the Middle Ages would weaken the Church and indirectly lead to the Renaissance and Age of Enlightenment.

In any case, Patrick was the most successful of Ireland's missionaries – and perhaps one of the most successful missionaries ever. Early Christianity had spread throughout the Roman world largely (although with notable exceptions) from the bottom-up, as the faith of slaves, women, and others who were not as fully vested in Roman society. In Ireland, Patrick took a top-down approach, targeting kings and cultural elites. Patrick also used his intimate knowledge of the Irish as well as his ample natural talents to "out-druid" the druids in matches of wit and song.

Patrick probably also won over the Irish by stressing the similarities in their religion to Christianity. For example, the Christian doctrine of the Trinity is considered one of the religion's more difficult concepts, but Irish Druidism already had the concept of trinity built into it (for example, the maid, mother, and crone aspects of the triple goddess or the ubiquitous *triskelion* triple spirals and *triquetra* symbols).

So, Patrick became the apostle of Ireland, and, in time, Ireland became the apostle to Early Medieval Europe. The Irish have always been a very spiritual, artistic, literary, and bold people, and they eagerly adapted these traits to their newfound faith.

The spirit of monasticism thrived in Ireland. Ireland was far more forested then than it is now, and it offered miles of lonely, windswept coast and desolate islands for the heavy soul to seek solitude. Monasteries and abbeys popped up everywhere, including one that Patrick himself founded in Armagh. This Armagh monastery was to become the spiritual heart of Celtic Christianity, and would by the Viking's time be a sprawling religious center with hundreds of monks, nuns, and priests. Celtic art was seamlessly infused into illuminating holy manuscripts, and Celtic music graced Christian liturgy. Celtic stories and sensibilities helped mold the literary work of the Irish monks, and these skilled scribes in turn worked tirelessly to preserve and perpetuate the endangered classics of the ancient world.

The energy of the Irish monks was too great for Ireland to contain, and Irish missionaries began spreading throughout Europe. Men like Aiden (Cuthbert's idol) began converting the Saxons in Britain, and men like Saint Columba began expanding the mission field to Scotland and beyond. The court of Charlemagne and other European kings gauged their appeal and sophistication by how many Irish scholars they had in residence. Even when the Vikings came to cold, remote, "undiscovered" Iceland, they would find Irish monks there, reading their books and pursuing their lives of the mind and soul.

This period is sometimes called the Celtic Renaissance or the Ireland's Golden Age. Almost all golden ages in history occur during times of peace and plenty. Even modern psychological theory, such as Maslow's Hierarchy of Needs, hold that human intellectual growth and self-actualization are all but impossible during times when the base needs of existence are in danger. But the flower of Irish monasticism and spiritual life may be an exception to this – because Early Medieval Ireland was anything but peaceful and prosperous. Ireland was – and perhaps always had been – in an almost constant state of civil war.

When the first dragon ship reached Irish waters (probably around 795) it approached an island with over a hundred principalities and petty kingdoms. These plethora of kings or chieftains were sometimes (and even then, often only nominally) in the liege of a High King at the mount of Tara in the east of Ireland. Even under the best of conditions, these many rulers disputed each other's borders, held long grudges and feuded over old slights, envied each other's success or sought to gain from another's failure, and engaged in almost-recreational raiding. Long before the Viking Age began, and long after it ended, the Irish considered venturing into neighboring territory to steal cattle or other movable wealth to be quite normal, and a good way to keep one's warriors sharp.

This warlike culture, and the true lack of centralized authority had always been what made Ireland so hard to control. With scores of petty rulers who were more than happy to keep fighting forever, any invading army would only inherit a quagmire. Once more, this was true long before the Vikings came and long after they left. Historically, the Romans knew that they would gain nothing by trying to take Ireland, and only the British Empire was able to establish any sort of lasting stability there (though not without guns and a great deal of brutality).

However, most of the Vikings did not want to control Ireland – they just wanted to exploit it – and the political discord and chaos of the land was exactly the environment that made the Vikings apex predators.

So, what historians would call The First Raiding Period of Ireland began around 795, with a few dragon ships crossing the cold seas, attacking a few monasteries and coastal villages, and disappearing back over the waves. Unlike Lindisfarne, few people noticed at first. The Irish chiefs were too busy fighting each other and were not going to interrupt their summer raiding to go chase dragon ships that could move several times faster than their war parties. But the problem grew exponentially, with each new Viking raid breeding several more. Soon it was if, as one 9th century chronicler wrote, *"The sea spewed forth floods of foreigners over Ireland, so that no haven, no landing space ... might be found that was not submerged by waves of Vikings and pirates"*.

So, while the lordship of the land stubbornly pursued their quarrels, the men of Norway (particularly) and Denmark came behind the armies and picked their lands clean.

Though Ireland had many monasteries where the treasure of the land aggregated, Ireland itself was probably not a rich land at the time – certainly not compared to Charlemagne's empire or the lands of the south. But, aside from gilded book covers, jeweled altar pieces and the heavy ransom the Vikings could gain from selling churchmen back to their congregations, Ireland had several things the Vikings were very interested in. These included cattle, wool, timber, and of course, slaves. It is said that after Saint Patrick, slavery was outlawed in Ireland, but now the sins of the long-dead Irish slavers were being visited upon their descendants.

Valued for their famous weaving skills as well as whatever carnal abuses the Viking slavers purposed, Irish women and girls were kidnapped at an alarming rate. As many as a thousand were taken at once, to be kept by their captors or sold in the markets of Scandinavia, the Baltic, or the Islamic world.

But then there was a new disturbing turn in the luck of the Irish – one that even the fractious Irish lords should have taken heed of – the Vikings began overwintering in Ireland. They did not all return home on the autumn waves, but instead hosts of Vikings carved out settlements for themselves where the local lords were afraid to drive them out. In the early 9th century, the Vikings came to Ireland to stay.

While overwintering, Viking forces did not have the safety offered by their dragon ships' superior mobility. So, they had to fortify their positions to discourage counter-attack from vengeful locals. The raiders – now invaders – were amassing so much loot that they needed stable places to trade and export all these slaves and stolen goods. So, the Vikings did not just make small burgs of wooden palisades, but built large, well-defended settlements they called *longphorts*.

These *longphorts* grew over time, as even local merchants followed the pull of trade and the settlements became the destination for more and more men from Scandinavia. The modern Irish cities of Cork, Wexford, Waterford, Limerick, and others began as Viking *longphorts*.

So, in the first part of the 9th century, the Vikings had gone from smash-and-grab raids on religious houses to taking land, building settlements, and exploiting the resources of Ireland at will. Some of our primary sources for the tale of Viking Ireland are *The Annals of the Four*

Masters, The Annals of Ulster, The Fragmentary Annals, The *Annals of Clonmacnoise*, and *The Chronicon Scotorum*. Almost always sparing of words, the glimpses they offer of this time are bleak. The "foreigners" win victory after victory over the Irish, and destroy religious houses one after another. They take hundreds of slaves at a time (710 from one abbey, illustrating how some of these institutions were sprawling campuses and not always little buildings housing a few bookish old men). The Vikings martyr abbots, kill kings, and drag some nobles back to their ships where they are later murdered. Whether these latter deaths were sacrifices to Odin, sadistic sport, or botched ransom attempts, the chroniclers do not say.

Meanwhile, the annals list numerous battles, raids, and assassinations between one Irish strongman and another, regardless of the growing threat from outside. In an uncharacteristic flourish of despondency, one of the chroniclers punctuates this grim list of losses, *"for the Irish suffer evils not only from the Norse, they also suffer great evils from themselves."*

So, the 9th century Irish were losing their sacred treasures, their clergy, their land, their food supply, and even their families; but things were about to get much worse.

Holy War Comes to Ireland

In 836 or 837, a Norwegian prince called Turgeis (a.k.a. Tuirgeis or Turgesius to the Irish and Thorkill, Thorgest, or Thorgils to the Norse) arrived in Ireland with a "royal fleet" of ships. Whether through kingly endorsement, personal charisma, or because of the number of ships he already had under his command, Turgeis received immediate clout amongst the Vikings in Ireland. More ships joined him, and soon he was able to launch 66 ships on an expedition upriver deep into the heart of Ireland.

So many ships mean Turgeis had probably between 2600 and 4000 men at a time and place where armies were numbered in the few-hundreds. Once again, unprepared for the mobility and reach of the dragon ships, rural Ireland was all but undefended from a threat of such magnitude.

As previously mentioned, Christendom had immediately reacted to the Viking incursions as events with religious implications. However, the average Viking had no such view, and did not consider himself to be in any kind of holy war. The Norse did not have an organized religion. While the Norse had a strong sense of the sacred, they did not attach this sense to institutions. They sacked monasteries because that was where the wealth of the land was most easily accessible. In *Ragnar Saga Lodbrok*, Ivar the Boneless and his brothers sack a pagan religious center for no other reason than it will bring them wealth and street-credit. In the *Saga of Hrafnkel Frey's-Godi*, even a temple to the Viking god of plenty is treated as personal property and subject to looting as the spoils of a feud.

In their raids on Christian monasteries, the Vikings slaughtered monks and other non-combatants for expediency and because failure to fight back was loathsome in Norse culture. There was no room in the Viking's world for men who turned the other cheek.

It is possible that Vikings also massacred monks because the monks made books, chanted, and prayed, and since all these things were associated with magic in the Norse world some Vikings may have considered the monks to be dangerous or, at least, bad luck. If that were the case, it is also true that the Norse considered magic as not fitting for men, but – at best – a woman's domain, making these monks further contemptible to the Vikings' perspective.

The way in which some monks, nuns, or abbots were murdered showed disdain for certain Christian practices, such as when the abbot of Skerry was starved to death as the Vikings ate and drank in front of him (a mockery of the religious practice of fasting) but overall no one really cared about the religion of their native foes. There were no "heathen" missionaries or attempts at proselytizing, and Viking toleration of the religion of peoples under their control or even in their own household was already underway. For the Vikings, the faith of their enemies only became more than a curiosity when it provided institutions to exploit, such as churches or holidays, and no Viking returned home bragging to his friends how many converts he won to Odin.

But Turgeis was one very big exception to this. Turgeis embarked on his expedition up the rivers of Ireland not just to take more wealth, as his predecessors had, but to take control of Ireland by attacking her religion. Whether this was because this young prince of Norway was a deeply devout follower of the Old Ways (his name is derived from "Thor" and he was married to a *volva* priestess) or simply that he perceived that crushing the faith of the Irish was the key to dominating them, we do not know. What we do know is that Turgeis's overwhelming army burned every abbey in its path as it made straight for Saint Patrick's own center at Armagh, the spiritual heart of the land. After that, he turned south, ultimately taking the famous Clonmacnoise Abbey.

Turgeis and his thousands fell upon these large religious centers and slaughtered whosoever they willed, but they did not just take the gold. They did not fire these magnificent (by the standards of the day) buildings as they had the lesser centers. Instead, Turgeis made sacrifices to his gods on the high altars. Armagh and Clonmacnoise were no longer abbeys devoted to God, but now temples devoted to the gods of the Vikings. Turgeis appointed his wife, the *volva* seeress and prophetess, as chief priestess at Clonmacnoise.

But even in this, Turgeis did not think he had gone far enough. The God of the Irish may be evicted from Armagh and Clonmacnoise, but that was no reason why the infrastructure that had supported such machines of wealth and leisure should shut down. Turgeis named himself abbot, to replace the one he had killed, and he sent his men round to tell everyone that their tithes, offerings, and other financial obligations to these repurposed temples were to continue.

To the Christian mind of the time, wealth given to the Church was given to God himself as a form of worship and devotion, and secured God's favor. Thus, for them to give wealth to a heathen temple was to involve themselves in blasphemy, for which there would be no absolution. Yet, if they did not do it, they would incur the wrath of the Vikings.

Turgesius's actions had profound, destructive impact on the Irish. In the face of this assault on their very identity, and the failure of their secular leadership, some Irish clergy led their congregations in armed resistance. Other Irish abandoned their church and their people and either joined the Vikings or simply imitated them.

The fabric of society was torn. People walked away from their lives, and banditry proliferated. Perhaps for many, the ability of the Church to secure God's favor was called into question. The chroniclers tell us that of the 14 attacks one abbey endured, only a few were at the hand of the foreigners. The rest were from roving bandits who no longer respected the sanctity of the Church. Others were from legitimate rulers who began to see the political alliances of these institutions to be fair game in their civil wars. Perhaps unrelated to Turgeis directly, but as a consequence of this social upheaval, slavery again became commonplace even amongst the Irish after centuries of Saint Patrick's abolition. The saint's very legacy, it would seem, was under siege.

Turgeis pressed this advantage, taking more and more territory. He soon needed a port fortress of his own, and so participated in the founding of Dublin around 841. Dubh Linn meant "Black Water" in Old Irish and it was on these black waters on the estuary at the mouth of the River Liffey that the Vikings built their greatest western settlement. In time, Dyflin (as the Norse approximated the Irish term) would become the center of a Viking empire, and would withstand scores of desperate attacks by Irish and Vikings alike. It was in Dublin that Turgeis declared himself "King of all the Foreigners in Ireland".

But Turgesius over-reached. He had been in Ireland for seven or eight years, and he seemed unassailable. Yet, his ambition had only just begun, and his reign lacked the legitimacy and stability it needed for him to match the emerging kings in Norway, Denmark, or Sweden. Turgeis did not want to just be King of all the Foreigners. He wanted to be King of the Irish, too, and to that end, he reasoned, he would need a high-born Irish wife.

He chose the daughter of one of the nearby Irish kings, Máel Sechnaill. Máel Sechnaill may have feigned goodwill towards the King of Dublin, but he was bold, cunning, and very ambitious in his own right. He accepted Turgeis's proposal, and promised his daughter's hand.

Ignoring or not receiving any advice from his other wife, the prophetess, Turgeis eagerly went to the wedding, bringing only his trusted household troops.

Ironically, Máel Sechnaill was inadverntenly following an old Norse legend of Thor when his daughter and her handmaidens arrived at the wedding in their veils and finery (see *Thrymskvitha* in *the Poetic Edda*, or the tale of *Freya's Unusual Wedding* in your favorite Norse mythology book). These few veiled maidens accompanying Máel Sechnaill's daughter were not maidens at all, but highly-trained young men. When Turgeis and his Vikings had drunk many mead horns, the young men produced weapons from concealment and cut their way to the gates. Máel Sechnaill's army burst in, killed Turgeis's berserkers and captured the King of the Foreigners.

Turgeis was bound, dragged away, and flung on a boat. Once out in the middle of the lake, Loch Uair (some sources say Loug Owel), his captors fastened heavy stones to him and cast him into the water. Thus, Ireland's first Viking king drowned. Some experts see in this form of execution something of the old "triple death" ritual of the Druids. It seems more likely that Máel Sechnaill and his priests had Matthew 18:6 in mind.[9]

Máel Sechnaill became High King of Ireland two years later. He immediately began imposing order. According to the Annals of Ulster, within a month or two of taking power he "*destroyed a large band of wicked men ... who were plundering the land in the manner of heathens.*" This "band" seems to be describing Irish outlaws or perhaps a mixed company. Then the next year, in 848, the annal reads, "*Máel Sechnaill won a battle against the heathens at Forach in which 700 fell.*"

But order was to prove elusive. Though Ireland finally had a High King who was willing to fight the Vikings by any means necessary, it would continue to have a great deal of internal division. Nonetheless, from the reign of Máel Sechnaill onward, we start to see more Irish victories.

We also see another phenomenon – one that should not surprise us – starting around the year 842, we start to see Irish and Vikings making alliances and fighting together on the same team. There were new generations of both peoples growing up side by side and intermingling with each other. *The Chronicon Scotorum* specifically mentions Máel Sechnaill being supported in his wars by Norse-Irish.

The Fair Foreigners and the Dark Foreigners

---

[9] "*If anyone causes my little ones to sin ...it would be better for him to have a millstone tied to his neck and cast into the sea.*"

It was in the year 849 that the beleaguered Irish received a mixed blessing. *The Annals of Ulster* tells us that a "*new king of the foreigners*" came with 140 ships to gain control of the foreigners who had been in Ireland before, and that "*they caused confusion in the whole country.*" Afterwards, we see vicious battles between Viking groups, some lasting days.

In 852, 160 more ships came from Scandinavia to further the fight between the Vikings. According to *The Chronicon Scotorum*, these ships were led by a king named Amlaib Conung, who is believed by many historians to be Olaf the White, from the Norse sagas.

The Irish took to calling these warring groups the "fair" (or sometimes "light") foreigners versus the "dark" foreigners. The most common opinion among historians is that the fair foreigners were Norwegian while the dark were Danish (and at least one annal specifically refers to them that way), though it is not unlikely that the "fair" simply referred to the established Vikings (who were "fair" because they had some Irish ties) and the "dark" referred to the new.

If the "fair foreigners" were Norwegian Vikings and the "dark foreigners" were the Danes, the timing of the conflict becomes interesting, for it suggests that the Danes were choosing to encroach on the territory of their former neighbors instead of pursuing gains in mainland Europe. Perhaps Francia's much-maligned *danegeld* policy was working a little, or perhaps Charles the Bald's defenses were taking shape. Or perhaps there were just too many Vikings trying to carve out a space for themselves for them not to start competing aggressively with each other.

Amlaib Conung – or Olaf the White – would go on to become a nemesis to Máel Sechnaill and his successors, fighting many pitched battles against the Irish and Norse-Irish after gaining dubious dominion over the Fair Foreigners.

Sometime before 857, Amlaib would be joined by an ally named Imar. One of the annals states that Amlaib and Imar were brothers, and that they were both sons of the king Gothfraid of Lochlann (or *Laithleind* or *Lathlend*, which may refer to part of Scandinavia or to the Western Scottish isles under Viking control) but other annals make no mention of this familial relationship. In Scandinavian sources, both men claim descent from Sigurd Fafnir's-bane and so they may have been cousins, so this may have been what the lone Irish source was referring to. The uncertainty has left room to follow other circumstantial evidence and conclude that Imar is none other than Ivar the Boneless, son of Ragnar Lothbrok.[10] In any case, Amlaib and Imar (or Olaf and Ivar) were successful at carving out a stable power base centered in Dublin.

Historians end the "First Raiding Period" of the Vikings in Ireland around this time. After 860, the rate of raids worthy of record

---

[10] Though 'Imar' and 'Ivar' appear different in transliteration, the pronunciation in Old Irish and Old Norse would not have been that different. The same is true of 'Amlaib' and 'Olaf.'

gradually slows. There were still many Vikings in Ireland, but things were starting to change, and relationships were becoming more interwoven and more complicated.

But there was another reason besides Irish victories or changing Norse allegiances that made the Vikings lose their former interest in the Emerald Isle: around 865, Ivar the Boneless was preparing to avenge the death of his father, Ragnar Lothbrok. The "Great Heathen Army" was about to descend on Britain.

Chapter IX: Bjorn Ironside in the Mediterranean

Ragnar Lothbrok along with his three sons, Fridleif, Ragbard, and Bjorn rode out ahead of their battle line to face their nemesis, King Sorle of Sweden. King Sorle was accompanied by his champion Starkad, along with the brute's seven sons – all elite Vikings with a long history of vicious raiding. But when Sorle offered Ragnar the choice between single combat with his champion or letting the armies fight each other, Ragnar proposed he face Starkad and his sons with just his three boys.

The details of the duel are not recorded, but Ragnar, Fridleif, Ragbard, and Bjorn were victorious. Sorle attacked with his army anyway, but Ragnar's Vikings routed them. Bjorn killed several of Starkad's sons and helped lead his father's Danes to victory, all while seeming impervious to harm. From that day on, he was called Bjorn Ironside.

Ragnar was never a man to stay in one place, and so he left his new Swedish kingdom for young Bjorn to govern. But while Bjorn was not as insatiable as his father nor as cunning as his brother, Ivar the Boneless, he exceeded both in wanderlust. Before long, Bjorn would leave Sweden with a force of 60 ships and head for Francia.

Instead of focusing his activity on Paris and the politically important northwest, Bjorn went far deeper, and either by river or by navigating around Moorish Spain he began raiding in the ancient territories of Provence and the rich sunny lands that are now known as the French Riviera.

The further Bjorn went, the more he realized that the view of the world held by most other Vikings had been far too small. There was much more wonder (and far more opportunity) to be had than just raiding Scandinavia's neighbors. The Mediterranean had always been the cradle of human civilization. Diverse cultures had grown to be highly-sophisticated, wealthy, and strong because of the perfect climate, abundant resources, and the influence (positive and negative) of each other. There was more war glory, more riches, and more trade than any one Viking could hope to see much less hold.

Bjorn was not the first Viking to reach the Mediterranean: raiding and trading by the Viking-led men of Rus was first mentioned in 839 (maybe 10-20 years before Bjorn's voyages). In 844, a Viking fleet sacked cosmopolitan Seville. Saxo Gramaticus mentions Ragnar himself going as far as the Hellespont in modern-day Turkey. In 860 – probably around the same time that Bjorn was in the Mediterranean – the Varangians (Byzantine term for) of Rus were even bold enough to lay siege to mighty Constantinople.

The Rus did not succeed, but their bellicose activity was only one piece of what made Bjorn's arrival in the Mediterranean so perfectly-timed for him and so badly-timed for the people of the region. The Byzantine and the Islamic powers were preoccupied with wars against each other. Bjorn's fleet was the ideal size to maintain the beloved Viking advantage of mobility while still landing a force of about 3000 elite warriors wherever it chose.

Bjorn's foray into the Mediterranean was, at first, abundantly successful. They raided along the coasts of Francia and Spain, down to the trade-wealthy towns of North Africa, the island of Sicily, and then all the way up to northern Italy. They took all the gold, jewels, weapons, and (unfortunately) slaves that they could carry from the unsuspecting and unprepared cities along the sea.

As they went, Bjorn's ambition and confidence grew until he became obsessed with conquering Rome itself. This was not a very realistic expectation. Rome had not been the center of an empire in 400 years, but it was still the center of the Church, and it still had its old defenses. The Goths and Vandals had taken the city in the 5th century, but only in exponentially higher numbers and even then, mostly by trickery or intimidation. Still, Bjorn Ironside was intent on trying.

When the Vikings reached the amazing, walled city on the central Italian coast, they saw what they were up against. But Bjorn's co-commander Hastein (or in some versions, his brother Hvitserk) had a plan.

Hastein was a Viking hero in his own right (some sources suggest Ragnar – who was still alive at this time – sent him to mentor young Bjorn) and as the fleet approached the imposing, impenetrable walls he showed his cunning and daring. Bjorn sent messengers to the city, stating that they were indeed the dreaded Norse fleet the residents had heard so many tales of, but that their leader had become sick and died. They said that their leader had made a deathbed conversion to Christianity, and only wanted that his body should be buried on holy ground. The unfortunate clergy and leadership of the city fell for the story and admitted the coffin along with a small retinue of pall bearers through the city and to the main cathedral.

Once inside, Bjorn Ironside (or Hastein, sources differ) burst alive and well from the coffin. He and the pall bearers whipped out their hidden weapons, cut their way through the horrified crowd, and opened the gates for the thousands of Vikings who had taken up battle formations while the city was so distracted.

Bjorn Ironside took control of the city swiftly. As the story goes (from a later Norman source), the citizens surrendered as soon as they could be allowed to; and upon hearing the Viking boasts that they had so easily conquered Rome they were at first afraid to say anything. An old man finally did stand up and tell Bjorn and Hastein that they were not in Rome at all – they had captured the city of Luna.

At this point, Bjorn realized that his luck was changing, and it was time to turn back. According to the *Ragnar Saga Lodbrok*, the Vikings were discouraged from pursuing their Roman campaign by a mysterious old man that convinced them that Rome was impossibly far away. It was not all that far away, of course; and so, the old man in the story was either a very clever Italian, or – to engage in the skaldic tradition – Odin was telling Bjorn his goal was unattainable.

Bjorn's fleet, mostly unscathed and heavy with plunder, chose to leave the Mediterranean by the maritime route that led past the Straits of Gibraltar. But such a successful Viking expedition in the center of the world was not to go unanswered. A sizeable navy from Moorish Spain was waiting for them.

Bjorn Ironside's fleet was blocked. The Vikings were ready and eager to fight – after all, they had been undefeated, and felt more than capable of taking on any navy in the world in ship-to-ship combat. What the Vikings had not counted on was that the Moors had acquired Greek Fire.

Greek Fire was one of the most prized weapons of the Byzantines – a petroleum-based compound of unknown composition that could be launched from tubes and would continue to burn even on the surface of water. Bjorn Ironside's wooden ships were up against a larger fleet armed with medieval flame throwers.

The battle was fierce. Forty of Bjorn's ships caught fire and sank.[11] This means that about 2000 Vikings and an unknown number of

---

[11] While all applicable sources agree Bjorn lost about 40 ships, some say that he lost only two ships to the Moors' fire and the rest were lost in a storm. While the details are not fully obtainable, and storm losses are likely, it is unlikely that Bjorn would have retreated from the Moors if he had only lost a few ships.

Mediterranean captives were killed. Bjorn and Hastein escaped the Moors with the remaining third of their ships. In yet another testimony to the versatility and mobility of the Viking dragon ship, they were able to leave the Mediterranean through the riverways of Francia.[12]

Bjorn soon joined forces with his brothers to avenge the death of their father, Ragnar, at the hand of the Northumbrian king, Aella (which we will describe soon). Thus, Bjorn led his rebuilt forces as part of "The Great Heathen Army" that conquered several Anglo-Saxon kingdoms and led to the establishment of the Danelaw – a permanent Viking presence in Britain.

Some sources dispute Bjorn's involvement in this invasion, saying that he merely returned to Sweden. He is not specifically mentioned in *The Anglo-Saxon Chronicle*, while several of Ragnar's other sons are. This claim, though, seems out of character. We are told that when Bjorn heard the news of Ragnar's death, he *"gripped his spear shaft so tightly that his fingerprints were left on the wood"*. It is unlikely that one of Ragnar's favorite sons (the only son Ragnar himself gifted with a kingdom) would fail to avenge him. We know that a Viking named Hastein was very involved in the later struggle with Alfred the

---

[12] The Fragmentary Chronicle of Ireland offers a parallel account of two sons of "Ragnall" that successfully raid the Mediterranean. In this account, the Vikings also lose 40 ships, but manage to break through the blockade and sail to Ireland. The account specifies that the Moors who intercepted Bjorn and Hvitserk (if we may make this assumption) were from Mauritanea (which in context also means Morocco and Algeria) and not Spain, though of course these forces had close connections at the time.

Great's Wessex, but there is no guarantee it is the same Hastein who accompanied Bjorn. We do know that, assuming Bjorn was involved, he played less of a role than Ivar and some of his other brothers, and that he did not stay to help rule the Danelaw afterwards[13].

In any case, after the war Bjorn decided that it was time to return to Sweden. He had at least two sons, and founded the Munsö Dynasty which ruled in Sweden for generations.

With two-thirds of his ships, crew, and loot at the bottom of the sea and the embarrassing conquest of the wrong city, Bjorn Ironside's Mediterranean expedition may not seem like much of a success. It appears that Bjorn did not consider it one, as he never returned. But Bjorn's contribution to the Viking story is highly meaningful. Bjorn's expedition expanded the "cognitive map" of every Viking. The Rus Vikings had reached the Mediterranean around the same time, but these Norse-Slavic hybrid of Kiev (Kyiv) were separated from the Norse of the West by land and sea. Vikings in Scandinavia, Scotland, Ireland, the Danelaw of Britain, and France now realized that their world could be so much bigger.

The rest of the Middle Ages would be increasingly characterized by Norse and Norman action in Sicily, Italy, and the Byzantine world. Some of our most colorful accounts of Viking life would come from

---

[13] A later Norman source specifies Bjorn was shipwrecked in England and had to retreat back to Scandinavia, thus explaining his low profile and early exit from the invasion.

Arab geographers. For better or worse, Viking descendants would be involved in the Crusades and in the formation of kingdoms far removed from their cold habitat. After 1066, Vikings leaving the demise of their age would find new homes for their talents by joining their Russian cousins as members of the Varangian Guard. To this day, there are archeological traces of the Vikings throughout Italy, Greece, Turkey, and the Middle East; and the history of those regions are rich with tales of Viking bravery. Perhaps this was all inevitable – fate, as the Vikings themselves would say – but it is hard to see how it would have happened without the daring and wanderlust of Bjorn Ironside.

Chapter X: Ivar the Boneless and the Great Heathen Army

Ivar the Boneless was leading elite crews of berserkers against the Irish when news reached him that King Aelle of Northumbria had trapped his father, the legendary Ragnar Lothbrok, and killed him by casting him into a pit of vipers. The *skalds*[14] tell us that Ivar quietly demanded the details of his father's death, and as he listened "*his face became red, blue, and pale by turns*". King Aelle had just made an enemy of perhaps the most dangerous man of the 9th century; and though he did not know it yet, this action would doom his kingdom and shape the history of England. For Ivar was more than just another rampaging Viking, testing his skills against the warriors or Ireland while seizing hold of their treasures and territory; he was a military genius and a leader of magnificent ability.

He also may have been a cripple. Historians argue over what the mysterious moniker "the Boneless" means, because our sources give us only conflicting clues. The *skalds* say that "*only cartilage was where bone should have been, but otherwise he grew tall and handsome*", whereas other tellers say that it was as if he "*had no bones at all*". In the *Ragnar Saga Lodbrok* (which we must remember was finally set down in writing a few centuries later) there is a story that he was born with deformed legs because of a curse; and there are accounts of his men carrying him on their shields. He was said to be very lethal, but is

---

[14] Skalds are Norse storytellers and poets. The reference here is from *The Saga of Ragnar Lothbrok and His Sons.*

usually mentioned killing with a bow or upon laying hold of an enemy. Paradoxically, he is said elsewhere to have towered over his enemies, and to have great strength; but this may simply be literary license typical of heroic poetry.

Many historians dismiss this idea, emphatic in the belief that the Norse would not have followed someone into battle who could not even stand. This is a valid objection, for before a Viking could even face his enemy in the ultimate physical test of prowess, he would have had to row, march, or ride great distances over violent seas and wild terrain. In fact, in Ivar's time many cultures (especially the Byzantines, but even the Irish) would maim an unwelcome political figure solely to disqualify him from rulership.

But however rare it may be for a physically disabled person to become a leader in pre-modern times, it was not unprecedented. As unlikely as it may be that the Vikings would follow someone with a severe physical disability, it is even more unlikely that they would tell stories about such a thing if it had not been the case.

The key to Ivar's acceptance lied in his birth, his ability, and his brothers. The sagas say that Ivar's brothers carried him with them wherever they went, and that he fully participated in all their actions. Ivar's intelligence, cunning, and wisdom where so great that – if we can believe the *skalds* – his brothers were reluctant to take on any significant challenges without his insight. Thus as the royal heirs of Lothbrok's legacy grew, so did Ivar's acceptance and value to his people.

Theories on Ivar's Name

The strange thing about Ivar's affliction is that many sources hardly mention it (focusing instead on his incredible victories or savage character). This may support the notion that it was not some glaringly obvious physical variance. Some believe that "boneless" refers to impotency, for it is mentioned that Ivar "never showed any lust" or had love for anything besides war, and *Ragnar Saga Lodbrok* says he had no sons. This lack of progeny is highly debatable, though because Ivar the Boneless is considered by many to be the founder of the Ui Imar dynasty of Irish Vikings that were major players of the next century. Family tree aside, the euphemism is anachronistic; and while the Norse knew little medicine they certainly had a very good understanding of gross anatomy.

A popular view is that Ivar suffered from *osteogenesis imperfecta*, a rare, genetic condition that hampers the formation of bone cells and can lead to deformities and fractures. Others take the opposite view, (attempting to reconcile "boneless" with other accounts of Ivar's battle prowess) and believe that Ivar was especially fast and flexible. If so, it may be possible that Ivar was on the opposite side of the spectrum of connective tissue disorders, having something like *Ehlers-Danlos syndrome*, as some contortionists do. Such abilities could potentially be a great benefit to a warrior enabling him to do things that his opponents could not anticipate (though there are associated maladies that could certainly make them miserable).

The *skalds* themselves offer one final suggestion (perhaps unwittingly) when they say that Ivar was occasionally afflicted by a sickness which made him temporarily unable to move. This could be a seizure disorder, some other type of neurological disorder like Guillan-Barre syndrome, or even a psychological condition. If it were one of these, where the disability fluctuates in nature, that would explain some tales saying his followers had to carry him while other sources making no mention of infirmity.

One final theory comes from archeology. A burial mound in Repton, England reportedly housed the skeleton of a 9th century warrior that was allegedly nine feet tall. The skeleton was at the center of the mound, with signs of great status (weapons, armor, sacrifices, et cetera) but also signs of posthumous mutilation. The archeologists were eager to tie this magnificent find to the legend of Ivar the Boneless. If they were correct, Ivar's moniker would be hyperbolically ironic – he was so tall and bony (as those with giantism usually have prominent knuckles and bony features) that his peers called him "boneless" as a joke.

It is our opinion that while the Repton man is certainly an interesting discovery and must have been a fearsome warrior, that the links with his case and the story of Ivar the Boneless have significant flaws.

As in the case of the shield maidens, we find modern experts refusing to accept what the Vikings themselves accepted enough to include in their stories. If the Vikings would not have followed a true cripple – that is, someone who needed help even to get from one place to another – then why would they have told stories about it? Epic poetry normally accentuates the hero's strength, not his weakness. Unfortunately, there is no way to solve the mystery; but it is important to keep an open mind to all possibilities.

Because medical conditions and injuries change over time, it is also possible to reconcile several different theories. Ivar may have been both a mighty warrior and litter-bound at different points in his life.

Ivar and the Great Heathen Army

Whatever his disabilities might have been, by the time Ivar was planning to avenge his father he was already a highly-respected leader. The *skalds* describe him both in terms of a bear but also as a cunning fox. Based on the conclusion that Ivar (skaldic source designation), Imar (Irish source designation) and Ingvar (English source designation) are all one in the same person, he had been leading Vikings in Ireland for some years; and though Ireland was a magnet for raiders because it was the center of medieval monasticism it was a rough neighborhood even by Dark Age standards.

How many years Ivar was active is another mystery. The most commonly regurgitated date of his birth is 794 – but the math on this does not work out well. The Imar of the Irish annals was a younger man, and was first mentioned around the 850's.

Up to the mid-9th century, the Vikings had come as raiders that would sometimes take swaths of territory. They had assailed Paris with 5000 men 21 years before, but had never come to conquer whole kingdoms. According to the *Anglo-Saxon Chronicle*, the Vikings first overwintered in Britain around 855, but were eventually chased off by Ethelwulf, the father of the future Alfred the Great.

The *Anglo-Saxon Chronicle* mentions another thwarted Viking invasion around 861. According to *Ragnars Saga Lodbrok*, Ragnar Lothbrok led a very reckless invasion of Britain, during which his fleet was scattered by storms and he was captured and executed in extravagant fashion by King Aella, the usurper of Northumbria. King Aella is thought to have begun his rule around 861 or 862, so it is possible that the invasion mentioned in passing by the *Anglo-Saxon Chronicle* was Ragnar's.

The *Anglo-Saxon Chronicle* mentions an army of Vikings landing in Kent in 865, which was only partially successful. This could have been the expedition to Britain by Ragnar's sons, which failed because Ivar was not involved, as *Ragnars Saga Lodbrok* describes.

In any case, when Ivar joined his brothers and landed in the English kingdom of East Anglia in 866, he was well-prepared to accomplish what no Viking had before him. From our various sources, we have reason to believe that this "Great Heathen Army" was gathered from far and wide, including major representation from Ivar's Vikings of Ireland as well as from far to the east (even as far as the river Danube in central Europe). The *Anglo-Saxon Chronicle* tends to call the Vikings Danes whenever it is not calling them heathens, and so it is reasonable to conclude that Danes were the majority, though our early sources tend to be indiscriminate regarding the specific ethnicity of the Vikings.

Whatever the particular make-up or organization, this Great Heathen Army was so big that most early chroniclers do not even try to count it. It was under a number of leaders (all the sons of Ragnar and then many more) though Ivar quickly became the most conspicuous leader of the early years of the war.

This was a far bigger operation than Ragnar's attack on Paris, and bigger than any Viking attack to date. It was clear that after years of fighting a quagmire in Ireland and dodging the imperial powers of the continent, the prize of prosperous, divided Britain was the incentive needed to unite the Vikings.

As Sir Winston Churchill puts it, "Saxon England was at this time ripe for the sickle." Divided into four competing kingdoms and defended largely by *fyrds* of citizen soldiers who only expected to mobilize for forty days at a time, the English were neither expecting, nor prepared for the Great Heathen Army that landed on their east coast in 866.

The people of the kingdom of East Anglia panicked, and promised Ivar and his brothers horses in exchange for peace. So, in the spring of 867, the Viking host left their ships safely behind and headed straight for Aella's kingdom of Northumbria.

Most Vikings were not cavalrymen, but the East Anglian horses gave them excellent mobility between targets. Armies had difficulty catching them, and when they did Ivar would order his men to feign retreat. When the English followed and overcommitted, they would be cut off and ambushed. Ivar used a variety of other stratagems to trap his foes, or to escape the traps they set for him.

Soon the Viking army was laying siege Northumbria's greatest city, the Roman city of Eboracum that the Saxons called Eoforwic. Eoforwic fell quickly, and the Great Heathen Army set up their base there. They called the city Jorvik, (from which its modern name, York, is derived). Jorvik would go on to play an important role throughout the rest of the Viking Age.

King Aella was already enmeshed in a civil war with King Osberht. Finally, recognizing the crisis that was upon them, the two put their feud aside and led a united army to repel the invaders.

Aelle and Osberht found the Vikings huddled in York behind walls that had obvious gaps and week points. The Northumbrian forces pounced. The Vikings retreated into the town, and English pursued them into the close streets. It was there that Ivar sprang his trap. The English rushed into carefully prepared kill zones, and all escape was cut off. Their forces were cut in half, unable to help each other. Ivar's Vikings slaughtered the Northumbrians.

Osberht died on the field, but according to Norse sources, Aelle was captured. Ivar and the sons of Ragnar performed the Blood Eagle ritual on King Aelle, ripping his lungs from his body and finally avenging the death of their father. This was the end of Northumbria as an independent kingdom.

Drunk on victory, Ivar the Boneless and his armies turned towards Mercia, the heart of Saxon Britain. But by now the English knew that they must unite or be destroyed. Wessex, under King Ethelred and Prince Alfred joined with Mercia, and forced Ivar to the negotiating table.

Peace only lasted a short time. Ivar broke the treaty of Nottingham, martyred King Edmund of East Anglia, and once more went on the war path. Later, Ivar changed course and joined his old friend (or brother, according to one source) Olaf the White in invading the Briton kingdom of Strathclyde in modern-day Scotland. Together once more, the veterans of Ireland's Viking wars permanently destroyed Strathclyde as a kingdom. The Great Heathen Army, now led by Ragnar's bastard son Ubba and a Norse king named Guthrum would continue to carve out a Viking kingdom in Britain without the help of their greatest tactician.

Ivar the Boneless returned to Ireland. As Churchill puts it, "Laden with loot and seemingly invincible, he settled in Dublin, and died there peacefully two years later"

Ivar the Boneless was an extraordinary warrior whose ferocity and cruelty at times reached psychotic levels. He was responsible for the death of three kings (two by ritual murder), to say nothing of soldiers, clergy, and civilians. But he was also a visionary and a true leader. Before him the Vikings were primarily raiders who hadn't done anything bigger than sack Paris. Ivar changed that, and in just a few years his Vikings had turned three English kingdoms into a large Norse state called the Danelaw. If in the first siege of Paris we saw Ragnar's dream, in Ivar's accomplishments we saw this dream fully realized.

We have evidence, too, that in those rare times when he was not fighting, Ivar may have been a good ruler. He showed religious and ethnic tolerance in York and other formerly-Saxon cities he controlled. We are told that he was generous to his subjects, *"giving with two hands"*. When he died, the pious chronicler wrote *"he slept in Christ"*. We do not take this to mean that the leader of the Great Heathen Army converted; but we do think that it shows that his subjects respected him – which is no small thing for a conqueror to accomplish. If he did all this despite a disability (or perhaps because of it) that makes it all the more amazing.

Chapter XI: Kenneth MacAlpin and the Viking Origins of Scotland

Scotland played an important role in Viking raiding, trading, and colonization; and the Vikings played an important role in the history and national identity of Scotland. While several references in surviving sagas and other Norse lore strongly state that Scotland was best avoided – being a land of fierce savages and abominable weather – many Vikings obviously ignored the advice. In addition to the rich supply of archeological evidence, Scotland boasts some of the highest Nordic DNA outside of Scandinavia, and shares many cultural similarities with Norway. Within a relatively short period of time in the early 9th century, Vikings had taken enough territory in Scotland to form their own kingdom there (called *Lochland, Lothlend,* or *Lochlainn*), which at its height extended influence from Dublin to York. For the natives of Scotland, it was not just the active influences of this Norse presence, but also their reactions towards it, that forged many disparate tribes into one people.

Why Scotland?

The motivation for Viking conquest/colonization in Scotland is immediately apparent upon studying any world map. Sailing out from Norway, Denmark, and Sweden towards the rich monasteries, fertile fields, and abundant resources of Ireland and Britain, the archipelago of islands that form the west of Scotland would make perfect base camps for armies to amass and trading posts to flourish. These 790 islands, including those of Orkney, Mann, Skye, Shetland, and the Hebrides are also perfectly situated to receive goods (and retreating forces) back from Ireland and Britain, as well as Iceland and lands further west. The fjords and hills of these windswept havens even looked a little like the homelands the Norse had left behind. Meanwhile, the natives of these islands – while certainly brave and hardy people – could rarely have possessed the military organization to resist Vikings that landed in any significant number.

The western isles off the Scottish coast, therefore, offered what we could call the Viking dream: in the pioneer days of the early 9th century, someone who owned a few ships could possibly win themselves their own island, and the freedom to pursue their ambitions as far as their fate would take them.

The mainland of Scotland was another story, though. Centuries before, a few failed campaigns had taught the Romans that it was better to build a wall to keep the natives of Scotland out than to try to conquer them. The Romans even had to pull back from their Antonine Wall to Hadrian's Wall further south. The Saxons had fared no better, and so their dominion stopped in Northumbria. By the time the Vikings came on the scene, what is now Scotland was a patchwork of competing kingdoms, and each of these kingdoms was a patchwork of competing tribes and clans.

These diverse tribes fell into three basic categories: Picts, Britons, and Scots. The Pictish territories of pre-ninth century Scotland are usually referred to as Pictland. The region of Strathclyde in the southwestern part of the territory was inhabited by a Britonic people, like those in Wales and Cornwall. The Scots inhabited Dal Riata (or Dalriada), a trans-marine kingdom stretching from eastern Ireland to the southwestern portion of this contested territory of islands, hills, and hinterlands.

The Picts were the aboriginal peoples of Scotland, especially the north (including the Highlands) and east. The Romans had called them *Picti*, which referred to their alleged tendency to run into battle "naked" and painted blue. In the intervening several-hundred years they had perhaps become more sophisticated but were still very frightening. They were a mysterious people of contested origin and language who left many standing-stone monuments and fantastic artwork that can still be seen today.

While the genetic deck is well-shuffled now, the Picts had been the majority in Scotland throughout its long history and so it is ironic that the place is now known by the name of the lesser-numbered, foreign Scotts. The same can be said for England, whose namesake Angles were only one of many tribes, and only a moderately-important one at that.

The Scotts were a Gaelic/Celtic people that most experts believe had migrated into Scotland from Ireland. The Romans referred to Irish raiders in Britain as *Scoti*, and this term still appears referring to Irish in contemporary sources, such as the *Anglo-Saxon Chronicle*. These two lands are very close to each other, of course, and there was a great deal of cross-pollination between Ireland and Scotland throughout history.

The Picts and the Scotts were constantly at war with each other, as well as with the Britons in the region, and of course the Saxons of neighboring Northumbria and Bernicia. Religion was one of the few areas where most parties agreed, and so monasteries (such as the famous abbey in Iona) thrived despite the discord throughout the rest of the land.

This all was – as we have seen in Ireland – the natural habitat in which Vikings become apex predators. The Vikings took advantage of the war and strife bubbling between native tribes, and while the Picts and Scotts fought each other the Vikings robbed the monasteries and snatched more and more territory.

Within about 50 years of the first Viking raids, there was enough Norse strength in mainland Scotland to threaten the existing powers there. That threat, however, had an outcome that no one – especially not the Vikings – could have anticipated.

How the Vikings Inadvertently Created Scotland

In 839, King Ailpín of the Dal Riata Scotts met a confederation of several Pictish kings in battle. Ailpín's Scotts were routed, and the king was killed. As the Picts impaled the hapless ruler's severed head on one of their spears, however, a large force of Vikings broke from cover and rushed them. It is not really known why the Vikings were there in such force, but it is likely that they were waiting to take further advantage of the turmoil to weaken the native resistance to their expansion. The Vikings smashed the Picts, killing all their kings and scattering the army.

Ailpín's son, Cináed (remembered to history as Kenneth MacAlpin) took his father's place as king of the Dal Riata Scotts. Taking advantage of the power vacuum the Vikings had just created amongst the Picts, Kenneth (who may have been half-Pict himself) began successfully taking over Pictish kingdoms. By 848, Kenneth MacAlpin was being called the *King of the Picts and the Scotts*.

This unification of Picts and Scotts (however incomplete it may have been) did not come a moment too soon, for a massive Viking fleet of 140 ships descended upon the Scotts' kingdom of Dal Riata. The Scotts were able to retreat east, into Pictish territory that they were now more welcome into, depriving the Vikings of total victory and further unifying Kenneth MacAlpin's kingdom. There, the combined strength of Picts and Scotts deterred the Viking armies from pushing any further, at least at that time.

Soon people did not speak of Dal Riata and Pictland anymore, but called the whole region Alba. While various political changes throughout the next few centuries led to the country being called Scotland, it is still called Alba in the native Scottish-Gaelic language today. While it would take many years, many wars, and many great leaders to turn a land of warring tribes into one people, it was the Vikings that initially catalyzed this change.

The Vikings in Scotland

Though the Vikings established supremacy in the western islands, and ended the Scottish kingdom of Dal Riata, the emergence of a more unified Alba changed their designs. Conquering the whole land no longer seemed possible, and so (as they had in Ireland), the Norse gradually became more enmeshed in the ethnic, cultural, and political landscape.

For example, the most successful Scottish ruler of the Dark Ages, Constantine mac Áed (Constantine II) crushed a Viking offensive led by Dublin's Ivar the Younger in 902, only to surround himself with Viking allies against King Aethelstan of England some decades later. Common cause and joint interest became more important than ethnicity, and Norse, Scotts, Picts, and Britons intermarried in Scotland on all levels of society. Eventually, it was not only the Picts and the Scotts that were Scottish, but the Vikings, too.

Once more, the islands were different, and remained a bastion of Viking activity and Norse customs long after the Viking Age ended. It was to islands like Orkney, the Shetlands, and the Isle of Mann that the Irish king Máel Mórda drew many of his allies against Brian Boru in the Battle of Clontarf (1014), and it was back to these islands that the Viking survivors returned. The Hebrides were officially territories of Norway, not Scotland, until the 13th century, as was Orkney and Shetland until the 15th. Today these places are still as rich in Norse culture as they are in Norse blood. DNA studies show that the Shetland Islands are 44% Norse, and Orkney is 30%, and offer firm evidence that these areas of Scotland were settled by Scandinavian families, and not just male adventurers. Other islands, like the Hebrides, are around 15-20% which is still very high considering this was a migration that occurred a thousand years ago.

Medieval Scotland was a wild land with a rugged way of life. There were a few great cities and cultural centers, but most of these were situated in the south. Large swaths of countryside were completely rural and open. In such an environment, local rule becomes even more important than the rule of any far-off king. Men and women live by their wits, tenacity, and courage, and ways of life are slow to change. Vikings who settled there fit right in, and maintained much of their character and customs while also learning new ones from their like-minded neighbors. They contributed to the history of the land, but due to the nature of Scotland so many of those stories are lost to the mists of time.

Chapter XII: Alfred the Viking Fighter, the Danelaw, and the Birth of England

It was late in the year 871 when the 23-year-old Alfred, newly-appointed king of the last free Saxon kingdom in Britain, sat down for peace talks with two sons of Lothbrok and other leaders of the Great Heathen Army.

For young Alfred, it would be impossible not to feel intimidated by the situation.

Halfdan Ragnarson and his half-brother Ubba were twice Alfred's age and had ten times his experience. Alfred had met these Viking champions three years before – but in 868 he had only been in the entourage of his older brother, King Aethelred, and they had been bargaining for the peace of neighboring Mercia and not Alfred's own home of Wessex.

Now in 871, when the Viking hosts had only been in the country for 5 years, Aethelred and all of Alfred's other once-powerful brothers were dead, and Mercia, East Anglia, Northumbria (with Bernicia), and Kent had all fallen. At least Ivar the Boneless had returned to Ireland – but more Vikings had come that summer. The kings of these reinforcements, including one named Guthrum, sat across from Alfred now, adding to the malice in the room and the sense that Alfred was a stag surrounded by a pack of wolves. But Alfred, as we shall see, was never one to show fear.

Wessex was the southernmost portion of Britain. It was wealthy and fertile, with the best trade-crossings to the continent, so of course, the Vikings could never consider their conquest complete until they had dominion over this territory. But unlike the other Anglo-Saxon kingdoms they had taken, Wessex did not have many wide, slow-moving rivers for the Vikings to exploit with their dragon ships. It had sea cliffs, mountain ledges, forests, moors, marshlands, and other challenges of topography to slow invaders. It had a strong warrior tradition and had until recently had a line of vigorous kings. Its political structure made it easier for ealdorman (the Saxon equivalent of jarl) to carry on the defense of the land without the king's direct involvement, making military action much faster. So, it was for these reasons that the Vikings saved Wessex for last.

Invasion finally came to Wessex as a surprise attack in the dead of winter, January 871. The Vikings won that attack at a place called Reading (which gave them an all-important winter base for their campaign), but just two weeks later King Aethelred and his little brother, Alfred met them on the slopes of nearby Ashdown.

The Vikings had the high ground (giving them about a 30 percent advantage, according to the military science rule of thumb) as well as the psychological edge of a five-year winning streak. The Saxons split their forces, but then on the fateful morning of the battle, Aethelred was reluctant to attack. We are told the pious young king was in prayer, but

Prince Alfred realized they could wait no longer. He led his men into battle "*charging in like a wild boar*." His brother finally joined him, catching the Vikings in a pincer attack. It was Alfred's first real command, and it was a great victory for the Saxons. The slopes of Ashdown were littered with heathen dead, including one of their kings (a Dane named Bagsac) and five jarls.

But the Vikings were back in the field for a rematch almost immediately. The two West Saxon brothers would repeat the strategy a few times, and fought well, but never with the same success as at Ashdown. Time after time, the Vikings "*held the place of carnage.*" By Easter that year, Aethelred – only in his mid-twenties with six years on the throne – was exhausted and succumbed to a fatal illness or wound.

Alfred took his brother's place and continued the fight. A total of nine battles were fought that year, with the West Saxons losing a little ground each time. There would be no way to sustain this war, and yet there seemed no way to turn it around.

But for the Great Heathen Army, it was much more than they had bargained for. They had expected Wessex to fall as everywhere else had. The kings and jarls had expected to make themselves and their men rich. But every gain was hard-won, and they were losing a lot of warriors to the sword or to desertion for easier gains elsewhere. What was more, the hard fighting that enmeshed them here was keeping them exposed in their other semi-conquered kingdoms, like Mercia and Northumbria.

It was time to talk.

So, when Alfred met Halfdan Ragnarson, Ubba, Guthrum, and the others at the close of that long, violent year of upheaval, both sides wanted the same thing – time. Though the course of the next hours or days were probably full of posturing, threats, boasting, intimidation tactics, and scabbard-rattling, the West Saxons and the 'Danes' (as Old English sources usually collectively call Vikings) finally came to an agreement – there would be a cease-fire for a period of five years.

Peace did not come before a *danegeld* was set, and this bribe must have been set high for it took Alfred a few months to raise it. But once the Vikings had their silver and gold, they returned north.

We know that Halfdan, Ubba, and Guthrum were as happy to have their cease-fire as Alfred was, because they did not find ways to bend their agreement. Instead they promptly moved to secure their holdings, unleashing more war in Northumbria, finally driving out Alfred's old battle-shy ally, King Buhdred of Mercia, and preparing for the re-invasion of Wessex in the near-future.

It was a mistake. Had Ivar the Boneless still been with The Great Heathen Army, he would probably have told them to kill Alfred when they had the chance.

Young Alfred had already shown himself to be a warrior king, but in the 9th century, warrior kings were a dime a dozen. Alfred was more than that. Alfred's name meant "Elf Wise" or "Elf Counsel." His parents gave him this old pagan name at a time when names were not given for the ring of their sound, but as a hope of the blessing they might convey. Alfred's name in our culture would basically mean "supernaturally intelligent," and he was to live up to it. The man had an uncommon amount of crystalized (static), fluid (dynamic), and emotional intelligence as well as a visionary spirit. He backed these attributes up with tremendous discipline in both his personal actions and his policies. These qualities would shape his every move in life, war, and diplomacy.

Bishop Asser's Life of Alfred

We know a lot about Alfred, not only because the many actions of his 28-year reign are recorded in the *Anglo-Saxon Chronicle*, but because of a biography written by a monk (later a bishop) named Asser. Alfred was a patron of Asser, as well as a great patron of the Church in general, and so Asser's biography is seldom objective and primarily preoccupied with the King's moral and religious qualities. But it does offer us a lot of details of Alfred's personal life, personality, and struggles that we seldom get for other Early Medieval figures. Even without Asser, though, Alfred's actions speak for themselves, and his influence is felt in England even now.

As Asser tells us, Alfred was a very pious person and would do nothing before praying, hearing mass, and receiving communion each day (insisting – even at times of great distress – that the affairs of heaven are always more important than the affairs of earth). In an age where kings often used religion to endorse their avarice rather than restrict it, Alfred's list of outrages, indiscretions, and atrocities is mercifully short. This is not to say that he was not a ruthless king – for the Middle Ages was such a time that the few gentle kings there were have been condemned by history as failures. Alfred loved his faith, though, and used it to both find his own strength as well as strengthen the bonds between his people. It is likely that he saw – as Constantine the Great had seen before him – that the Church could be used to drive common purpose and to build up networks in his age of fractured kingdoms. Towards this end, as well as for the sake of his personal piety, Alfred was quick to advance the interests of the Church and to make large gifts to religious institutions from Ireland to Rome.

This advanced his name and his control of Britain, too. For Alfred, the throne and the Church had a symbiotic relationship. He had come by this realization early, for his father Aethelwulf had brought him along on a pilgrimage to Rome when Alfred was 10, where the Pope not only impressed the Saxon prince with the grandeur of that station but also allegedly made quite a fuss over him. Perhaps Aethelwulf, who had several other sons who could (and would) be King after him, intended Alfred for the Church.

But there was one thing that might have saved Alfred and England from this alternative destiny: Alfred may have had a learning disability.

Though Alfred would go on to be one of the more learned kings of his day and would even translate Roman philosophers into English, throughout his childhood he could not read. While this was normal for most of the population of Medieval Europe at the time, it was not typical for a royal household.

It was not until Alfred was 12 – almost a man by the standards of the day – that he was able to teach himself (with a little help) to read and write. Asser's several assertions that Alfred "*wanted to learn but could find no master to teach him*" is generally taken to mean that there were no educated people around, but in monastery-rich Wessex, it is unlikely that there were no monks available to teach a prince his letters. Instead, it seems that Alfred had to overcome his own blocks and find a way in which his mind could be unlocked to the written word.

Asser's story on how this happened has at least two points of interest. Alfred's mother (Aethelwulf's first wife and not the Carolingian princess, Judith, he would later marry) told the 12-year-old that he could have her book of Saxon poems if he could learn to read it. His motivation suddenly fired, Alfred found people to read him the book until he memorized every word, and then used his knowledge of the poems to decipher the book. Once he had done this, he had "learned how to learn" and would go on to read in several languages as well as gradually acquiring skill in the essential academic disciplines of the day (rhetoric, astronomy, music theory, grammar, logic, arithmetic, and geometry). Alfred teaching himself what no one else was able to teach him gives us a glimpse of his unusual, adaptive mind, but it also gives us insight into his character.

Because of his reputation for intellectual and academic pursuits, Alfred is sometimes interpreted as a figure in the continental, neo-Roman, or even proto-Renaissance mold. People are sometimes tempted to think that he is a perfect juxtaposition of high European culture against the barbarism of the northern invaders. But this does not really seem accurate. Alfred found his motivation in a book of Saxon poetry – not in a book of saints' lives, classical philosophy, or what scriptures he may have had access to. Though Alfred was eager to apply knowledge from the world-over to perfect and expand his kingdom of Wessex, in his heart, he was driven by the distinct spirit that was embodied in the poetry of his people.

Alfred's intellect was not only oriented towards the theoretical and academic. He was an inventor and made developments ranging from improvements to the hand-held lantern, to coming up with candles that could precisely mark time, to designing a fleet of ships for coastal defense.

Alfred began working on his ships the moment the Vikings left Wessex, though the project would take years. His ships were twice the size of dragon ships, with 60 oars or more, and their sides and decks were higher to give their crews the advantage when vessels came broadside to fight.

But though they were fast, Alfred's ships did not have the maneuverability of dragon ships, were expensive to build, and were hard for his Saxon and Frisian sailors to handle. So, while the young King was right that sea power would one day be a key to British military superiority, Alfred's fleet never made much of an impact in his Viking wars.

Alfred was an innovator of policy and would eventually find solutions to some of the biggest problems Vikings posed to his people. He reorganized the *fyrd* – the citizen soldiers who were called out to fight for set periods of time – from a single body into two groups of alternating attackers and defenders. This reduced the soldiers he had available to him at any given time, but for once his soldiers no longer needed to worry that their families and homes were being destroyed by Vikings while they were away. This greatly cut down on desertion. It also helped ward off the famous feints of the Viking strategists.

Alfred's other answer to Viking attacks on his heartland was a state campaign of building *burghs. Burghs* were forts set up in strategic places. They not only housed troops but were refuges people could quickly flee to with their movable wealth, thus frustrating the smash-and-grab tactics of raiders.

Asser tells us that King Alfred's constantly-active mind and the near-perpetual crisis of his times came at a high personal cost to him. Implacable on the exterior, the King was consumed by stress within, and his time spent in religious pursuits were as much to seek solace and find fortitude as they were to set any examples for onlookers. Probably because of the amplification of these stresses by his intense mind, Alfred suffered from chronic physical pain.

Though Asser goes on at length about the King's affliction, he is vague in his description. One gets the sense that it might have been something like ulcerative colitis, bleeding peptic ulcers, or diverticulitis. Whatever the case may be, Asser tells us that "*there was not an hour that went by that the King did not live with pain or in fear of that pain.*" Despite this, Alfred was healthy enough to hunt and to lead his troops, and in keeping with the peculiar bent of the Medieval Christian mind, both Alfred and Asser felt the disease was a sign of God's hand in his life.

And Alfred was going to need God's hand, for in the spring of 877 the peace treaty between the West Saxons and the Vikings was to end, and all of Wessex was about to collapse.

The Last Kingdom

When the treaty ended, King Guthrum of the Danes wasted no time before invading Wessex with an overwhelming force. Alfred's preparations had not come to fruition yet, though, and the Saxon King met the Vikings with his own army while waving the banner of truce. New terms were drawn up, new gold surrendered to Guthrum (Halfdan Ragnarson seems to have stayed in Northumbria), and new oaths were taken. The Vikings swore an oath of peace upon a sacred arm ring.

This ring, though, it would seem, had been misrepresented in its power, for the Great Heathen Army took advantage of the West Saxons' good faith and immediately raced to attack Exeter.

It was the first colossal embarrassment of Alfred's young career. The walled town of Exeter fell to the Vikings – who were following their familiar pattern of taking a fortified city by treachery and then using that fortress as a base of operations for deeper incursions.

But Guthrum's oath-breaking was to be punished by divine hands. As his massive fleet moved to join him near Exeter, a terrible storm blew in from the cold Atlantic.

This violent storm wrecked 120 or more ships, dashing them on the rocks of Britain and drowning 5000 Vikings. The Great Heathen Army had swollen to "incalculable" numbers, but no army of the day could shrug off such a loss of men and ships, nor ignore the spiritual implications of such a disaster. The Vikings were forced to make peace and to accept that they were being punished by their gods for their duplicity in breaking the treaty. They swore stronger oaths and moved further off from Wessex. Peace again reigned.

This time, Guthrum would wait five whole months before breaking his word again.

And so, it was not until the twelfth night of Christmas (January 5, 878) that the Viking army attacked the unsuspecting and drink-sodden West Saxons at the height of their revelry. The attack was so well-timed and well-planned that the Saxons could hardly mount a defense at all. Alfred, his *housecarls* (personal retinue), family, and some of his followers escaped into the wild. There was no friendly refuge they could reach, and they were forced to go into hiding. Almost every major city was besieged, every ealdorman's lands hemmed in. Guthrum and his Danes saw to it that each Saxon force remained isolated and could not join together in any strength.

Many surrendered. Some ealdorman fled. As Asser records,

"And they drove many of that people by their arms, by poverty, and by fear, to voyage beyond sea, and reduced almost all the inhabitants of that district to

subjection."

In the cold months of 878, it seemed certain that the last kingdom in Saxon Britain had fallen.

The Outlaw King

This was the greatest disaster that Alfred (now aged about 30) had ever experienced. In a single night he had lost his entire kingdom, his army was scattered, and all Saxon Britain was under the dominion of the Vikings. Few kings have ever recovered from such a catastrophe. Alfred did not quit, though. He was a king in exile within his own lands, hiding "*in the fastness of the moors*" and in the swamplands of southern Britain – the wilderness that would be hard for anyone to cover much less control.

Perhaps the Vikings hardly cared. They were busy taking the wealth of Wessex and mopping up resistance. Alfred could not hide forever, and every day he was gone, their hold on the land strengthened.

Always moving, Alfred would lie in hiding throughout the winter. Many folktales commemorate this time, passed down from mothers to children about a wandering king in disguise, a proto-Robin Hood waging a guerrilla war against an invading power. We hear of Alfred posing as a harpist at a Viking feast so that he could learn their plans. Another famous tale tells of a housewife who scolds the King when he lets the bread burn, unaware of who it was that sheltered in her house. Probably the West Saxons in the winter of 878 were also encouraging each other by spreading these rumors. They did not want to face the facts that all seemed lost and that instead of the England that people had once imagined – a united kingdom of Saxons, Angles, Britons, and others – there was instead to be a patchwork of Danish principalities.

But a new rumor silenced any hopeful stories they could tell. Twenty-three more ships had just arrived in Wessex from Dyfed in Wales, carrying well-over a thousand Vikings. This new force was led by one of the sons of Ragnar Lothbrok, and he carried with him the Raven banner.

Both the *Anglo-Saxon Chronicle* and Bishop Asser call this Viking leader "the brother of Ivar and Halfdan" but do not name him. He has generally been assumed to be Ubba, but Ubba's name was known to the *Anglo-Saxon Chronicle*, and so it seems strange that they would not name him here if it were him. In any case, Ubba or one of the other sons of Lothbrok besides Ivar, Halfdan, Sigurd Snake-in-the-eye, or Bjorn (who all have historical alibis) led his large force into Britain's southernmost peninsula, looking to break the last strongholds of West Saxon resistance.

Ragnarson's army caught an un-named Saxon ealdorman in Devonshire. The Saxons were besieged, but instead of surrendering or giving themselves up to a slow death of starvation they rushed as one from the gates of their stronghold and fell upon the Vikings with all the desperation and fury that evil winter had engendered. The son of Ragnar and 840 of his Vikings were slain, and the legendary Raven banner was captured.

This victory had a profound effect on the West Saxon morale, and Alfred did not waste the opportunity. He had already been gathering strength, even leaving the wilds to build a wooden fort at Athelney, near Somerset. As summer drew near, King Alfred marched his *housecarls* and the survivors of his winter war out into the open. From all corners, the Saxons gathered to him.

King Alfred and his new army attacked Guthrum's Danes near Eddington. This time, the Saxons would not be beaten, and the Vikings were put to flight. Those that survived the battle took refuge in the fortress there. Realizing that they could not long endure the siege, Guthrum surrendered after two weeks.

Wessex was saved. Alfred had learned his lesson well, though, and would not be appeased by a few oaths and hostages from the Vikings. He, Guthrum, and other leaders sat down to draw up a lasting treaty. It was not enough for Wessex to keep its independence while the Vikings carved up the rest of Britain – a boundary was set for each domain. This boundary line was the old Roman road that ran diagonally from Dover in the southeast all the way to Wales. In the 9th century, this *via* was called Watling Street. To the south and west of the road would be Wessex's dominion, which included much of Mercia (Wessex's old rival). Everything to the other side of the road would be the Danelaw, a place where the Vikings could make their rules, fight their wars, worship their gods and do whatever they decided to do. The Saxons and the Vikings were to each keep to their own side of the tracks, as it were.

The Danelaw

As the treaty was being decided on, many people must have realized the implications. Britain had been many kingdoms – Pictland, Dal Riata, and Strathclyde (all now Alba) in the far north; the Saxon kingdoms of Northumbria, Bernicia, Cumbraland, East Anglia, Mercia, Kent (or Cent), and Wessex; and the Britons of Wales and Cornwall. Most of these territories still existed in peoples' minds, but in practicality, the formation of the Danelaw was reducing all of Britain into really just four domains: Alba, the Danelaw, Wessex, and Wales. The idea of an England may have seemed unlikely when there were so many kingdoms, but now the balance of power was almost simple.

Alfred was probably the most aware of this. Though peace and protection for his people was his first concern, there is every reason to believe that he dreamed of creating an England. While England would not exist until the time of his grandson's reign, several times the *Anglo-Saxon Chronicle* refers to Alfred as *"the King of the English people."* This was not at that time an official title, but it appears to be how people were beginning to think of it.

The 878 treaty was sealed with the baptism of Guthrum and at least 30 jarls. Baptism was frequently a condition of surrender in

Christian/Non-Christian conflict. The intent was that the Christianized enemies would be more likely to live in accord or at least be influenced by the constraints of the Church. It often did not really work that way, but at the end of the 9th century, it was gradually starting to. Whereas one of Guthrum's men boasted that he had been baptized 20 times, and then complained that the free white baptismal garment was not up to the usual quality this time, Guthrum himself seems to have taken his baptism and his treaty seriously. Now King of East Anglia within the Danelaw, and Alfred's godson, Guthrum would never again fight Wessex. A few decades later, another political conversion would yield similar results when Rollo the Walker was baptized in France.

The conversion of Viking leaders that began to accelerate about 100 years into the Viking Age showed that the Norse invaders were increasingly interested in being part of the established order rather than just disruptive outsiders. The next century would see several of these Norse kings, particularly in Scandinavia, becoming very active in attempts to forcibly convert their neighbors and using Christianity to extend their rule and legacy over larger and larger territories.

But not all conversion happened this way, and it was both a top-down and bottom-up process. The Vikings had been taking Christian slaves for almost a century. The confusion and contempt with which Vikings met that religion was slowly fading as Norse settlers began to live in proximity and intermarry with Christians. We see many examples in the sagas of Vikings having different religions in their own families. The archeological record gives us evidence of this gradual religious drift, with Mjolnir amulets and crosses being found in the same areas and sometimes even in the same graves. Doubtlessly, these religious changes gave rise to new confusion and discord at times. Overall, though, the slow, steady shift from Norse paganism to Christianity did much to blend the Vikings with the natives, but it did little to change their character.

Faith was only one of many changes for the Vikings of the Danelaw. The resurgence of Wessex and newfound political solidity changed the nature of the war in Britain. The Vikings had failed in Wessex, but they had got what they wanted elsewhere.

But many Vikings found that getting what they wanted was not what they wanted. These restless men left the Danelaw to go join Rollo in France or to take a gamble raiding the Holy Roman Empire in what is now Germany, Belgium, Luxemburg, and the Netherlands.

Most of the Great Heathen Army settled down to enjoy their dominion, though. They divided up their conquered lands equitably, and Viking raiders became yeomen farmers. They married local women and let the similar languages of Old Norse and Old English blend along with their bloodlines. Winston Churchill would point out that these Vikings gave rise to an independently-minded people in the north and east that would be a driving force in English history for hundreds of years.

England

This is not to say that the Vikings of the Danelaw and the Saxons stopped fighting after the treaty of 878. Far from it! The *Anglo-Saxon Chronicle* follows the movements of "the army" for at least 30 years. Alfred would go on to wrestle London from the Danes, and fight incursions for the rest of his life (he died of illness – perhaps the culmination of his chronic illness or the cancers that can arise from these types of conditions – around the age of 50). New Vikings were always coming in, and new Viking leaders were always trying to exceed the glory of their predecessors. Alfred would never live to see a united England.

Alfred's effective 28-year reign was followed by effective successors. His son, Edward, began the conquest of the Danelaw's Five Burrows, reducing Viking power in Britain and adding territory to what was increasingly thought of as a common country. Alfred's daughter, Aethelflead, married the client-king of Mercia, but when that king died, Aethelflead ruled Mercia herself. She was not called Queen, but rather The Lady of Mercia by her subjects who adored her, and this change in title further shows the consolidation of the Anglo-Saxon kingdoms.

Aethelflead was not only a female ruler at a time and place where there were none, but she was also a Viking fighter in her own right. She led her troops against Viking incursions and then began to conquer parts of the Danelaw. The Vikings of Jorvik (York) even surrendered to

Aethelflaed in advance of her arrival there, but the Lady of Mercia died of illness before accepting their submission and before she was 49 years old.

It was Alfred's grandson Aethelstan who would finally realize his dream. Aethelstan was a great statesman and warrior who would wrestle control from numerous warring factions and instill order over the island of Britain. His career culminated in a stunning victory at the Battle of Brunanburh in 937, in which he defeated an invading force of Vikings, Scots (under the Scottish King Constantine II), Irish, and Welsh. For most of his reign, Aethelstan was called the King of the English, and after the Battle of Brunanburh England would more-or-less have the borders it has today.

Alfred the Great

Alfred the Great is often thought of as the man who united England and kicked out the Vikings. Those are both extreme oversimplifications. As we have seen, Alfred did – against all odds – break the momentum of the Viking conquerors of Britain and push them back into a confined territory that his progeny would eventually retake. Alfred also united the Saxons and other tribes of Britain into a common cause, and ultimately, they would meld into a single people. In that, Alfred can safely be called the father of a nation, though the title of the first King of England belongs to his grandson, Aethelstan. In that Alfred did all this against all the odds, and not only avoided the political annihilation and material subjugation of his people but put them on the path of ultimate success is why he deserves to be called Alfred the Great.

But it was not only the Saxons that were melding into the English – it was the Vikings, too. Alfred did not drive the Vikings out, and neither did Aethelstan. Most of the Vikings stayed, put down roots, and they also became English. In fact, in the years after Aethelstan, England would always be united as one country – but sometimes that country had Danish kings. Vikings like Cnut (pronounced and sometimes spelled Canut or Kanut) and Harthacnut would trade places back and forth with Saxon kings like Edward the Confessor, Aethelred the Unready, or Harold Godwinson for the English throne. Though they followed a long history or war, these transitions of power themselves were often bloodless. Much evidence suggests that the English did not see these changes as disastrous upheavals and reversals of Alfred the Great's legacy. They were just the shifting sands of politics, and only when England was conquered by the Normans in 1066 was it seen as a real defeat and lasting change. This attitude was not one-sided. *The Saga of Ragnar Lothbrok* refers to London as "*the finest city in Scandinavia,*" and the *Russian Primary Chronicle* refers to England as a Scandinavian country.

In Britain, the Saxons, Danes, and earlier natives became one people – the English. Without the vision, tenacity, and valor of Alfred the Great and his scions it probably would not have happened that way.

It is also true that without the Vikings, Britain would have continued as a land of warring tribes for a long time to come. Vikings were the catalysts that led to the birth of England, and their legacy would always be felt strongly there.

Chapter XIII: Rollo the Walker and the Second Siege of Paris

Inspired by the success of the 845 Siege of Paris, the vigor of Scandinavia became increasingly focused outward. Raids on the Carolingian Empire continued; but the big story of the middle 9th century occurred in Britain. There the sons of Ragnar Lothbrok avenged their father's death by invading with an unprecedented host of Vikings. This "Great Heathen Army" forcibly took the lion's share of Britain's several kingdoms, leaving only Wessex intact. Had it not been for the arrival of a visionary leader of extraordinary ability – who would be known to history as Alfred the Great – all of Britain might have fallen. But Alfred and his Saxons eventually prevailed in both battle and diplomacy. As the 9th century waned, the Vikings found it expedient to observe the peace of their new Danelaw and again turn their full attention east.

However, the toils of Charles the Bald had made the Carolingian domain more secure in the last 40 years; and if the Vikings were going to harvest the wealth of that land, they would have to go through Paris. The very virtues of geography and politics that had made Paris so prosperous (even after the disaster of 845) now made it essential to any meaningful Norse campaign on the continent. So, in 885 a new fleet – exponentially larger at up to 40,000 men – sailed up the River Seine.

This great host recruited from all over the Norse world was under brave new leadership: a great warlord named Siegfried and his second-in-command who would eclipse him thoroughly in the eyes of history – a man named Rolf Ganger. Rolf is better known by his French name, Rollo. The monicker Ganger means "the Walker," as he was supposedly so big it was hard for him to find a suitable horse.

Rollo's back-story is extraordinary to us – but it may not be atypical of his time. It is largely believed that he was born in Norway sometime just before 860, when Harald Fairhair was forcing that land into a single monarchy. We will meet Harald Fairhair more properly in the next chapter and see his ambition to force the disparate tribes and principalities in Norway to bow to one king (himself) just as Denmark and Sweden would also each bow to one king. Harald's force of will did not only truly found a unified Norway – but it led to the founding of Iceland by those fleeing his rule. By 872, Rollo – who may have been related to Harald – was ousted from Norway, too (reportedly for stealing the King's own cattle).

Rollo went to Orkney in the western Scottish Isles, where his father Ragnvald had connections. Rollo the Walker took part in the wars and raiding that racked Scotland at this time, led several expeditions to Frisia, and may have even gained experience fighting Alfred the Great alongside King Guthrum. Rollo is mentioned specifically by the *Anglo-Saxon Chronicle*, though whether this merit was because of his activities in Britain or because of his later fame is unclear.

But by the 880's the Danelaw did not have enough to offer a man of Rollo's energy, and so he and thousands of Vikings like him followed their fortunes to Francia.

The Second Siege of Paris

The rich, green lands these men now entered had already mourned the death of Charles the Bald about eight years before and were now under the rule of Charles the Fat. Charles the Fat cared not for war, but he was wise enough to appoint men who did; and so, as the Viking horde sailed upriver they soon came across the cunning defenses of Count Odo.

The city Rollo and Siegfried now surrounded was different from Ragnar's Paris of only forty years before. It was well-garrisoned and fortified specifically to deal with the Vikings. These fortifications – drawn from this region's thousand years' experience with siege warfare – had one particularly notable feature: bridges. These were not ordinary bridges, but castled structures of stone and heavy timber, with battlements, arrow slits, guardhouses, and traps. Paris is still known for its bridges today, but in 885 the bridges meant one thing to the Vikings: they could go no further unless they took the city. The Franks had chosen their ground.

Paris had changed, but the Vikings had also changed. The Norsemen had learned siege craft during their campaigns in Britain; and they now approached the walls of Paris not merely with axes and shields, but with covered rams and massive *ballista* crossbows, with rolling towers and *mangonels* catapults. So, as autumn was waning in the year 885, the people of Paris looked out over the largest horde of Norsemen ever assembled and saw to their horror that it was an army that had evolved.

Yet in terms of character, the Vikings were the same as they always had been – terrifying, relentless, single-minded, and ferocious. A monk who was eyewitness to the events gives us this dazzled description of what the men, women, and children of Paris beheld:

> ... *a frenzy beyond compare. They were an evil cohort, a deadly phalanx, a grim horde ... a thousand stood shoulder to shoulder in the fight, all bare-armed and bare-backed. With mocking laughter they banged their shields loud with open hands; their throats swelled and strained with odious cries ... Fear seized the city. People screamed and battle horns resounded.*[54]

So, the battle for Paris commenced, with the Vikings fighting for treasures beyond their dreams and the defenders fighting for their very survival. Yet there was more than that – what was at stake in this clash of cultures for the Vikings was whether they would go forward or backwards as a people; and what was at stake for Paris was whether the shining city could protect its identity, law, learning, and refinement, or whether it would be just another of history's victims.

Siege warfare is one of the most brutal, cruel, and demanding forms that war can take. Death is indiscriminate. A valiant hero with a dozen victories can be slain by a housewife chucking a rock from a palisade. It is a diabolical chess match of siege engines against fortifications, where men die until their massed bodies form barriers against their brothers' advance. At the walls of Paris, both sides assailed each other with arrows, bolts, and stones. Vikings scaling the walls with ladders were met with showers of boiling oil or red-hot sand. For the Vikings, the *Norns* (the three spinners of fate) would decide if the wounded died a slow death or lived a pain-stricken life. For the defenders, their only hope was in God, or that their king would send an army to their aid. It was this type of battle that gripped Paris as the icy rains gave way to snow.

Both the Vikings and the defenders had largely spent their energy after a few weeks of relentless death. Now winter had fully set in, and retreat was impossible. Maneuvers continued, but mining and blockading largely took the place of reckless frontal assault. At this stage of the siege, the greatest enemies became starvation and disease. The Vikings increased the radius of their foraging parties (a murderous staple of medieval warfare which serves to feed the army; break the will of the people; and to deplete the resources of the defending nobility). All the while, the soldiers and citizens of Paris remained resolute.

Spring finally came, and with it came the promise of a relief force; but Charles the Fat's army had to come all the way from Italy. It was slow in forming, and when it did it was impeded by floods and misfortunes.

Meanwhile Siegfried tried to double-cross Rollo, and so the Vikings army began to fracture.

In the late summer, even as the relief force was nearing Paris, Rollo's Vikings finally breached the walls and poured into parts of the city. Encountering resistance in street-to-street fighting, and fearing the approach of the Frankish army, the Vikings only looted for a short time before anticlimactically returning to the safety of their camp.

The Vikings had surrounded Paris; but by early autumn, 886, the Vikings found themselves surrounded by the Frankish army. But as Charles beheld the Norse in their battle array, their bright-painted shields locked together, and he sensed their indomitable fighting spirit, he lost his nerve. He chose diplomacy.

After a series of talks, the Vikings agreed to an arrangement King Charles borrowed from the ancient Romans – the Norsemen accepted gold to transfer their war to Charles's enemies, the rebellious Burgundians in the southeast.

The Siege of Paris was finally lifted. But as a testimony to their character and their outrage at their king's cowardly fecklessness, the

Parisians still refused to let the Vikings pass. Instead, Rollo and Siegfried had to move their dragon ships overland (probably on log rollers) to get past the exhausted but incensed defenders.

In many ways, the 885-886 siege of Paris was a draw. The Vikings entered parts of the city after almost a year of fighting, but never really held it. The people of Paris suffered greatly, but their city endured (it would be almost a thousand years before another foreign army took the city). Count Odo became a national hero, while Charles' slow response and failure to fight the Vikings ultimately cost his throne. Odo replaced him as king, thus breaking the Carolingian dynasty in Francia.

The Count of Rouen

Siegfried died fighting far-off battles; but Rollo continued to be active in Francia. When he came again to Paris years later (911-912), a new king, Charles the Simple, preempted another siege by giving him choice lands in Normandy in return for allegiance to the crown. Charles the Simple sweetened the deal with official titles and even the hand of his daughter, Gisele. There were only two conditions. The first was easy – Rollo and his Vikings would be on stand-by to fight Charles' enemies. The second was perhaps more difficult: Rollo would have to be baptized.

Baptism was becoming the cost of entering lucrative alliances with mainstream nations, and if Rollo had served with Guthrum all those years before he may have been expecting it. Rollo determined that the price was well worth it. He was probably nearing the age of 60, and decades of being on the move in a depleted and exhausted countryside had to be leaving its mark. Rollo had several children, including at least four from his "Danish wife" (a euphemism for concubine or polygamous relationship, common enough in Sea Kings but almost absent in Norse frontier culture) Poppa, the daughter of the slain Count of Brittany. But the prospect of being the son-in-law of the King of Francia had to be appealing.

In 912, when Rollo was baptized Robert, with his former enemies looking on, he probably had a sense that he was making the greater choice for the good of his people and the sake of his legacy.

However, the transition was not seamless. After the baptism, when it was time to kiss Charles' feet in submission (literally), Rollo balked and had one of his warriors do it instead. But instead of kneeling down, this Viking pulled the King's foot up to his lips. Charles the Simple lost his balance and fell sprawled on the church step. More than a few of the witnesses probably saw prophecy in the physical comedy – and history would prove their fears correct.

Thus, Rollo the Walker became the Count of Rouen, the first of what was later called the Duke of Normandy. He went from being one of the most feared raiders of his day to the protector of the realm. He kept his word to defend Charles' domain by defeating or deterring Vikings, his former friends. Rollo was a good ruler, who built edifices and works of engineering, and made his city of Rouen and his duchy of Normandy a place of law and order.

Rollo's bigger dynastic ambitions may not have been satisfied in his lifetime, for he and Gisele had no children to compete for the throne of Francia – but Rollo's great-granddaughter Emma would be married to two kings of England (Aethelred the Unready and Cnut the Great) and her son would be one of the last kings of Saxon England, Edward the Confessor.

Rollo's more-famous descendent (through his marriage to Poppa) was of course William the Conqueror, and through him Rollo's descendants are still on the throne of England today.

Around 927, Rollo (now ancient by the standards of the day) left his throne to his son, William I "Longsword". William Longsword was the first of several successors who would strengthen Normandy's resources, boundaries, and reputation and secure Rollo's legacy.

Rollo himself lived until 933, showing in his final acts the duel nature of civilized western ruler and Viking that had characterized his career: according to legend he donated 100 pounds of gold to surrounding churches – but only after he had sacrificed 100 prisoners to Odin.

In the fertile fields and long coastlines of Normandy, Rollo's Vikings would further evolve by melding the Frankish ways of war (armored cavalry and castles) with the Viking spirit of restless daring. Less admirably, perhaps, Rollo and his descendants discarded the desire for freedom and self-determination that continued amongst their cousins in Iceland for a more stable system they could exploit for the grander goals of the elite – Medieval Feudalism.

But with all their adaptations to their changing goals and changing world, this new breed of Norseman – the Norman – would soon set out to conquer, and to leave their mark on all of Europe and beyond.

Chapter XIV: Floki of the Ravens and the Founding of Iceland

"Floki, the son of Vilgerd, was the name of a man, a great Viking," the *Landnámabók* (*The Book of Settlements*)[15] reads.

We do not know any of Floki's back-story, but when we meet him he is leading a single ship crewed with men looking for *Garðarshólm*. *Garðarshólm* means Gardar's Island, a name given by the Norse explorer who claimed to have circumnavigated it. This Gardar had only heard of it from a man named Naddod, who had reached it entirely by accident and named the uninhabited place *Snæland* (Snow-land).

So Floki and his few followers were looking for a place that was only a rumor. They knew that there was no wealth to be taken and no people to fight. They did not know where the land was, exactly, but they would have known that it was hundreds of miles of iceberg-infested waters from the nearest friendly land mass (the Faroe Islands). They were betting a lot on this journey – for they were bringing their animals, and at least some were bringing their families. It is not unreasonable to believe that men and women who would take such a risky journey with the intent to stay were running from the world they had known.

---

[15] *Landnámabók* (*The Book of Settlements)* is a unique book attributed to Ari the Learned in the 12th century. It describes the discovery and settling of Iceland, giving accounts and partial genealogies of over 3,000 individuals and 1,400 specific locations.

In the latter part of the 9th century, when Floki undertook his voyage into the unknown, there was a lot to run from. At that time, the Vikings had awakened an endless war in Ireland and laid siege to Paris; they had invaded Britain as a great army, and had forced the mightiest kingdoms in Europe to cede them silver and land. A man who had lived through that, as our great Viking had, would have experienced much victory, but also much suffering. We also know that Floki's daughter, Geirhild, had recently drowned in the Shetland Islands. So whatever Floki's role in the tempestuous, violent events of his time had been, he had found no home there. He sailed away looking for what he had been unable to find anywhere else.

But how do you find something that no one had ever found before except by luck? Gardar's Island was far away, and though the Vikings were consummate sailors, they had no real instruments by which to navigate. They used the sun by day and the stars by night; and they used visual cues (like the color of water) and followed the flight patterns of birds. They learned to use a crystal to see where the sun was in cloudy, northern skies; along with shadow sticks and cleverly-designed discs (like the *Uunartoq* disc found in Greenland) to offer directional clues; but they had no compass, sextant, or anything else to offer certainty.

So Floki did something unusual. He brought three ravens with him. Ravens are Odin's birds, and Odin is both the far-seeing god and a god known for wandering the earth. He is also the Allfather to the Vikings, and so we can perhaps see in Floki's choice of birds an appeal for divine help.

The first raven simply flew back to the Faroes. The second flew in the air and then returned to the ship. The third raven flew away, though, and Floki headed after it.

From the story, we do not know if Floki released his birds all at once – presumably it was sequentially, for a raven cannot fly 400-500 miles without landing. But whatever the details might have been, Floki's third ravens did not let him down. In time (perhaps about two weeks), he saw land in the distance. From that point on, Floki was called *Hrafna-Floki* – Floki of the Ravens.

Floki and his followers came ashore on a wide land of startling, austere beauty. It was not only a land of mountains and rivers, but of glaciers and many active volcanoes. When we consider that the Norse believed the world was created from a place where fire and ice met, the sight of their new home must have seemed like the birthplace of the earth.

They made their fledgling settlement on a bay that was so teaming with fish that all summer and autumn they were never hungry. But it was there that their luck changed for the worse. Hinting to their background as better warriors than farmers, Floki and his followers were so preoccupied with fishing that they neglected to cut and store hay for the animals that they had brought. Winter soon came – cold and dark and brutal – and the animals starved.

Slowly beaten down by cold and hunger, the settlers decided to turn back. But turning back was not so easy, and the next summer was almost over before they had managed all the repairs and the preparations for their return voyage. At one point, their ship broke away from its mooring with only one man (named Herjolf) on it, and he drifted until the vessel came to rest. Weeks passed before Floki and the others could find him. By that time, it was winter again, and they could not leave. They spent another long, dark season watching the mountains cough out black ash over the glaciers.

Finally, summer came and Hrafna-Floki and his fellow survivors departed from the place they had renamed Iceland.

When Hrafna-Floki returned to the land of men, he had little good to say of his ordeal in Iceland; but Herjolf was eager to spread the word of the land's potential.

This news could not have come at a better time. Up until then, Norway (like so much of Europe) had been a land of petty kings and jarls. But a king by the name of Harald had been struck with great ambition. As the story goes, Harald requested the hand of a Swedish princess named Gyda. Gyda shamed Harald, saying that she would not marry a minor king of Norway when Sweden and Denmark were each dominated by singular, strong kings. Harald vowed to not comb or cut his hair until he was king of all Norway. Harald was the first man to ever do this, and – though Harald's borders were smaller than Norway would become – from that time on Norway began to move towards becoming a nation rather than a land of small kingdoms and divided peoples. It took him 10-12 years (during which time he became known as Harald Shock-head), but Harald succeeded, was shorn, and was afterwards known as Haraldr Fairhair.

Amusing as this story may be to us, it was not amusing for the jarls of Norway who had to contend with the meteoric rise of a tyrant. Harald was not simply a king of more territory than the kings of the past – the nature of national-level kingship was fundamentally different from the old northern model of small kings and chieftains. What Harald, and his counterparts elsewhere in Europe, was rolling out was an early form of feudalism. It was a tiered structure in which the peasant lived for the lord and the lord lived for the king, basically. It glossed over and then swept away the personal freedoms and self-determinations of the small landholder, and did away with the more democratic, traditional Germanic government structure, such as the *Thing* or the *Folkmoot*. Harald and his successors, along with the kings of Sweden, Denmark,

France, and elsewhere were forging nations where there had once been tribes, but these nations were to be under absolutist rule.

Those who found themselves on the wrong side of Harald Fairhair were looking for a place to continue their lives (and in some cases, their own rule) in peace. This fierce, beautiful, empty place called Iceland seemed like a better option than the suddenly-ordered kingdoms of Scandinavia, the precarious Danelaw of Britain, or the "sword lands" of Ireland.

Iceland drew Vikings from other areas besides Norway and the Faroes. DNA research shows that up to half of the women and a quarter of the men comprising the founding population of Iceland were Gaelic. A proportion of these were likely slaves, though the high Gaelic representation suggest that these settlers may have come by way of Ireland and Scotland, where Norse and Celt had been mixing enthusiastically for a few generations.

Given the events there at the time of settlement (between 870 and 930) this distribution makes sense. The Vikings had achieved great success in Ireland, but around that time things were not as easy for them as they used to be, and Vikings need room.

Similarly, rapid changes in other old hunting grounds, such as the establishment of the Danelaw in Britain and France's use of Rollo the

Walker for their watchdog meant that it was far more challenging for maverick groups of Vikings to plunder territories without having to face the wrath of other Vikings or other capable resistance. The sense of restlessness and even anxiety amongst unaffiliated Viking bands is evident in the various annals and chronicles of the period.

So, from many locations, and in increasing numbers the Viking settlers came to Iceland. It was not a place to seize riches and slaves, it was a place to make a life for oneself and one's family and to live that life in peace and freedom. These early settlers included "*a great multitude*" that had been disenchanted, disenfranchised, or dispossessed by the rule of Harald Fairhair and other autocrats.

Not surprisingly, the culture that developed in Iceland was conservative and hearkened back to the old ways in government, organization, and ideas of social justice. While it would eventually become Christian (due in part to changing times and in part to the large number of Christian Celts in their midst), Iceland maintained Nordic paganism for a long time. This new island kingdom, far away from everyone, would become the greatest repository for Norse culture, language, poetry, and mythology in the world. The saga itself (that is, the long telling of an epic story in prose form rather than verse), as a literary form, was said to be invented and refined in Iceland.

As it turns out, Iceland was not completely empty – a small number of Irish priests had formed a religious community there. When they saw the Vikings, the poor men (who probably had some experience) fled so fast they left some of their books, bells, and staffs behind. Iceland was also not completely treeless, either, but had a fair amount of forests which the Vikings quickly used to build their settlements (to this day, the land is bald from their clearing).

The *Book of Settlements* and the *Book of the Icelanders* tell of many different colonists and the challenges that they faced. In the beginning, settlers simply made a land-grab. As the ships came near shore, the chief of the company would throw a beam of his ship into the sea, accompanied by certain rites and prayers to the gods. The sailors would then follow this beam as it was carried on the currents, until it came ashore. The dragon ships (or perhaps more commonly the *knarr* merchant ships) would then beach, and the company would climb the nearest hill to survey the land. They would apportion the land equitably and then consecrate it by burning a ring of fire around it.

The homesteads of the company would have a "town" in the middle, with a temple and a place to meet and conduct the common business. It was a well-ordered but rustic life of pastoralism (animal fodder would grow, but not much else due to the high amount of ash in the soil) and cottage industries, along with fishing, trapping, trading, and going *viking,* as needed. This model would persist throughout Iceland's history, and it was always said to be a place that "knew neither great wealth nor wide poverty."

One of these early settlers was Hrafna-Floki, who eventually returned to Iceland along with a wife, a son, and another daughter. He and some friends settled by a river; and both the river and the town that developed there bore his name. Floki and his family would spend the rest of their days in Iceland.

By 930, the land was said to be fully settled. The population at that time is estimated to have been around 25,000. It would eventually climb to 50,000 before the end of the Viking Age. It would peak around 70,000 people by the time of Snorri Sturluson (the great Icelandic "Homer of the North") before the Little Ice Age would gradually cut that population in half.

Also in 930, the jarls of Iceland met for the *Althing* – an ancient Norse meeting of self-government. They appointed a *Lawspeaker* to recite law from the Law Stone. Lawspeakers memorized, recited, and passed on laws – not created them. They served three at a time for short periods of time, so that no one could gather too much power. So, it was that by reinforcing time-honored democratic Norse institutions like these in defiant contrast to the growing autocracies in the mainland that the commonwealth of Iceland was fully born.

Iceland is considered the world's oldest commonwealth and maintained this democratic structure hundreds of years before any other European country. It was eventually forced by various necessities to submit to the rule of Norway. Still, men and women remained freer in Iceland, well out of easy reach of continental kings, than they were anywhere else in Europe throughout the Middle Ages. A direct descendent of the *Althing*, Iceland's parliament is still considered to be the oldest such body in the world.

Iceland was to become one of the most important Viking countries – not because of size or power, but because Iceland became the vessel of so much Norse culture. Viking descendants in France, England, or Russia gradually set aside much of their past in order to keep pace with the constant change around them, and both the Church and society in general did not encourage the fostering of their myths or culture. But far away from the wars, religious struggles, and politics of continental Europe, the Icelandic yeomen and their families could spend their short days working as they always had, and their long nights recounting the great lore of their people. It is through Iceland that most of the sagas, beliefs, and lore we know have come to us. For that, we are all lucky that Hrafna-Floki followed his raven.

<u>Chapter XV: Rurik, Igor, and the Kievan Rus</u>

It may be an oversimplification, but it often said that the Vikings of Norway pushed west and the Danes pushed south, but the Vikings of Sweden pushed east. To the east of Sweden lies Finland, inhabited by a people that were culturally and linguistically different from the Norse. To the southeast were the Baltic peoples and beyond that were the open lands of Eastern Europe and Western Asia.

The peoples of Sweden had trod those lands before when the Goths, Heruli, Vandals, and others had migrated in the early centuries of the Common Era. These migrating Scandinavians had picked up other peoples along the way, adapted their customs and ways of life to suit their new environments, and eventually wound up at Rome's back door. Now, in the mid-9th and 10th centuries, a similar occurrence would again transpire.

But at that time, the lands of what are now Ukraine, Russia, Belarus, Latvia, Lithuania, Estonia, Moldova, and the Crimean did not have the many wealthy monasteries that Francia, Britain, Ireland, or Alba offered. The Slavs, Balts, Finns, and Turkic peoples who lived in these lands were for the most part no richer than their Scandinavian neighbors, and there would only be meager gains from raiding. But there was something else to attract the Vikings – trade routes to the grandeur of the empires of Byzantium, the Islamic East, and by extension, even China.

The hallmark of the modern world is globalization, or international trade. Every day, people in countries like the United States, England, or Norway eat food shipped in from Mexico, wear clothes made in Indonesia, drive cars from Japan featuring German innovations, and play on technology made in China. We are used to this, and it is difficult to imagine life without it. But our age of planes, trains, reliable sea travel and safe highways was not the first occurrence of globalization. Almost two thousand years ago, a Roman citizen living in Britain may also eat olives from Tunisia, drink Spanish wine, wear silks procured from trade with Persia, and wear amber jewelry from over the Rhine set in gold by Greek craftsmen.

When Western Rome fell apart, so did this trade (in the west), and the archeological record shows stark differences in the quality of life in the centuries after that time.

Though globalization would remain elusive until recently, world trade would be re-established to varying degrees at different times in history, by disparate peoples ranging from the 13th century Mongols to the 18th century British. In the 9th century, the Vikings would make the first post-Roman move to effectively re-establish this large-scale east-west trade.

Of course, it is unlikely that the Vikings thought of it that way. What they knew was that there was wealth to be made by importing the luxuries of the far south and east back home to Scandinavia and other markets in Western Europe. Beyond the largely open lands southeast of the Baltic, empires were teaming with silver, silk, wine, jewelry, textiles, and things the Norse had perhaps not even thought of but yearned for once they saw them. There was also new knowledge and culture in these distant lands that the sons of Odin would eagerly pick up as well, but this would be a by-product of material exchange.

The riches of the east had always been impossibly far away, though. Trekking thousands of miles across hostile territory was neither a practical nor enviable business, and the greater the wealth, the higher the uncertainty of profit or even survival. But – once again – with the advancement of the dragon ship that changed. The Vikings of Sweden could sail across the Baltic Sea and enter the riverways of central Europe. The Volga River would bring them to Bagdad. The Dneiper would bring them to Constantinople. Travel had suddenly become much swifter and surer than it ever had been.

But the luxuries of the east were expensive, even in their home countries. The Vikings had some goods to exchange – crafts, textiles, animal furs, honey, amber, maybe some ivory from walrus tusks (a prized commodity) – but not enough to cause the Viking stampede seen in western Europe.

The Vikings always had something that was in high demand – their willingness to fight and skill in warfare made them sought-after mercenaries and bodyguards. But to bring the riches of the Orient home, they would need more than that. So, the Vikings entered the east with an unexpected and grim business model. The dragon ships departed from the waters of Sweden and Gotland almost empty. The Vikings planned to fill them as they go.

Though it is a repulsive feature of human history, before the advent of machines civilizations operating above subsistence levels depended on exploiting cheap labor. The Islamic world was enjoying a golden age and was an eager market for slaves. So, as the Vikings traveled along the riverways towards these markets, they stopped to raid the countryside not for the sparse goods they may find but for people to kidnap. By the time the dragon ships arrived in the sun-drenched southern ports, they would be fully laden with men, women, and children to sell. According to one late-ninth century arrangement between the Vikings and their buyers, a young man or a "grown girl" was worth ten coins, a middle-aged person eight, and a child fetched five.

The Viking's eastern trade was a booming success. Archeologists have found thousands of silver coins from Arab lands, along with many other goods (even shirts with Arabic embroidery) in hordes within Scandinavia. More evidence for the gradual re-establishment of east-west trade by the Vikings include the findings of a few human skeletons within Scandinavia that date from the 10th century but have drastically different DNA from Norse remains. These findings are especially concentrated in Sweden, though the western Vikings traded with the Moors and Berbers of Spain and Africa as well.

The peoples of the east called the Vikings "Rus," possibly from the Old Norse word, *róðsmenn* or Finno-Ugric word, *"ruotsi"* which both mean "oarsmen." The word Rus and its derivatives were applied to these men in Arabic, Byzantine, Frankish, Persian and later Russian sources. Just as western histories use the term 'Vikings' for Norse adventurers of the era, eastern sources often use the term 'Varangian,' from the Old Norse *"væringi"* meaning "sworn companion." They were called this in the context of their later service as mercenaries or bodyguards.

Just as the term 'Viking' as it is often used is not true to the original meaning of the word, so it is with the word 'Varangian.' Viking and Varangian both refer to Norsemen, but it is an occupational, not ethnic, description and not every Norseman was a Viking of Varangian.

Contact with the Muslim and Byzantine world has given us some of the best and most colorful accounts of the Vikings we have. Arab geographer, traveler, and eyewitness Ibn Rustah describes the trade of this period thus,

"The only occupation of Rus is the trade with sable, squirrel and other furs. They harry the Slavs, using ships to reach them; they carry them off as slaves and sell them. They have no fields but simply live on what they get from the Slav's lands."

Another Arab eyewitness, Ahmad ibn Fadlan, describes the physical features of these new northern traders as, *"tall as date palms, blue-eyed, blonde, and ruddy."* Ahmad later describes the funeral rites and cremation of a Rus chieftan in lurid detail.

As was the case with the Vikings in the west, success spawned imitation, and the number of dragon ships embarking eastward grew exponentially. More trade encouraged more ports and bases, and more Viking activity farther and farther afield. In fact, archeologists have found more Viking Age Norse artifacts in the east than in the west. Every adventurer kept his ears open for rumors of more opportunities, and every ship's leader was ready to follow his nose as he tried to make the most of their risk and effort and to out-compete other Vikings.

These traders probably could not have imagined where their adventures would eventually take their people.

Rurik and the Beginning of the Kievan Rus

According to the *Russian Primary Chronicle* (formerly known as *Nestor's Chronicle*, which dates to around the 12th century), the Viking impact on the Slavic lands southeast of the Baltic was so great that in the middle of the 9th century the Slavs united to drive them back. The Slavs were successful in this, but once they did, the resulting power vacuum ushered in so much violent chaos that the Slavs turned back to the Vikings for help. According to the chronicle, a Swedish Viking named Rurik, along with his two brothers, re-established order with their armies and made a capital in the city of Novgorod. This capital was later moved to the city of Kiev (Kyiv), now the capital of modern-day Ukraine.

Rurik's two brothers died, leaving Rurik as the sole ruler of a rapidly-mixing Norse-Slavic culture, the Kievan Rus. Rurik founded a dynasty that would rule Russia and much of the rest of the region until 1610, and include such famous figures as Ivan the Terrible.

If it seems strange to you that people would beg a foreign power to rule them, you are not alone. "History is written by the winners," and the explanation offered by the *Russian Primary Chronicle* of how a Scandinavian dynasty and nobility came to rule is likely the propaganda of their descendants. There are not many other historical examples of an indigenous people voluntarily giving up self-determination, especially not to a power known to be as aggressive and heavy-handed as the Vikings. There are many historical models, however, of an endangered indigenous power (kings, nobility, chiefs, or usurpers) inviting a foreign power in either as allies or mercenaries and that invited foreign power taking over everything. This happened most notably with the dawn of

China's Qing Dynasty when the Manchu people crossed through the open gates of the Great Wall built to hold them out and then ruled China until the 20th century. The Rurik Dynasty may have had similar origins, where Vikings were hired as mercenaries for local rulers and then quickly turned those local rulers on their heads, seizing power for themselves.

In either case, the *Russian Primary Chronicle* repeatedly emphasizes the Slavic majority, and the Scandinavian ruling elite quickly became one people, and these *"were called Rus because of the Varangians."*

Like Ragnar Lothbrok (who, as you may recall, also had eastern adventures and whose son, Bjorn Ironside, founded Sweden's long-ruling Munso Dynasty), Rurik is semi-legendary. That is to say, there are more stories about him than written records, and we do not know much about him for sure. Rurik established his dynasty around the time Ivar the Boneless and the Great Heathen Army carved out their Danelaw. Rurik did not live long after this accomplishment, and by around 870-880 he had left his fledgling kingdom to a relative named Oleg (Old Norse, Helgi), who would guard it for Rurik's descendant, Igor (the Russian form of the name Ingvar or Ivar).

According to the *Primary Chronicle* and legends, Oleg was a man of extraordinary ability. He swiftly united the Slavs, Balts, and

Finns under one banner and attacked the mighty Byzantine Empire with 2000 ships. Oleg and his large force unleashed great slaughter amongst the Greeks of the Eastern Roman Empire (or Byzantines), and by the year 911 or 912, he forced them to sign a treaty, essentially recognizing the Kievan Rus as equals. These events are not mentioned in any other sources, however, and Byzantine chronicles of the time are preoccupied with far more mundane affairs such as icons and iconoclasts, and so many historians regard Oleg's accomplishments as apocryphal. In any case, the Kievan Rus were off to a good start, and Rurik's steward was able to both prepare the young heir Igor and hand him a broad domain that was reasonably secure.

Oleg himself met a tragic end. While still in the prime of life and at the height of his success, the steward had a horse that was said to be the finest in the land. But a seer told Oleg that the horse would bring about his death, and so Oleg feared to ride it. Instead, he put the animal out to pasture. Years later, he thought of the horse and asked what had happened to it. When he was told the horse had died, Oleg asked to see its bones.

Oleg was led out to the field where the horse had fallen and looked over its withered skeleton. The king laughed heartily in both relief and self-reproach, and then he derided the wisdom of his seers and the uselessness of their magic. Then Oleg kicked the horse's skull in final dismissal of his paranoia – but when he did, a serpent that had been sheltering under the horse's skull bit him. A few days later, Oleg was dead.

Igor, Grand Prince of Kiev, and the Assault on Constantinople

Despite no shortage of sources, we are not really sure exactly when Igor began his reign or really how long it lasted. What we do know is that the Prince of Kiev (as he was called) wasted no time in consolidating his dominion and increasing his demands for tribute on his neighbors. Slavic tribes, such as the Drevlians, had been paying the Rus tribute since Rurik's time to avoid the dragon ship raids, but now saw that tribute go from Rurik's "*one black marten fur*" per family per month to several times that value.

Igor had more powerful – and far richer – neighbors further afield. The Volga Bulgars were a major power to the southwest and were often at war with the Byzantines. To Igor's southeast were the lands of the Khazars – A Turkic trader people who controlled much of the Silk Road and acted as middlemen in the East-West Trade. The Khazars, whose ruling and cultural elite practiced Rabbinic Judaism, were experiencing strife with the Byzantine Empire over recent religious intolerance there.

On this patchwork of established and entrenched powers, Igor's fledgling Rus kingdom was a cultural, economic, and military upstart.

Igor wanted to change that, and the entrance of one more transplanted people gave him the confidence to do that. For in Igor's time, the fearsome, fated Pechenegs entered the Eurasian Pontic Steppe.

The Pechenegs were a mysterious, nomadic people from the wide, grassy wilderness steppe further east. They were a Turkic people, apparently with an Iranian cultural elite, who were religiously heterogeneous. There were 2-3 million of them, and they were extraordinarily hardy and fierce. They tended to shift alliances easily, as we shall see. Like almost everyone on the steppe, the Pechenegs fought on horseback as mounted archers or with lance and sword.

Pecheneg forces also had an interesting feature – they used heavy battlewagons, which they would circle into movable strongholds. These portable fortresses proved very difficult for most armies to assail.

Igor immediately made friends with the Pechenegs, but within a few years, he was battling these aggressive people. He put the hostilities on hold, though, when the Khazars approached him with a proposition. According to one source, the Khazars enticed Igor to use his military might and boundless energy to mount an attack on the Byzantine Empire. The timing was perfect – for the Byzantine navy was away fighting Arabs in the Mediterranean, and the empire had been experiencing rapidly-shifting leadership. If ever they would be vulnerable to a Viking-style attack, it was now.

The hope of glory and unimaginable riches was enough for Igor to make peace with the Pechenegs and everybody else around him. In 941 he embarked down the riverways of Eastern Europe with a massive force. Byzantine sources say there were 10,000 or even 15,000 ships, but these improbable figures are balanced by one eyewitness who puts the number at "*a thousand and more.*" In any case, Igor's forces included more Vikings brought in from Scandinavia, his Varangian-led Kievan Rus, a Pan-Slavic army, other Finno-Ugric and Turkic peoples, and even the Pecheneg allies traveling by land.

By the time Igor entered the Bosphorus (having used rollers to bring his ships over the stretch of land separating this sea from the rivers, as Rollo did in Paris and Mehmet II would later do) his ships "*blackened the sea*" and the presumed-impregnable city of Constantinople was under the threat of its life.

But the city of Constantine had not survived all those centuries to fall easily, and today the word, "Byzantine" is still a synonym for trickery. The Byzantine navy was indeed far away when they were needed most, but the city's defenders had a ruse in mind. They took 15 old, scrapped ships and set them afloat against Igor's armada.

The Vikings and others pounced, greedy for glory and eager for the battle to commence. But the Byzantines aboard the ships had submerged pipes under the water. When the dragon ships came in range, the Byzantines jetted Greek Fire out at them, engulfing them in *"winged flame."* The chemical compound continued to burn on the surface of the water, so as Igor's hapless navy jumped ship they either burned anyway or were dragged to the bottom of the sea by the weight of their armor.

Never ones to risk their precious ships, the surviving Vikings and Rus withdrew. Constantinople was saved. But Igor was enraged. His army did not leave the area but instead raided the countryside of the prosperous Byzantine Empire. Unstable government within the Empire failed to check his advance at first, and many monasteries, towns, and even cities fell, and many treasures and prisoners were taken away.

Eventually, Igor fell back – but only to regroup and collect even more allies from the Scandinavian Vikings, the Slavs, and other indigenous tribes. He approached Constantinople once more in 944. This time, the Byzantines met with him and bought him off with an expansive and generous truce. Igor returned home, perhaps without the glory and bloody vengeance he had meant to achieve, but he had forced one of the greatest powers in the world to the table with his fledgling Rus nation. An Empire with 1700 years of history (even then) that had at times controlled much of the known world acquiesced to the demands of the third-generation ruler of a mixed people from the northern wildlands.

The treaty ensured that the Rus would be treated as honored (but mistrusted) guests in the future, and opened the possibilities up for the thriving trade and cultural exchange that was to shape the future of Igor's people. The Rus – who would become founders of today's nations of Ukraine, Russia, Belarus, and others – would be forever profoundly influenced by the Byzantines, including their written language, culture, and orthodox faith.

But Igor could not have known that as his ships and riders traveled north and disbanded. Moreover, though the treaty would someday increase the wealth and standing of the Rus, Igor's followers were not feeling the silver jingle in their pockets now. The next year (945) Igor gave in to some of their murmurings and went out in arms against his neighbors, the Slavic Drevlians. The Drevlians already paid the Rus tribute, but Igor and his retinue demanded more and took it *"through violence."*

For the Vikings and others like them, every leader had to be a gold-giver. That is, he could expect loyalty only in as much as he could bring prosperity to his followers. Igor had done that for his personal army by oppressing the Drevlians, but as he rode home, he was not satisfied with it. The year before he had been so close to greatness – now he was shaking down peasants for animal pelts.

Igor sent his army back to Kiev, and with only his small personal retinue of bodyguards he turned around and went back towards the Drevlians to demand even more money. From this erratic and ill-advised action we can assume Igor was looking for glory, or perhaps he was just trying to take out his frustrations on the only ones he could strike out at that moment.

It proved a terrible decision.

The Drevlians saw Igor coming and knew that they had to do something or that he would continue to become bolder in his oppression of them. So, the Drevlians attacked Igor, killing his men and taking him prisoner. They dragged the Grand Prince of the Rus into a nearby forest, where two tall, straight birch trees had been bent down and fastened to the earth with ropes and stakes.

They tied Igor's limbs to the two trees, and then – either as an extemporaneous execution or as a sacrifice to their gods – they cut the ropes holding the treetops. The birch trees sprang back to their original height, tearing Igor to shreds in an explosion of blood and body parts.

The fledgling Viking state of the Kievan Rus was not going to face its greatest early threat from the powerful Byzantines or the Islamic caliphates. It was going to face these threats from their own lands.

Chapter XVI: Olga, Blood Saint of Varangian Kiev, and Sviatoslav the Brave

It may be that Igor's blood was still raining down from the treetops when the Drevlians fully realized there was no going back. But the prince of this Slavic people was a man named Mal, and he intended to press his advantage over the hated Rus with their Varangian aristocracy. The *Russian Primary Chronicle* tells us that Mal immediately dispatched an armed envoy to Kiev (Kyiv), where Igor's wife and young child awaited their lord's return.

Igor's wife was a princess named Olga (or Helga in Old Norse). Though sources differ, she was probably quite young. Her son, Sviatoslav (Norse, Sveinald), was but a boy. Without Igor, Olga was in a very delicate position – and Mal knew it. Sviatoslav was far too young to rule, and the Slavs did not expect that the Rus would follow a woman. Sviatoslav would be vulnerable to any Rus with backing who wanted power, and both he and his mother could very likely end up dead. Olga's only hope was to find a male protector, and soon.

Mal's delegation informed Olga that her husband and the ruler of her people was dead, and they conveyed Mal's offer to marry her and become the guardian of her son, the heir to the Rus throne. The Drevlians believed that not only had they killed Igor but that they would be able to take over the kingdom of their enemies as well.

Though Mal's reasoning was sound enough, he did not know Olga. Her position may be a delicate one, but there was nothing about the Varangian princess that was delicate, and though she would one day be remembered as a saint, at this time there was very little about her that was saintly.

Olga agreed to Mal's offer, stating that she could not bring her husband back to life by wishing and that it was only prudent to find a protector for her son. She told the delegation of Drevlians – who had arrived upriver via boats – that she would afford them a triumphant procession into the city to show the Rus who their new masters were. But, she specified, they should wait until the next day so that the city could be made ready, and that instead of entering the city on foot or on horseback, the citizens of Kiev would carry them on their boats like the heroes they were.

The Drevlians liked the arrangement and spent the night on their boats. Meanwhile, Olga's people dug a deep ditch in the center of the city.

The sun rose the next day, and a crowd met the Drevlians at the boat launch. They dragged the heavy wooden vessels out of the water, and hundreds of hands lifted them onto hundreds of shoulders. The Drevlians stood and brandished their weapons in exaltation as they rode into Kiev.

When they reached the ditch, the Rus dropped the boats into it. Olga stood at the edge, taunting the Drevlians as her men buried them alive.

Olga then sent a message to Dreva, saying that if Mal really wanted to marry her, he should not send a few warriors but rather a delegation of the best governors and chiefs. Assuming their first delegation was still alive and well in Kiev, the Drevlians complied.

When this new delegation of Dreva's nobles arrived, Olga invited them to take a bath in the bathhouse before they came to her court. Once the men entered the bathhouse, Olga's retainers locked them in and then stoked the fires until the Derevlians were steamed to death.

Olga sent a message to Prince Mal, informing him that she and little Sviatoslav were on their way. She asked Mal to meet her in the place where Igor was killed and to have much mead ready to hold a funeral for her husband – for it would be unseemly to get married before properly mourning him.

Olga and her son arrived with a relatively small band of retainers and servants. Mal was very taken with her beauty, virtue, and her excellent manners. As Olga's followers built up a burial mound over Igor's grave, Mal asked his prospective wife where all the men were that he sent to fetch her. She told the prince that he would see them soon, but that she had been so excited to see him that she travelled faster than those men could keep up. When the burial mound was finished, she urged the Drevlians to join her in toasts to her late husband Igor and then urged her followers to serve them. When the Slavs had thus become very drunk, Olga gave the word, and her servants butchered them all, including Prince Mal.

Olga then descended at the head of a Rus army and met the Drevlians – now finally aware of their peril – in a field of battle. Sviatoslav cast the first spear (possibly the traditional Odin-sacrifice spear cast), but since he was only a few years old, the spear did not go very far. Still, his Varangian tutor, Asmund, cried out to his men that their lord had entered the battle and that they should fight to be worthy of one so brave as he. The Rus took the field, and the Drevlians fled to their city, Iskorosten, and barred the gates.

Olga besieged the city for a year. Finally, the starving citizens begged for terms. Olga told them that she was tired of the siege herself, and since she had already thrice avenged her husband that she would let the Drevlians alone if they but paid her a simple tribute of three pigeons and three sparrows per household. If they followed this simple request, then there would finally be peace.

The Drevlians complied, for the city was full of birds, and every house had pigeons living in the thatch or the rafters. When the birds were collected and turned over though, Olga told each of her warriors to take a bird and tie a piece of sulfur to it with a strand of cloth. That night, as the Drevlians believed the Rus were preparing to depart the next day, Olga's men lit the sulfur and released the birds. Panicked, the thousands of birds flew to where their instincts took them – their nests within the city of the Drevlians. The entire city was soon alight with raging fire. The Drevlians fled through the gates, where the Rus cut them down or gathered them up to sell into slavery. So, the siege of Iskorosten and Olga's retribution on the Drevlians finally ended.

Olga and her army traveled through the land, ensuring that all other tribes and peoples knew that she ruled in her son's name. She further emphasized her strength by building fortresses. Olga did not only have a mind for revenge, though; she was also a capable administrator. As she re-instituted tribute amongst the Slavs and others, she changed (and standardized) the way that tribute was collected, lest future rulers make the same mistakes that her late husband had.

Though she became the most powerful woman of her region and had many suitors Olga never remarried. The *Russian Primary Chronicle* offers an amusing tale of how Olga met with the Byzantine Emperor at Constantinople, and how it was like when the Queen of Sheba met Solomon in the Bible, but the only thing we know to be true of Olga's concourse with Constantinople is that she did convert later in life to Christianity, and sought to further that religion in the lands of the Rus.

Her son, who by then was growing to be a man, refused to convert though, saying that his men would never follow him if he were a Christian. Byzantine accounts would later mention Sviatoslav and his warriors making oaths in the name of Perun and Veles. This suggests that even the Scandinavian elements of the Rus had taken on the Slavic paganism of their neighbors. However, Perun is a sky god and a god associated with thunder, and so it is likely that the Rus had simply syncretized their Thor with their new subjects' Perun – or perhaps it was not their syncretization but that of the Byzantine chronicler who related what he saw with what he knew of the Slavs. Similarly, Veles was a Slavic god of the underworld and the dark, so he has been associated with Loki by modern experts – but a close inspection of Veles reveals many similarities to Odin's darker elements. Like Veles, Odin was also a god of the dead and a god of magic. Veles was the god of music while Odin was the god of poetry. Both are crafty, both are often depicted with a spear, and both have wolves as their familiars. So, perhaps Perun and Veles were Thor and Odin to Sviatoslav's people, or perhaps it was just another way the Vikings adapted to their surroundings as they later would in the west.

Young Sviatoslav had other things on his mind than religion or even administrating. In fact, Sviatoslav was happy to let his capable mother run all the mundane aspects of his kingdom for him – like his father, he was interested only in war, expansion, and glory.

Sviatoslav the Brave

Sviatoslav inherited his father Igor's blonde hair, blue eyes, and lust for glory. We are told by Leo the Deacon (a Byzantine chronicler who met him) that he was of average height, but powerfully and ruggedly built. While these physical features belied his Norse ancestry, Sviatoslav's dress and customs were solidly on the Slavic side of the Rus character. He shaved his head, except for a long lock of hair on the side, and kept a full, bushy mustache but no beard. He dressed identical to his fighting men, except that his tunic and breeches were white "and cleaner," Leo says.

Since growing into manhood, Sviatoslav had drawn many valorous warriors to him (says the *Russian Primary Chronicle*). He went everywhere with this *druzhina*, or company or comrades, risking their dangers and sharing in their privations. While on campaign – and Sviatoslav was always on campaign – he stretched no tent over his head, but slept outside on a horse blanket and used his saddle for a pillow. His *druzhina* had no baggage carts or supply lines, we are told, but lived on what they could take from the land or from their foes.

Sviatoslav and his company of professional killers galloped on small, lean steppeland horses over the rolling hills and open prairies of Central and Eastern Europe, looking for more peoples to conquer. The *Russian Primary Chronicle* sums up his personality and the hunger of his ambition, "*he stepped as light as a leopard.*" He may have had Viking blood, but he had completely adapted to his new home in a way that few could match.

As Olga administered for her son, Sviatoslav picked fights with anyone and everyone. He defeated the Alans, who had raced their horses over the Pontic Steppe and around the Caspian Sea since Roman times. He continued to subjugate his Slavic neighbors and to put down any rebellions to Rus rule, and he continued to fight the Pechenegs whenever it suited him.

But the real economic power in the region was the Khazars, and Sviatoslav grew jealous that his neighbors seemed to take them more seriously than they took the Rus (and paid them more tribute). So Sviatoslav raised a large army to accompany his rough riders, and he made war on this rich, sophisticated, and powerful people until he wholly conquered and deposed them. Atil (or Itil), the capital of Khazaria, was utterly destroyed, and much of the cultural treasures of this advanced civilization were lost or went into stark decline. The Rus took over the Khazars' territory, their trade routes, and their influence in the region.

But Sviatoslav was not yet satisfied.

To the southwest, in the Balkan region, the Bulgarians were thriving, in defiance of their natural enemies, the Byzantines. Impressed with Sviatoslav's disposal of their Khazar competitors, Byzantium paid Sviatoslav to raise and lead as many as 60,000 men (including Pecheneg forces) against the Bulgarians.

Sviatoslav jumped at the chance. His massive army arrived in the Balkans on horseback and on dragon ship and made brutal war on the Bulgarians. Overwhelmed, the Bulgarians lost 80 towns along the Danube to Sviatoslav between 967 and 969. The Bulgarian Empire was pushed back to a fraction of what it had been. At that moment, Sviatoslav was in control of the largest domain in all of Europe.

Sviatoslav liked the Balkans. He made his new capital at the city of Pereyaslavets (now the community of Nufaru – formerly Prislav - in modern-day Romania) saying, *"all the riches would flow* [there]: *gold, silks, wine, and various fruits from Greece, silver and horses from Hungary and Bohemia, and from Rus' furs, wax, honey, and slaves."* Sviatoslav's ambition, vision, and ability had come together. He was only in his late 20's, and he already had three sons to secure his line. He was ready to become one of the most powerful men of his century.

But his enemies were not going to let him achieve that without a fight. The Bulgarian Emperor, Boris II bribed Sviatoslav's Pecheneg troops to leave him and go attack Kiev. The Rus perhaps did not think much of it when the battlewagons of the wily tribesmen rolled away, but a few weeks later they were receiving desperate messages for help from the Rus homeland.

Sviatoslav had other problems – relationships with Byzantium were starting to break down. The Byzantines had – rather foolishly perhaps – thought that Sviatoslav was only an eager soldier and that he would cede to them the Balkan territories he won. They had not meant to raise up an even more powerful emperor in place of the Bulgarians they were trying to contain.

Sviatoslav had no intention of giving up an inch of the land he had taken, and he knew that if he ran home to answer the Pecheneg threat that the Byzantines and the Bulgarians would both take full advantage of his absence. So, instead, he sent a general named Pretich back with 10,000 men to rescue the Rus heartland.

The Death of Olga

Meanwhile, the Pechenegs had surrounded Kiev with "*an innumerable multitude*." Conditions deteriorated rapidly in the great city, and by the time Pretich's dragon ships were seen on the river it seemed that death by starvation and thirst was only a few days away. Pretich was hopelessly outmatched though and was reluctant to attack the overwhelming numbers of the Pecheneg warriors.

Olga managed to get a message to him through the desperate actions of a daring young citizen of Kiev and told Pretich that if he did not act immediately, the city, its regent, and Sviatoslav's three sons were all doomed.

With a mix of extreme valor and trickery, the Rus attacked and chased back the Pechenegs. The Pecheneg chieftain was so impressed with their bravery and craft that he made formal oaths of friendship to Pretich and rolled back his siege.

Olga's first action as a free woman was to write her son a scathing letter rebuking him for not coming to the aid of his mother and sons himself. Upon receiving it, Sviatoslav pulled as many forces as he could spare out of his new territory and finally returned to Kiev. There he unleashed war on the traitorous Pechenegs, but when he was satisfied that they were pushed back into the steppes, he again readied himself to return to the Baltic.

"You behold me in my weakness," Olga protested, for whether from the hardships of the siege or the hardness of the years she was in failing health. *"Let me die, and then go wherever you want."*

Maybe Olga was broken-hearted, too, that her son only cared for war and that his wars were so obviously taking him on a collision course with Olga's beloved Byzantium. Whatever the combination of reasons, Olga was dead three days later. Sviatoslav ordered that she receive a full Christian burial and be interred in one of the churches she had built.

A long time later, Olga would be named a saint by both the Orthodox and Catholic churches for her attempts to unite her people under one Christian faith. Saint Olga was even given the title, Equal to the Apostles, a title given to only four women in the long list of Church heroines. While not everyone would agree on the holiness of this woman who had taken so many lives, her extraordinary leadership in the early history of what was to become Ukraine, Russia, and Belarus is undeniable. Had it not been for Olga, the Kievan Rus may have just been a footnote in history, and not the genus of several great nations.

Loving son though he was, Sviatoslav wasted no time before dividing regency of his northern realms to his three juvenille sons and then leading his *druzhina* south. Sviatoslav earliest memories were probably of losing his father and then being pulled front and center into his mother's extensive revenge (he was probably present at the funeral massacre, threw the first spear at the later battle with the Drevlians, and lived in his mother's camp during the siege that culminated in a fiery slaughter of an entire city). Somewhere in all that, perhaps, he learned that the answer to life's pain was more action.

We might have expected that the Pecheneg's nearly-successful seizure of the Rus heartland while he was off adventuring would have taught Sviatoslav the importance of consolidating his holdings, administering his domain, and moving more slowly. It did not.

War with Constantinople

When Sviatoslav returned to his capital of Pereyaslavets, he found the Bulgarians already in possession of it. Incensed, Sviatoslav stormed the city and took it (but only after hard fighting and heavy losses). He then sent word to the Byzantines that he was coming for them (it was always his custom to tell his enemies before he attacked them) and he said that he would capture Constantinople just as he had taken Pereyaslavets.

The Byzantines pretended that they wanted to make a peace treaty and pay tribute instead of fight, but only so that they could assess Sviatoslav's strength (which was nowhere near the 60,000 he once allegedly had but was now closer to 10,000). Satisfied that they could overwhelm his numbers, they marched against him with a great host.

The Rus were terrified, says the Chronicle, but Sviatoslav implored them to fight, saying, "*Let us not disgrace Rus, rather let us sacrifice our lives lest we be dishonored... and I will march before you. If you see my head fall,* [only] *then look to yourselves.*" Rallying, his men swore, "*Wherever your head falls, we too will lay down our own.*" Such was the bond between Sviatoslav and his warriors, a bond forged from a lifetime of shared adversity and total commitment.

The Rus met the Byzantine attack and cut straight through it. The Byzantines fled. Sviatoslav was in full rampage as he tore into Byzantine territory. He looted and burned his way through Thrace, sweeping aside any forces sent against him. No army had ever taken Constantinople, but Sviatoslav was drawing close, and the Grand Prince of the Rus was undefeated.

The Byzantines turned to diplomacy. This failed at first, for the Rus were drunk on victory, and Sviatoslav was driven by forces that few of us can fully understand. Eventually, though, the Rus began to realize that they had lost a lot of men, were deep in enemy territory and that it may not take long for the lands they won so quickly to fold back in around them. Winter was coming fast, and the Rus were risking everything by expanding too greedily.

Sviatoslav agreed to talks and tribute. A new treaty was drawn up, less favorable than Igor's but fitting to the purposes at hand.

One piece of the tribute given, we are told, was a fantastic sword that Sviatoslav – usually a man who was difficult to impress – took a keen liking to.

The Rus returned to Pereyaslavets, but Sviatoslav still felt he was too vulnerable after his losses. He decided to head back north to Kiev before winter to raise more troops and support before consolidating his holdings in the spring.

But as he and his *druzhina* sailed up the river Dneiper, the Pechenegs ambushed them at the cataracts. Sviatoslav and his men escaped to the city of Belobereg, where they spent a brutal winter with hardly any food or supplies.

In the spring, Sviatoslav attempted to reach Kiev again, but the Pechenegs were still waiting for him. They ambushed his exhausted *druzhina* again, and this time all of them were killed, including the Grand Prince.

The leader of the Pechenegs, a chieftain named Kurja, had Sviatoslav's skull inlaid with gold and kept as a drinking cup. Barbarous though it may seem, this act was considered a high honor amongst the wild and strange Pechenegs.

In 2012, a Ukranian fisherman pulled up a sword from 22 meters under the Dnieper. It was not the first 10th-century sword that had been discovered there, but this one had an *Ulfberht* inscription (which were the most famous and sought-after swords in the Viking Age) and had a hilt inlaid with copper, silver, and gold. It is quite possible that this is Sviatoslav's sword, perhaps even the one gifted to him as part of the Byzantine diplomatic tribute.

The Kievan Rus after Sviatoslav

The Rus were different after the death of Sviatoslav. They were still very warlike, and as a people, they were still on an upward trajectory towards greatness. They continued to carry the marks of their Varangian heritage, and tutors for their noble sons and royal brides for their princes were often sought in Sweden or other Scandinavian lands. But the Viking traders and Varangian mercenaries that filtered through the lands of the Rus were no longer part of the ruling elite but instead were foreigners.

Some modern experts hypothesize that the reason for this shift from a two-layered culture of Varangian and Slav was that most of the Norse ruling elite died fighting with Sviatoslav, and were replaced by new regimes as his descendants vied for power. While this may be true, the *Russian Primary Chronicle* already answered the question: "*the Rus were one people.*" The Vikings were extremely adaptive people, who blended with indigenous populations and changed to fit their environment while not betraying their inner spirit. We see in Sviatoslav's character how within just a few generations, the Grand Prince of the Rus had taken on local dress, customs, and fused or syncretized his gods; but still had Viking ethos and appreciated his ships and his *Ulfberht* sword. The Rus never really stopped being Viking, but they went on to take on their own identity, as the Normans and other Viking evolutions would. They went on to find their own fate.

There is one last thing to mention before we leave Central and Eastern Europe for a time. Sviatoslav left three sons. The sons immediately started warring with each other, and to escape his murderous brother, the younger son, Vladamir, fled to Sweden. He returned with several thousand Varangian mercenaries, overthrew his surviving brother in monstrous fashion and seized the throne.

Vladamir had both the effectiveness and longevity of rule to be remembered as "Vladamir the Great."[16] Though his brutality and avarice are difficult to overlook, the pious chroniclers of his age celebrated his efforts to unite the Rus under Christianity. Finally, with at least their

---

[16] Vladamir the Great is still celebrated as a founding father in Russia, Ukraine, and Belarus. He should not be confused with the many other Vladamirs and Vlads (such as the 15th century Romanian impaler, etc.).

faith more-or-less in common, the diverse peoples of the Rus lands could better move towards unified goals.

But once Vladamir had his throne and was free to work his will on the land, his Varangians proved to be too much trouble for him to occupy and restrain. Vladamir sent 6000 of these Varangians to Constantinople – not to attack it this time, but as a gift to strengthen the ties between the Rus and the Byzantines through service to their emperor. This was the beginning of the famous Varangian Guard, which would play a significant role in the future of the Viking Age and the final centuries of the Roman east.

Chapter XVII

Erik the Red and Leif the Lucky: The Vikings in Greenland and America

If American schoolchildren know one Viking by name, it is Leif Erikson, who was the first known European to set foot on North American soil. Leif's fantastic voyage to Vinland was almost 500 years before Columbus and the Age of Exploration. But Leif was just part of a whole family of intrepid Viking discoverers. His father, Erik the Red, started the first permanent Norse settlement on Greenland, and Leif's brothers and sister played a part in Norse America's ill-fated early history as well. These stories come to us primarily from two sources – The *Saga of Erik the Red* (*Eiriks Saga Rauða*), and the *Greenlander's Saga* (*Grœnlendinga*). These two works have some confusing and contradictory passages, but they present an incredible account of life on the Norse frontier and offer the first ever written reports of Native Americans.

Most assume that Erik was called "the Red" for his hair or for his ruddy complexion (the sagas do not explicitly say). He may have been more aptly called "the Red" for his charisma, his fiery temper, or his bad habit of killing people. Erik was from Norway but had been exiled from that land along with his father for violent feuding.

Erik the Red settled in Iceland and attempted a reformed life of peace. Some years later, though, two of Erik's slaves were killed by his neighbor, Eyjof the Foul. Erik went to demand justice (probably in the form of *wergild*). Eyjof the Foul was less than repentant and brought some muscle to back him up – a man ominously called Hrafn the Dueler. Erik's temper got the best of him, weapons were drawn, and Erik was the only one left standing.

Eyjof's kin brought charges against Erik, which in Iceland meant that he had to be convicted by at least 30 men from a jury of 36. The jury ruled against him, and he was banished from his region. Erik moved to another part of Iceland, and managed to live there quietly for an unspecified amount of time, but when a third neighbor refused to return some property Erik loaned him, a new quarrel erupted.

Erik the Red once again found himself with fresh blood on his hands and in the midst of a rapidly-escalating feud. The vendetta became so bad that he or his foe never went anywhere without their armed men around them, and the violence began spilling out to the whole area. Erik's peers had soon had enough, and at the next *Thing* (the local democratic assembly) Erik the Red was made an outlaw and banished from all of Iceland for three years.

Perhaps Erik, too, thought that he should get further away from neighbors, or that he needed to find a place where the laws were more lenient towards men of passion such as himself. He had heard of land in the midst of the cold northern seas – a barren and forbidding place called Gunnbjarnarsker (Gunnbjarn's Rock). Only one settlement had ever been made there, but it had fallen away into calamity and violence, and only two men returned home. Erik the Red thought he may be able to find the land, though, and so his dragon ship set out across the frothing North Atlantic waves. Erik's luck and sea craft held, and after about a week at sea he saw stark, barren hills rising from the ocean.

The land Erik came to is the biggest island in the world – more massive than all of Scandinavia put together – and yet, very little of it is habitable. Most of the land was covered in glaciers, and only the southernmost fjords offered enough shelter from the winds to even attempt the pastoral, agrarian lifestyle the Norse knew. Even there, the first frost would fall in August, and the fjords themselves would freeze in October. There were almost no trees, and most necessities would have to be imported from Iceland or elsewhere.

Yet, aside from the freedom which Eric craved, this place was full of valuable commodities for trade, like animal pelts and fox furs, polar bears (both for hides or even to bestow as live gifts to Viking lords), white hunting falcons, and of course there was one of the most sought-after commodities in the Norse world: ivory.

The ivory the Vikings traded came from walrus tusks, as well as the "horn" or tusk of the narwhal. These objects were valued in the natural state, or fashioned into works of art. An excellent example of Norse ivory art is the famous Isle of Lewis chess set.

Erik realized that his new land would not only allow him to rise above trouble, but it would also make him very rich. All he had to do was find more people who would leave Iceland to follow him into this bold new venture. To help with this, he called his new home Greenland, because "*more men will want to go there if the land has a good name.*"

His banishment ended, Erik the Red returned to Iceland and told everyone he could of the opportunities of Greenland. He was not disappointed. That summer 35 ships left Iceland for Greenland. Yet only 14 arrived. The rest turned back or were lost. Greenland was not to be a land that welcomed all in – even to reach it was a true test of courage.

Because these were ships of colonists, we gather from the sagas that they may have averaged about 30 men each (half of what we would expect from a raiding ship, because of all the livestock and supplies that must be brought along). There were also women who came, but there were not as many women as there were men in the initial stages. The lack of women in the early formation of settlements was not only a common source of strife, but could even doom a colony.

Erik the Red finally had his small realm, where his followers could live in peace while growing wealthy on trade. From what we can tell, these first Greenlanders – especially Erik – took to their new life and met the arduous demands of their new home with resolve and ingenuity. Erik and his wife, Thodhild, raised three sons, Thorstein, Thorvald, and Leif. But it was Erik's daughter, Freydis, who inherited much of his charisma, vindictiveness, and fiery character. Thorstein was close to his father, and it was said that not many in Greenland were so well thought of as he. Erik's youngest son, Leif, we are told, *"was a great and strong man, grave and well-favored, therewith sensible and moderate in all things."*

Greenland was set up like Iceland, in that it was democratically-governed, and so Erik was no king. Nonetheless, as firstborn, Thorstein would inherit the lion's share of his father's wealth, leaving his younger brother Leif to seek his fortune elsewhere. So, as the 10th century closed, Leif sailed back to Norway and served in the personal guard of King Olaf Tryggvassan.

He could not have possibly imagined where that adventure might ultimately lead him.

Leif the Lucky

King Olaf Tryggvassan was the grandson of the famous Harald Fairhair, the tyrant who had united all of Norway. Like his ancestor he was ambitious, but Olaf's ambition was to make all of Norway Christian, by force if necessary. Olaf was very impressed with Leif, and (after Leif converted) asked his bodyguard if he would return to Greenland to spread Christianity there. Leif told his king that Christianity would be a hard sell in Greenland, but Olaf insisted, saying *"I believe you would have good luck in it."* Leif graciously replied, *"That could only be if I carry your good luck with me."* This was to prove prophetic, for when Leif left, King Olaf (age about 36) was killed in battle.

Leif and about 35 men, however, where on the high sea, and at first it may have seemed that luck was against them. They became lost in a fog for days. But when they finally did see land, it was not the barren hills of Greenland but a land of tall maple trees.

They explored the coast and several islands (experts think they may have found Newfoundland, Nantucket, and/or the Labrador Coast of Canada). Winter was coming so the party built a longhouse from the abundant timber. They ate well on salmon and they found wild grapes (or some other berry) in abundance. A German in their company helped the Vikings make wine, which made Leif and his men merry through the winter. The weather was warmer than any winter they had experienced in Greenland, Iceland, or Norway, and the explorers noted that there was abundant grazing for animals if they were to make a colony.

Leif was not the first Viking to see North America (that distinction belongs to a man named Bjarn Herjulfson, who was too busy to stop and explore and was forever after ridiculed for that) but he was the first recorded European to set foot on these shores. After overwintering, Leif and his men loaded their ship full of timber and grapes and set sail for Greenland.

On one of the North American islands they passed, Leif's keen eyes picked out a shipwreck in the fog. There were about 15 survivors clinging to life on this island, who could not believe their luck that another Norse ship should come by in time to rescue them. They were also Greenlanders, and the leader had even known Leif as a child. Leif took all the men aboard his ship and was able to salvage some of their cargo. From that day on, Leif Erikson was known as Leif the Lucky.

Leif Returns Home

Returning to barren Greenland with a boatload of lumber, wine, and rescued men, Leif the Lucky achieved instant fame. Everyone was eager for his tales of these fertile new places, Markland and Vinland, and to hear all that had befallen him serving a great king in Norway and exploring the unknown end of the Midgard.

Leif found that his new popularity opened doors for him to fulfil his promise to King Olaf, too, and many Greenlanders accepted Christianity. Among those was Leif's mother, Thodhild. Erik the Red was happy to see his son but did not think much of his new religion. When Thodhild refused to sleep with Erik until he converted, the saga says, "*this was a great trial to his temper.*"

Erik's older son, Thorstein, was hungry to mount his own expedition to America immediately, perhaps being uncomfortable with his little brother eclipsing his own fame (and he was right, Leif would later be selected over Thorstein to be the leader of the Greenlanders). He urged Erik the Red to go with him. Erik was reluctant, but eventually decided to go. On the way to the ship, though, he fell off his horse, injuring his ribs and shoulder. So, Erik stayed home, and it was just as well – for Thorstein's voyage was ill-fated. The ship blew around on the waves all season without finding America, and so they returned home empty-handed.

That winter, there was a plague in Greenland and Erik the Red died. He was about 51 years old. Leif the Lucky was made leader of the Greenlanders after him.

Further Expeditions to America

The Greenland Vikings mounted several more expeditions to America. The year after Leif's return and Thorstein's unsuccessful expedition, their brother Thorvald set out with one ship. He found Vinland, but quickly got into trouble with Native Americans there. Thorvald was shot with an arrow, and the other Vikings buried him at the spot where he had said he wanted to build his home. Thorvald Erikson was the first recorded European to be killed on American soil.

Another expedition involved 160 Vikings and was led by men named Karlsefni and Thorhall the Sportsman. Erik's daughter, Freydis, and his son-in-law (also named Thorvald) accompanied this expedition. They found Leif's lands and explored further, having some success. But they had many problems (including religious strife) and Thorhall's men split off on their own. Thorhall's ships were ultimately blown off course

276

to Ireland on the return journey, and Thorhall and his explorers were killed or enslaved by the warring factions there.

The hundred and forty explorers who stayed with Karlsefni soon encountered Native Americans, whom they called Scraelings or *Skrælingar*. While there was at least one episode where the Vikings and the Scraelings traded peaceably, most of the encounters ended with violence or bilateral apprehension.

At one point the Greenlanders' expedition was attacked by a great host, and despite their shield wall and their iron weapons, they were very nearly destroyed. But Freydis Eiriksdottir grabbed a sword and – stripping herself half-naked – beat her breast with the blade and shouted at the Scraelings so fearsomely that the Vikings rallied, and the Natives fled.

Karlsefni's expedition tarried a while longer in America. Karlsefni's wife had a son, named Snorri who was the first recorded European born in America. Eventually, though, this colony began to lose pace with the demands placed on them by the wild new environment. They returned to Greenland, though some perished along the way.

Some archeologists believe that the definitive evidence of Norse settlement found at L'Anse aux Meadows in Newfoundland is Karlsefni's colony (possibly the camp the saga calls Hop) because that was the longest-standing settlement the skalds have told us of.

The last expedition the sagas report was far grimmer than Karlsefni's expedition. Freydis Eiriksdottir was not back in Greenland for more than a few months when she hungered to return to America. Having a shrewd head for business (and living in one of the few medieval places where a woman was free to do so) she entered into a partnership with two brothers from Norway.

Freydis and the brothers agreed they would take two ships with no more than 30 fighting men each (lest one party have an advantage over the other) but as many colonists as they liked, and set up a colony in Vinland at the very spot where Leif had wintered (now ten years before). They would use this colony to export goods back to Greenland, and would split the profits 50/50.

Whether she entered into the pact duplicitously or simply for her own security, Freydis snuck five additional fighting men aboard her ship, giving her the advantage should the parties ever fight each other. The colony reached Vinland, and at first progress was good. Not surprisingly, though, there was the gradual growth of strain between the two factions as the stresses of life in a difficult environment mounted. Soon the parties were not on speaking terms, and the colonists with the brothers from Norway moved further off.

Isolation and hardship do strange things to people, and the annals of explorers throughout the ages have been filled with dark episodes where seemingly ordinary people lost their minds. This may have been the case with Freydis Eiriksdottir, or perhaps the "zeal" she had shown in defeating the Scraelings years before was an earlier manifestation of her deep psychosis. Whatever the reasons, one morning Freydis set up an elaborate scheme to drive her Vikings into a rage and attack the other camp.

Not only were the Norwegian brothers killed, but Freydis herself butchered five surrendered, non-combatant women with an axe. She then threatened her own men, who by this time began to realize that they had been lied to and were implicated in something truly horrible, that if they ever spoke of these events that she would kill them, too.

Not surprisingly, Freydis's colony failed. They returned to Greenland, almost empty-handed. Leif found out about the massacre, and tortured three of Freydis's men until he heard every detail. He refused to raise a hand against Freydis though, instead laying a curse at her feet. After that, Freydis and her husband were ostracized by the community.

There were probably more expeditions to North America. Archeologists are finding artifacts spread over various parts of Newfoundland, New Brunswick, and beyond. There are also hints in the historical record of more journeys to Leif's lands for lumber or raw materials, and there is the possibility that some small numbers of people may have attempted colonies there as conditions in Greenland deteriorated. We will probably never know the full extent of Viking involvement on North American soil. But we do know that the journey was treacherous, the conditions difficult, relations with the natives adversarial, and life on the frontier very uncertain. When it came to the exploration of the unknown world, the Vikings were ahead of their time, and so their efforts here were not fated to last.

The End of Viking Greenland

During the lifetimes of Erik the Red and Leif the Lucky, Greenland grew and flourished on trade despite their stark environment. At the height of its known population, about 3000 people were living in 30 farms (for comparison, Iceland had about 77,500 at the end of the Viking Age or about 15 times as many people as Greenland). But there was something that neither Erik or Leif could have known – they were living in what scientists would later call the Medieval Warm Period.

Just before the Viking Age, climates had been trending cold and wet. This – along with the geography and ordinary conditions of Scandinavia had honed the Viking ethos, culture, and character, for as Herodotus said, "*Hard lands make hard men.*" But from around the year, 950 to about 1250, temperatures in the Atlantic region of the world were considerably warmer. This period of warm temperatures is called the Medieval Warm Period, or the Medieval Climate Optimization. It was a very good thing for the Vikings in general because it was accompanied by population growth and easier trade routes, and it was perfect for the Greenlanders.

But what goes up must come down, and around the year 1197 the glaciers began to advance, and the Atlantic pack ice began to grow (possibly due to increased volcanic activity decreasing the sunlight there). It was not the worsened cold that the hardy Greenlanders noticed most – their sea routes to Iceland and the rest of Europe were becoming choked with floating ice. The shortest route to Iceland was three days hard sailing, but by the 1300s this way was blocked. For sailors to go to or from Greenland, they had to go far to the south and then head up – but even here, as one eyewitness wrote in 1364, *"now the ice is come from the north, so close to the reefs that none can sail by the old route without risking his life."*

In time, the trade routes that Vikings had established through Russia and Eastern Europe were considered far safer and swifter than venturing to Greenland. With the end of trade, the Greenlanders had to be entirely self-sufficient.

They were not the only human population on the island. Even during the Little Ice Age, the Inuit peoples expanded in Greenland, with an aggressive tribe known as the Thule taking over coastal territories from Inuit and non-Inuit alike. The Inuit were adapted by thousands of years to living in polar environments. Unlike the Norse who brought their Northern European way of life with them and depended on trade, the Inuit's lifestyle of fishing and hunting marine mammals did not need any help from the outside.

There are some Inuit legends of armed conflict between the Inuit and the Norse in Greenland. But the end of Erik the Red's people was a quiet one. The last record from Greenland was of a wedding held at Hvalsey Church in 1408.

In 1492, as Columbus prepared to seek out his path to the Indies, the Pope remarked that no one had been to Greenland in more than 80 years. In the 1700s, the King of Denmark read the *Saga of Erik the Red* and realized that the Greenlanders had probably not heard of the Reformation. The Danish mission the King sent found only long-abandoned buildings and freely-roaming herds of Scandinavian sheep.

Archeology just after World War I determined that Erik's people had made a brave struggle for survival to the end, but that the elements, famine, and isolation had made the last Greenlanders "severely crippled, dwarflike, twisted, and diseased."[59] At last, Erik the Red's independent kingdom at the edge of the world collapsed, though scholars and archeologists still wonder how many of the Greenland Vikings left for Markland (Newfoundland) and the Americas before it was too late.

PART THREE: RAGNAROK – THE DEATH AND REBIRTH OF THE VIKING AGE

Chapter XVIII: Brian Boruma and the End of Viking Power in Ireland

In the year 1004, Brian Boruma (better known as Brian Boru) mac Cainaidie, High King of Ireland, strode up to the altar of Saint Patrick's shrine at Armagh and laid a hefty gift of gold. The King, wearing his robes of state or perhaps the royal armor that had seen him through more than 20 battles against the Vikings and competing kings, told the wide-eyed scribe recording the donation to register it under the title, *Imperator Scottorum.* This was not the title of the High King of Tara (which was called *Ard Rí*), the ancient office of an appointed regent who would help moderate and instill some relative order on the numerous other kings of the island. *Imperator Scottorum* meant "Emperor of the Irish." By putting that title forward at Ireland's spiritual capital, as well as showing off the money and arms to back it all up, Brian Boruma was sending the message that Ireland was now one nation.

Nor was this idea all a delusion of grandeur for the aged king. Irish chroniclers would refer to Brian as the *"Augustus of the West,"* and would claim that his court received tribute from England and Scotland. The many kingdoms of Europe were coalescing into nations under strong, central leadership, and in 1004, Brian had pulled Ireland out of one of the bloodiest and most chaotic epochs of its long history.

The crowd of supporters who accompanied him to Armagh included men that had helped him win, but also men he had beaten.

Brian was invincible in battle, and he was generous and munificent in peace. He had been ruling in Munster since his brother, King Mathgamhain, had been murdered in 976. Brian had bloodlessly supplanted Mael Seachnaill II (also called Maelseachlainn or sometimes Malachy) around 1002. In all the lands that he controlled, there was rule *"not* [merely] *by strength, but by constitution and law."* The *Annals of Ulster* records with tragic awe that in Brian's Ireland, forts could go un-garrisoned, there were no dragon ships on the waterways, people could let their cows graze unguarded, and that a woman could safely walk outside unaccompanied.

Brian Boruma's Rise to Power

It had taken Brian Boruma time to accomplish all of this. The *Annals of Ulster* say that he was born in 941 (making him about 63 in 1004), but all other sources say he was 15 years older than that. He was a younger son of the King of Munster in southern Ireland. When Brian grew to manhood, his brother Mathgamhain (a.k.a. Mahon) was king. At that time the Vikings – both Norse-Irish like the Ui Imar, as well as influxes of new Vikings driven out of Scandinavia by the ongoing dynastic struggles there – were active in Ireland with renewed energy. The Irish slave trade was in full swing. Cattle raiding was accentuated under increased pressures from famines and natural disasters. Though many of the Norse were Christian by this time, church attacks accelerated.

Though some kings, like Mael Seachnaill, were bravely fighting back against the Vikings, others – including Mathgamhain – were afraid and eager to make peace at almost any cost. During his brother's reign, Brian Boruma took his own men and fought against the Vikings, killing them *"by twos, by threes, by fives, by scores, and by hundreds."*

Brian eventually convinced his brother to do his duty to his people and fight those who were exploiting them. King Mathgamhain then became an active Viking fighter himself. Together they beat the Vikings at the Battle of Sulcoit in 968 and shortly after that drove Ivar of Limerick (another of the Ui Imar clan of Ivar the Boneless[17]) out of his city.

Ivar escaped and took to the waves for about 8 years but managed to exploit Irish enmities and eventually orchestrate Mathgamhain's murder. Mathgamhain was killed while meeting with other Irish kings, and Brian took his brother's place around 976.

The assassination of Mathgamhain was a bad decision for Ivar. With the full power of Munster now under his command, Brian Boruma went on the warpath. He followed Ivar and his two sons to their hide-out on the monastic island of Scattery around 978. The *Annals of Tigernach* then complains that Brian violated holy ground by killing Ivar of

---

[17] In Old Irish, Ui Imar means "grandsons [descendants] of Imar" and was the clan of Imar who in the latter 9th century was called "King of All the Foreigners in Ireland." This Imar is thought by many to be the Ingvar of the *Anglo-Saxon Chronicle* and the Ivar the Boneless of Norse sagas. See chapter 10.

Limerick in single combat there. In the subsequent battle that ensued, Ivar's two sons were also slain, and the Ui Imar was thus weakened before the events of 980.

The year 980 saw the defeat of Amlaib Cuaran Sichtricson Ui Imar by Mael Seachnaill II at the Battle of Tara, and the rise of Mael Seachnaill as High King. Amlaib Cuaran (Norse, Olaf Kvaran) was a descendant of Ivar the Boneless and the King of Dublin and at times Northumbria, too. His transmarine Norse-Irish empire had built on the work of his father, Sichtric One-Eyed.

If the name Mael Seachnaill sounds familiar, it is because the High King of Tara who defeated Amlaib Cuaran was the descendant of the man by the same name who had drowned Turgeis, the first King of Dublin. Brian Boruma soon started working with the High King in his attempts to drive out predatory factions of both Norse and Irish.

The traditional narrative, advanced by such works as the early-12th century, *Cogadh Gaedhel re Gallaibh* (*The War between the Gaels and the Foreigners,* one of the most colorful primary sources of the Middle Ages) and the early 17th century historian, Geoffrey Keating, is that Brian and Mael Seachnaill were trying to rid Ireland of a Viking scourge. While inspection of the sources makes it clear that quelling the outbreak of Norse-backed violence was a high priority of the two kings, other historians would add that both Mael Seachnaill's and Brian Boruma's campaigns of the 980s and 990s rapidly consolidated their control and removed Irish opposition. Some have even accused Brian of being a Machiavellian usurper because as Brian acted in concert with Mael Seachnaill, he was gradually absorbing Mael Seachnaill's political clout until Brian was able to claim the High Kingship for himself around 1002.

There was an armed showdown between the two, but finding that his own clan (the ancient, powerful Ui Niel's) refused to support him against Brian, Mael Seachnaill made a grudging but bloodless submission. Brian gave Meal Seachnaill a gift of more than a hundred fine horses, but the deposed High King re-gifted the animals to Brian's son Murchardh and stormed off to fight Vikings on his own.

But as Brian Boruma prepared his army for a victory lap around Ireland before sending them home to start the hard work of peace in 1005, Mael Seachnaill was not the only one nursing grudges against the new *Imperator Scottorum*. Even though Brian was such a good ruler that even Norse sources praise him and some Vikings would later join in his defense, someone in his own home allegedly hated him – his wife, Gormlaith.

Seven Degrees of Gormlaith

Gormlaith ingen Murchada (also spelled Gormflaith in some Irish sources and Kormlada in Norse sources) is an intriguing character. She was the daughter of the Irish King of Leinster, who – around the age of 15 – was married to Amlaib Cuaran, the Norse King of Dublin and

Northumbria. Gormlaith bore Almaib a son named Sytric and two daughters named Máel Muire and Gytha. But just five or six years after she married him, the Irish Viking transmarine emperor of the Ui Imar clan was defeated by Mael Seachnaill at the Battle of Tara (980), his older sons were killed, and Amlaib retired broken-hearted to the monastery at Iona where he died a year later.

Amlaib's death left Gormlaith grieving and vulnerable. However, not only was Gormlaith an Irish princess, she was stunningly beautiful and alluring throughout her entire life. Fairly or unfairly, though, she is also remembered as being cold, calculating, and evil. As *Brennu-Njáls Saga* (the *Saga of Burned Njal*) puts it, *"she was the fairest of all women and best gifted in everything that was not in her own power, but it was the talk of men that she did all things ill over which she had any power."*

The timeline of what happened next is difficult to reconstruct, and there are several claims that seem at odds with each other. According to the *Annals of the Four Masters*, after Amlaib's death, Gormlaith married Mael Seachnaill and Brian Boruma both at different times. It credits Gormlaith not only for bearing Amlaib's eventual successor, Sytric, but also Mael Seachnaill's son Conchubar, and Brian's son, Donnchadh. The *Annals of the Four Masters* back up this odd claim by appealing to poetry (of course) with this verse:

> *"Gormlaith took three leaps,*
> *Which a woman shall never take again,*

A leap at Ath-Cliath, a leap at Teamhair,
A leap at Caiseal of the goblets over all."

Ath-Cliath (Dublin), Teamhair (Tara) and Caiseal (Cashel) are taken to mean Amlaib, Mael Seachnaill, and Brian Boruma respectively.

It appears that marrying the widow of the king you just killed was something of a 10th-11th century convention, for the Drevlian prince had expected Olga of the Kievan Rus to marry him, and the Danish King Cnut the Great would marry Rollo's great-granddaughter, Emma – the widow of the English King Aethelred the Unready. It served as a "p-r stunt" conveying the bringing together of the two sides, though in those patriarchal societies it also emphasized which side was dominant.

If the *Annals of the Four Masters* is right that Mael Seachnaill married Gormlaith immediately after Amlaib died in 981, then she must not have stayed married to him long if she were also the mother of Donnchadh mac Brian (who is thought to have been born in the early 980s and was a war leader by 1013). Perhaps the old Celtic tradition of hand-fasting (a "trial marriage" lasting a year and a day) was still in effect, and Gormlaith dropped the charade as soon as she was able to. In any case, the marriage would make for awkward family history, since Mael Sechnaill later married Gormlaith's daughter, Máel Muire. Or, since none of the other annals say that Gormlaith was married to Mael Seachnaill the "leap" at Tara may refer to her daughter's marriage and not her own.

Some sources say that Gormlaith married Brian as part of a treaty after the 998-999 uprising of her son, King Sytric Silkbeard (a.k.a. Sigtrygg Silkenbeard), Viking King of Dublin and scion of the Ui Imar clan, and his Leinster ally, Gormlaith's brother, King Mael Morda. Brian defeated this uprising and ran Sytric out of Dublin. But showing his usual magnanimity, Brian accepted an offer of peace from Sytric (rather than leaving him to become a lightning rod for further Viking activity). The treaty was sealed with Brian (already a double widower) taking Sytric's mother and Mael Morda's sister, Gormlaith, as his wife and giving his own daughter, Sláine, to marry Sytric Silkbeard.

There is further controversy in the sources. Annals mention Gormlaith as Queen of Munster in her obituary in 1030, and so Brian must have been her last husband, though the Norse sources say she divorced Brian, too. *Brennu-Njáls Saga* says she bore none of Brian's children, and this seems more plausible given everyone's respective ages (Brian possibly in his 70s and Gormlaith about 40 in 999, and Donchadh around 30 in 1013).

Or, if Donnchadh was indeed Gormlaith's son and Sytric's half-brother, then perhaps Gormlaith and Brian were married much earlier (in the 980s) and it only became a double wedding alliance when Sytric married Sláine in 999. If Sytric had already been Brian's stepson, it would explain why Brian exiled the rebel instead of killing him, and why they reconciled so easily a few months later.

Brian giving his daughter to marry the Viking lord of Dublin instead of a king of a bigger territory shows the importance he placed on peace with the Norse-Irish. Of course, Brian was feeling the confidence of plans coming together, and he had ample prospective heirs already – or so he thought.

But aside from being traded around like a trophy between the powerhouses of Ireland, who had all played a hand in destroying her first love, Gormlaith had other causes for resentment. Gormlaith's home kingdom of Leinster had strong Viking ties and had already rebelled against the increasingly power-hungry High Kings. Meanwhile, her son was the last Norse-Irish king in the country, and her daughter Gytha was married to King Olaf Trygvasson (Leif Erikson's mentor) in Norway. Gormlaith's husband Brian and ex-husband (and/or son-in-law) Mael Seachnaill, on the other hand, had either killed or had a hand in killing her first husband Amlaib, her stepsons, Ragnal and Aralt, their cousins Ivar of Limerick and his two sons, and others of the Ui Imar clan.

Some people are good in public but bad at home, but it may be that Gormlaith's much-older arranged husband Brian was never less than kind to her – the cause of her hatred for Brian could be simply that she had become Ui Imar. Her blood may be Irish, but her heart was Viking.

So, as a decade passed between Brain Boruma claiming the title *Imperator Scottorum* in 1004 and the incredible cataclysm of 1014 these several kings, queens, and princes – all connected by blood or marriage by a single woman – thrived or brooded as their natures dictated until, as legend has it, a single conversation threw the door open to a tragic climax at Clontarf by the sea.

The Second Leinster-Dublin Rebellion

It was late in 1012 or 1013, the *Cogadh Gaedhel re Gallaibh* tells us, that Brian Boruma invited his brother-in-law, King Mael Morda of Leinster, to come to his court at the Rock of Cashel. Always the good politician, Brian liked to use gifts and visits to keep his friends close and his enemies closer, but with 15 years having passed since Mael Morda's last rebellion (and now that they were family) this visit may have seemed much like any other. Brian had asked Mael Morda to bring with him three of the large, straight trees that grow so well in Leinster because he was building some ships that needed masts (Brian had been known to take on the Vikings in naval battles, too).

Mael Morda and some of his kin along with their entourage were nearing Cashel when a friendly quarrel broke out between them. We do not know what the nature of the dispute was, but it probably had something to do with Mael Morda's age or physical fitness, for he won the argument by deadlifting the end of one of the masts by himself. Mael Morda had proven he was still strong as an ox, but in the process, he burst one of the silver buttons from the fine silk, gold-embroidered tunic Brian had gifted him on a previous occasion.

The Leinstermen arrived in Cashel, and after the pleasantries, some mead horns, and feasting had concluded for the evening, Mael Morda visited his sister Gormlaith to see if she would sew his silver button back on for him.

Now, as weaving and working with fabric was one of the seven consummate feminine skills in the Middle Ages, it was not considered impertinent to ask a queen to sew a button – at least not when the garment was as expensive as the one Mael Morda offered.

But Gormlaith grabbed the offered tunic from her older brother's hands and tossed it into the fire. Then she upbraided her dumbfounded sibling, calling him a beggar and a lackey for being so submissive to Brian and pointing out that Brian's son would go on to hold the same authority over Mael Morda's son. Leinster and the other kingdoms of Ireland were letting one man rule the whole country, which had never been done before (as the ancient position of High King was really just a 'first among equals' arrangement). Gormlaith's tirade ended, and Mael Morda sulked off with neither his shirt nor any answer to give his vehement sister. He stewed on her words all night.

The next morning, the men of the court were in the great hall, passing the time and trying to stay warm. Brian's son and heir-apparent, the accomplished warrior Murchadh, was playing chess with his relative,

Conaing. Mael Morda sat down next to Conaing and started coaching him. Murchadh did not like to lose at anything, and so as another ivory piece was toppled he growled at Mael Morda, "This was probably how you coached your foreigners, too [referring to the first Leinster rebellion in 998-999]. Of course, I beat you then, when it mattered."

"You won't beat me the next time," Mael Morda shot back.

In a moment, the hall was in an uproar as barely-concealed animosity and old wounds were brought to the fore. Murchadh cursed Mael Morda as a traitor and Mael Morda stormed off, his men scrambling to follow.

Brian Boruma had not been in the hall but soon heard of the affair. He ordered a messenger to rush after Mael Morda and implore him to come back, telling him that the High King knew it was just a misunderstanding and that there were gifts of cattle that Brian had not had the chance to give him yet.

But when the messenger caught up with Mael Morda, riding towards Leinster in a fury, the King answered his peace offer by striking the messenger. Either from the blow or from falling off his horse, the messenger suffered a cracked skull. The luckless boy had to be carried back to the castle, where he later died.

A sister's upbraiding and heated words over a game had led to a young man's death. There seemed to be no going back – and the truth was, Mael Morda did not want to. Gormlaith was right. He must free Leinster from Brian's control, or he would be the one that gave his kingdom away. Mael Morda and his men raced back to their strongholds and prepared for war.

Brian also realized that the peace was broken. Men like Murchadh, Donchadh, and Brian's brother, Wolf the Quarrelsome, urged the old King to prepare for war or he would appear weak. So Brian did, calling for a muster of the warriors from all parts of Ireland that were his to command.

Around this time, we gather from the Norse source, *Burnt Njal's Saga*, Gormlaith fled to Dublin and urged her son Sytric Ui Imar to collect all the help he could and join his uncle, Mael Morda. Gormlaith sent her son on a tour to Scotland, Britain, and all the isles, and instructed him – that if land and plunder in Ireland were not enough to entice the Norse lords to attack Brian Boruma – then to offer her hand in marriage to any king or jarl that would kill the *"Imperator Scottorum."*

Sytric Silkbeard left Dublin and went on a wide circuit to raise support. He may have been far less sure of success than his mother and uncle were because he did not hesitate to offer Gormlaith's hand in marriage to several different kings (perhaps not expecting them all to survive long enough to realize his duplicity). *Burnt Njal's Saga* tells us that Gormlaith later approved of her son's tactics.

Sytric found a lot of help.

The Danes – who's king, Sweyn Forkbeard, the son of Harald Bluetooth – had just taken England from Aethelred the Unready, and though it was not a good time for him to commit his full strength to invade Ireland, sent a thousand of his elite warriors who were all *"encased in glittering corselets"* of heavy mail or scales.

But in the 11th century, the Viking Age was waning, and continental Scandinavia was – as in Sweyn Forkbeard's case – enmeshed in its own dynastic struggles and empire-building. In a testament to the changing times, most of the Vikings Sytric found were from the islands and faraway places of Europe's periphery. He brought men from Iceland, the Faroes, and Scotland's Western Isles. Jarl Sigurd of Orkney was one of his main allies, eager to have Gormlaith's hand and Munster's crown.

King Brodir from the Isle of Man led a smaller force, but one that was disproportionately feared. Brodir, according to the saga, was an apostate Christian who had gone back to the Old Ways. Some claimed he was a sorcerer. He was a big man with impenetrable armor. Irish sources say he fought with a double-headed ax, so Brodir of Man was like an image from a fantasy movie.

Sytric also garnered support from many (but not all) of the Norse-Irish.

According to the *Annals of Loch Cé* and the *Cogadh Gaedhel re Gallaibh,* the rebellion of Sytric and Mael Morda was also joined by adventurers from all over Europe – Normans, Saxons, Britons, Flemish, Welsh, men from the Holy Roman Empire (Germans), and even two princes of France. In all, 3000 Vikings and mercenaries would join Mael Morda's 3000 Leinstermen.

Sytric Silkbeard returned to Dublin and assembled his own army. All forces had agreed to meet there by Palm Sunday.

King Brodir of Man's brother, Ospark, had always been his partner in all his Viking expeditions, but Ospark *"refused to fight so good a king"* and so he took his 10 ships to join Brian. King Brodir sailed to Dublin with his 20 ships. His 3-day voyage was fraught with bad weather and bad omens, and according to the saga, every night a man in each dragon ship died. But Brodir cast the rune sticks and saw that if they fought Brian on Good Friday, Brian would die. If they fought any other day, then the rebellion would fail. As any sorcerer will attest, though, the answers magic renders are full of double meanings.

Whatever their future might hold, the massive armies of Brian Boruma's Ireland and the Leinster-Viking alliance met each other at Clontarf, just on the other side of Dublin Bay, April 23, 1014.

The Battle of Clontarf

When winter ended, and preparations were completed, Brian Boruma's forces marched towards where they knew their enemies would be waiting for them: Dublin. Brian was at least 73, and maybe even 88 years-old at this time, but he rode at the head of his army. He had 6000 warriors from all over Ireland, as well as a thousand Vikings (including

Ospark and his men) who fought as mercenaries or to protect their own interests. Their confidence started high – for it was rumored that Sytric Silkbeard's Vikings had quarreled and sailed away. That meant that Mael Morda's rebels would be outnumbered more than two to one, and that was even before Mael Seachnaill's men were counted.

But Mael Seachnaill did not show up outside of Dublin in April, as had been arranged. The once-High King had assembled his hosts of experienced warriors and had marched out of his home kingdom of Meath, but then had stopped and made their own camp some distance away.

Mael Seachnaill appealed to some current political motivation for his reneging of his oaths (allegedly, Sytric had already attacked him, and Brian had been unable to help), and indeed he risked Brian's wrath when the rebellion was over.

Some see the military wisdom in Mael Seachnaill's strategy of holding forces back and avoiding the risk of all of Ireland's might on one cast of the dice, as Brian seemed to be doing. But it seems equally likely that Mael Seachnaill had found his opportunity to get back at the man who had replaced him 12 years before; or perhaps that he just found he owed more loyalty to his brother-in-law, Sytric Silkbeard than he did to the autocrat who was pushing Ireland in new directions. Given the extensive political efforts Sytric had put forth to garner support, it seems unlikely that he would not have tried to secure peace with Meal Seachnaill if it could be had.

Undeterred by the loss of the warriors of Meath, Brian and his vast army arrived at Dublin a few days before Easter and prepared for battle.

On the morning of Good Friday, they awoke to see that Mael Morda's army of Leinstermen had sallied from the city and arranged themselves in formation with the bay at their backs. But as Brian's forces assembled, they received a grim surprise – a vast fleet of dragon ships filled the harbor, heading towards them at full sail. The disbanding of Sytric's allied forces had been a ruse. Hundreds of keels cut into the sand, and 3000 Vikings and mercenaries from all over Europe leaped out onto the beach to join Mael Morda's men. In all, 13,000 warriors were about to fight for the future of their world. Nothing on this scale had ever happened in Ireland before.

Both armies arranged themselves in three wings. Brian's forces had the forest to their backs, and the rebels had the sea at theirs. Brian himself did not lead the fighting, but instead, the elderly King prayed fervently for victory in either a tent removed from the field (Irish sources) or in a small shield wall of his own in the back of the line (Norse sources). On the far wing was Wolf the Quarrelsome's Irish against Vikings led by Brodir of Man. Irish sources say Murchadh mac Brian, heir to the throne, led the center, while Norse sources refer to a hero named Kerthialfad (who may or may not be the same person). Opposing from this main body was Mael Mordha and his 3000, as well as Sigurd of Orkney and his Vikings. On the near side to Dublin was Ospark and Brian's Vikings facing King Sytric Silkbeard.

The Battle of Clontarf began in the morning after the tide went out. *"A spirited, fierce, violent, vengeful, and furious battle was fought between them, the likeness of which was not to be found in that time,"* says the *Annals of the Four Masters*. Six shield walls smashed into each other, pushing and heaving as the sun climbed in the sky. Cavalry harried the backs of the lines and rode-down any who separated from the ranks.

In the center, Murchadh, crown prince of Ireland rode a white charger, armed with a sword in each hand. He killed 50 men with his left hand, and 50 men with his right, the *Cogadh Gaedhel re Gallaibh* says, striking with such speed, power, and accuracy that he never had to cut an enemy more than once. No armor or shield could stand against him.

Burnt Njal's Saga records, *"Earl Sigurd had a hard battle against Kerthialfad, and Kerthialfad came on so fast that he laid low all who were in the front rank, and he broke the array of Earl Sigurd right up to his banner, and slew the banner-bearer."*

It is thought by some that this banner may have been the Raven banner of Ragnar Lothbrok, that was believed to bring victory when the raven in its borders moved, but would be the death of whoever tried to force victory by waving the banner. This happened at Clontarf, for the banner changed hands several times, with each man who waved it being cut down until men were afraid to touch it. Finally, Sigurd took it himself and was soon pierced through with a spear.

The elite Danes in their heavy, gleaming armor inflicted great slaughter on Brian's Irish, but as the fury of the battle intensified and as the day wore on, the weight of their armor began to work against them. The tide was coming in, and the center was pushed back, and warriors were knocked over by the roiling waves. Men on both sides drowned, including Brian's own grandson, Toirdhealbhach, who died in the water *"with a Dane above him and a Dane below."*

Toirdhealbhach's father, the crown prince and veteran warrior, Murchadh, also finally met his end fighting a *"stout, furious, bloody, crimson combat"* with a Viking prince named Ebric. Soon Murchadh was dismounted and disarmed, wrestling on the beach. As they grappled, Ebric pulled his *seax* free and eviscerated Murchadh, but the Irish prince pulled the Viking's chain mail up over his head and impaled him with Ebric's own sword. Ebric died in the surf, but the disemboweled Murchadh was pulled from the beach by his men. He died of his grievous wound some hours later.

On the near flank, Ospark of Man and Vikings loyal to Brian fought a desperate battle against the Norse-Irish of Dublin. Ospark himself was wounded, and two of his sons were slain, but they broke the Dubliners and put them to flight.

Sytric Silkbeard fled the field and sped on a waiting horse to his stronghold (which may have been as little as three miles away by land, and just a mile or two across the bay, as the crow flies). Sytric watched the rest of the battle from his ramparts, as his wife, Sláine, ridiculed him. Sytric was neither a fool nor a coward, though. He had tried to beat Brian Boruma and bring back the promise and strength of his father Amlaib Cuaran's Dublin, but he had failed. By retreating back to his stronghold he and his men escaped the worst of the slaughter, and he would be one of the few leaders to survive this dread-filled day.

Sytric Silkbeard's flight had a domino effect throughout the battlefield. The forces of Mael Morda and his Viking allies lost their cohesion utterly and looked for any path out. But the tide had come in and separated the Vikings and other foreigners from their ships. There were forests on one side, and a river to the other. Some of Sigurd's men tried to swim the river, and many drowned there.

But on the far wing, Brodir of Man and his Vikings were still fighting viciously against Wolf the Quarrelsome and the warriors of Munster. The sorcerer-king dealt great slaughter with his double-headed ax. He seemed impervious to harm, and no weapon pierced his armor. Wolf, fighting from horseback, fought his way to Brodir and engaged the Viking hero in combat. According to Norse sources, Wolf knocked

Brodir down three times, and then Brodir fled into the woods with some of his men.

Between Brodir's retreat and the infectious rout that was spreading through the invading armies, the Vikings of the far wing also turned to flee wherever they may. Wolf led the charge after them, and the Irish followed, cutting down the Vikings.

As anyone can see from the family ties of the people in this story, the Vikings were deeply integrated and ingrained in Ireland from more than 200 years of history there. But there was still a great deal of resentment between the two peoples. As the *Cogadh Gaedhel re Gallaibh* says if every tongue spoke with a hundred voices, still they could not describe all the evils the Irish people had suffered at the hands of the foreigners. So, Wolf and his warriors pursued the fleeing Vikings with a vengeance.

But it was at this moment, Norse sources say, that Brodir of Man saw that Wolf's over-eager men had left Brian Boruma exposed. Brodir and his few remaining warriors tore Brian's shield wall asunder. In the fight, Brodir himself cleaved off the head of the *Imperator Scottorum*. Brian's forces had all but won the Battle of Clontarf, but their High King was dead.

The Irish sources are somewhat different. Brian was in his tent with his chaplain, praying for victory in the battle and the future of his country. Brodir, fleeing the field, stumbled across the King's tent and (because a Viking's eyes are always open for an opportunity) went in, accompanied by one of his warriors. Brodir thought Brian was a mere priest because the High King was dressed plainly. But Brodir's sidekick recognized Brian, because he had once served in his army, and he betrayed the identity of his former lord now.

We can imagine the briefest moment where everyone simultaneously realizes what they must do – and then a flurry of action. Brian was not so foolish as to be completely unarmed, and he grabbed his sword. As he drew the blade, he killed Brodir's attendant (who was probably standing closer) and then swung at Brodir – not aiming for the Viking's impenetrable armor, but below it. Brodir also swung his heavy ax at the same time. The sword of the old Irish warrior king chopped right through Brodir's leg and bit into his other calf, but Brodir's ax decapitated Brian. The *Annals of Loch Cé* confirm, Brodir exsanguinated, and both kings died by each other's hand.

The Norse sources of Brodir's end are more colorful. Wolf the Quarrelsome and his men realized – albeit too late – that their king was in danger. They caught Brodir and subdued him, and then Wolf the Quarrelsome tied Brodir of Man to a tree using Brodir's own entrails as rope.

Only nightfall stopped the slaughter.

The End of the Viking Age in Ireland

Of the 13,000 men who took the field in the morning at Clontarf by Dublin Bay, 10,000 were dead before the next morning. This 77 percent casualty rate is many times higher than that of most Medieval battles and demonstrates not only the magnitude of the event (and the strategic errors made there), but the passion felt on both sides. The Viking ethos and Irish spirit collided with nowhere to go but into the sea.

Brodir's runes did not lie. Brian's forces held the field of slaughter, Sytric was walled-up in his fortress, and Mael Morda was dead – but the *Imperator Scottorum* was no more, and his vision of a united Ireland was gone with him. While Norway, Denmark, Sweden, England, France, the Holy Roman Empire, and so many other dominions were uniting into nations, Ireland would not. Arguably, Ireland would not have unified home rule until 1922, when the Republic of Ireland was founded and at peace. Fittingly, the national symbol of that republic is Brian Boru's harp. But in 1014, when the bodies of Brian, Murchardh, Toirdhealbhach, Conaing, and numerous others were brought to the church at Armagh for burial, there was no one to take up the cause of unification.

Brian's remaining sons, including his son (allegedly) by Gormlaith, Dunchadh, immediately began battling for the throne. Losses at Clontarf had been so high the armies of Brian's sons were made up mainly of wounded men. When Meal Seachnaill finally stepped forward and took the role of High King back, many of the wounded warriors in the service of Brian's sons – according to legend – finally released their passion and gave up the ghost where they stood.

Mael Seachnaill held the country together, even making peace with Sytric Silkbeard. In 1022, more than four decades after defeating Amlaib Cuaran at Tara, Mael Seachnaill died. Though others after him may claim the title, High King, it never had the same power that it had from 1002-1022.

While the Viking Age catalyzed other lands into nations, Ireland seemed to just shake it off. After the Vikings, Ireland went on to be what it had always been.

Usually, the story is told that Brian Boru drove the Vikings out of Ireland at the Battle of Clontarf, but this obviously is an extreme oversimplification or misunderstanding of events. Brian Boruma was an avid Viking fighter his whole life but had achieved relative peace and stability by the time he reigned as High King. Only about a third of the forces represented at Clontarf were Vikings, and these fought on both sides of the conflict. Clontarf was the culmination of yet another Irish civil war. But it is true that after Clontarf, Viking power quickly waned in Ireland. There was no other major Norse incursion, and the Norse-Irish were mostly assimilated into the landscape of clans and kingdoms.

Sytric Silkbeard, the great architect and survivor of Clontarf, went on to reign for several decades, living the Viking lifestyle of raiding and shifting alliances. But this was now the Viking lifestyle of the 11th century, not the 9th, and things were far more complicated. Sytric would plunder some churches and build others. He would massacre men and then go on pilgrimages to religious shrines. His time as King of Dublin saw him ally with Mael Seachnaill and later even Donchadh mac Brian while renewing old feuds with his own Ui Imar cousins. While his forebearers, Sytric One-Eyed and Amlaib Cuaran, had a vision and a plan, Sytric Silkbeard's life – and the lives of so many Vikings of that time – was only about survival.

In 1035, Sytric Silkbeard finally cornered, captured, and executed Ragnall Ui Imar, King of Waterford. The next year, Ragnall's son Echmarcach, King of the Isles, would force Sytric to abdicate his throne and to flee into exile. He died in 1042. Dublin would continue to be Irelands biggest and wealthiest city. It would continue to be ruled on-and-off by Ui Imar kings until the Anglo-Norman invasion of Henry II in 1171 made Dublin the English capital of Ireland.

Historians favor the Battle of Clontarf as the close of the Viking Age in Ireland because it culminates in a conflagration, while the further adventures of Sytric and his kind sputter and flare out.

Chapter XIX: Harald Hardrada, the Last Viking

Harald Sigurdson was only 15 years-old when he served in the army of his half-brother, King Olaf II of Norway. Olaf the Stout (or Olaf the Big) as he was called in life would later be remembered as Saint Olaf because like Leif Erikson's mentor, Olaf Tryggvason, he was intent on converting Norway to Christianity. Saints usually die abruptly, though, and King Olaf the Stout would follow his predecessor to the grave on a fateful September day in 1030.

Young Harald was there at the battle at Stiklarstaðir, where Olaf's army was taken unawares and outnumbered 2:1 by forces loyal to Cnut the Great. Harald fell wounded by his half-brother's side, along with two-thirds of the revered king's army. Had Harald not been pulled to safety and hidden in a farmhouse a few miles away, he would probably have died, too.

Cnut the Great (who was not there, as far as we know, but ruling in his other kingdoms of England or Denmark) now firmly added Norway to his North Sea Empire. The legacy of Harald Fairhair (whose ambition to unite Norway was best-realized under his great-great-grandson, Olaf the Stout) was suspended, and Norway would lie under Danish dominion. For the next few decades the rule of the two lands would be intertwined.

Injured and hunted, young Harald Sigurdson fought death on two fronts while hidden in a farmhouse. In the early spring, he had recovered enough to try to escape Norway with the help of a few followers. Going west was too obvious – he and his Vikings would undoubtedly be caught. But his late half-brother had once found safe harbor in the land of the Rus, and so it was there that Harald's men ventured.

Harald Saga Sigurdsonan (found in volume 3 of the *Heimskringla*) tells us that the fugitive prince traveled by back roads to the Norwegian coast, where by good fortune he encountered men loyal to King Olaf's memory. Some joined him and equipped him with a ship, and so Harald crossed the sea to the Baltic and then traveled upriver until eventually reaching Novgorod and then Kiev.

Harald and his fugitive Vikings were welcomed at the court of Yaroslav the Wise, great-grandson of Saint Olga. Yaroslav was the son of Vladamir the Great, who had married into the imperial family of Byzantium and sent Basil the Bulgar-slayer his 6000 Varangians. Yaroslav took a liking to Harald, who was now 16 or 17 and had proven his mettle in battle, through surviving his wounds, and through traveling the perilous journey into the heart of Medieval Eastern Europe. Yaroslav invited Harald to fight for him, and within a few years, the Viking exile was leading Varangian and Rus armies against Yaroslav's enemies.

But Harald's ambition was a hungry wolf, and could not be slated in the relatively-secure (at that time) kingdom of Rus. Yaroslav encouraged him to take his men to seek service in Constantinople. Harald (now aged 20 or so) took the opportunity and rowed down the rivers of eastern Europe to the Black Sea, crossing into the lands of the famed Roman East.

As they drew closer to the Golden Horn where the great city lies the evident civilization and prosperity astounded the Vikings. Reaching the suburbs of "Miklagard," the well-cut stone buildings were so close together that they seemed like walls, and the streets of Constantinople itself were hung with silks.

Harald ordered his men to close their gaping mouths and to act as if none of this impressed them at all, and with that, they sought service with the Byzantine Empire as Varangian Guardsmen.

For the Byzantines, they had come at a good time. The Fatimid Caliphate controlled much of North Africa and the eastern Mediterranean. Saracen forces had dominion of Sicily and were threatening Byzantine holdings in southern Italy. The Italians themselves were usually in revolt, and now there was a new disturbance in these western holdings – some upstarts called Normans. The Holy Roman Empire in the Germanic north was always a threat, and the Turkic Pechenegs and Seljuks to the north and east were perpetual trouble. The Bulgars missed their former power, and so the Balkans, to the west of the Black Sea, were unstable. The Rus were friendly, but that could easily change.

There was no end of enemies, and so no end of opportunities. A Viking like Harald could only be limited by his own ambition, his courage, and his luck. Harald had more of all three of these than almost anyone else of his time.

Harald climbed the ranks of the Varangian Guard meteorically and was soon in command of most of the Varangians on campaign. This may have been due to his status as an exiled prince of Norway and half-brother of the already sainted (though not-yet officially canonized) Olaf.

Harald himself was no saint, but a shrewd, cunning, hard-fighting battle commander who always led his men from the front. Whether because of the magic imbued in his own raven banner, that he called "Land Waster" or because of his luck and personal prowess, he always seemed to win.

Doubtlessly, his ascendency and warrior's popularity were also due to his ample charisma and bearing. The *Heimskringla* describes Harald as tall, broad, fair-haired with a thick beard and impressive mustache, huge hands and big feet, and a booming voice. While he was anything but humble, Harald's choice of things to boast of was perhaps unusual in one so successful. He said he had eight accomplishments: that he could shoe a horse, ride, ski, swim, shoot a bow well, throw a javelin, play the harp (or perhaps the more-Norse lyre) and compose poetry. His poetry was not always on point, and there are a few passages in the Heimskringla where Harald struggles to find the right verse. His most-prized possession of all the treasure he ever amassed was Land

Waster, and Harald modestly attributed his many victories to it and not to his own merits.

Harald earned his nickname, Hardrada, which is usually translated "hard ruler" but also means "hard bargainer" or maybe "ruthless contender." Like every Viking's role model would be, Harald was full of violence and rapine, was gold-grabbing, duplicitous, conniving, hot-headed, and not above cruelty or murder; but he was also generous with his friendship, wealth, and (at times) his mercy. In his saga, we see an embryonic stage of the Medieval concept of chivalry – with all its imperfections and double standards – gradually forming. While skaldic verse relishes in his destroying whole towns, gloats over women dragged off into slavery, and commemorates his killing of priests (Christian though he reportedly was) his saga also repeatedly depicts episodes of honor and restraint, and says he offered quarter *to anyone who would ask for it.*

Campaigning with the Byzantine Army, though, Harald Hardrada served under a supreme commander who was anything but chivalrous. The Byzantine general George Maniakes, accompanied by a 23-year-old Harald Hardrada, set out on a campaign to take advantage of Saracen disunity in Sicily and North Africa and to re-establish wavering control in Italy. The Byzantine historian Michael Psellus, an eyewitness to many of these events, describes George Maniakes as ten feet tall, with a countenance like a tempest and hands made for smashing apart doors of bronze. Psellus closes his long, hyperbolic description with the statement, "*Those who saw him for the first time realized that every description they had ever heard of him was an understatement.*"

Though Maniakes had started out as a heroic general (years before in Syria) this Mediterranean campaign was to see him become an increasingly-psychotic war criminal. The campaign was highly successful at first, but when Maniakes was recalled after beating up the Emperor's brother-in-law (his co-commander), the change in leadership led to defeats and severe loss of momentum. The emperorship changed hands later, and in 1042, Maniakes was returned, at which point he unleashed a war of genocide, sadistic butchery, and terrorism on the peoples of Italy and Sicily.

Once again, the emperorship changed hands, and Maniakes was recalled. This time the messenger was Maniakes's mortal enemy – an aristocratic neighbor who had allegedly stolen his villa and slept with his wife. Maniakes stuffed this rival's mouth, ears, and eyes with horse dung and tortured him to death. His devoted soldiers now declaring him emperor, the dreaded commander rushed towards Constantinople, but even as he smashed through an intercepting army in Greece, George Maniakes (perhaps being too big to miss) was caught through the throat with a lance. What would have certainly been a history-altering change in the world order was avoided.

This all happened over four or five years. George Maniakes was a legendary general to his followers and a monster to his enemies, but despite any number of battles he won his overall influence in the region was negative for Byzantium. His boundless cruelty polarized support away from the Byzantines, while his successive disengagements created space for his enemies. Within a few years, southern Italy and Sicily would be the domain of Normans and be lost to Byzantium forever.

Some sources say Harald was already heading back to Kiev by the time Maniakes returned for his atrocious final chapter in 1042. According to the *Heimskringla*, George Maniakes (whom the skalds call Gyrgir) and Harald hated each other, and almost came to armed fighting on at least one occasion. The cause of this quarrel was primarily that Maniakes thought he could order the Varangians in both large and small matters, while Harald understood the Varangian Guard's allegiance as belonging to the Emperor and Empress alone. The saga goes on to say that the Varangians under Harald preferred to both camp and fight on their own. The *Heimskringla* describes (and Byzantine historians do not oppose) that Harald basically ran a parallel campaign in Sicily, North Africa, and some of the Holy Land, being tasked with taking cities in both Muslim and rebellious Christian territories in the name of the Empire.

And take cities Harald did. The Mediterranean was the cradle of human civilization, and thus the people there had centuries of experience in war and fortification. An average Mediterranean city of that time was generally designed to survive sieges lasting months or even years. In his relatively short time in the Mediterranean, though, Harald Hardrada had 80 cities surrender to him.

By definition, a siege makes an attack into a matter of attrition – the defenders behind their fortifications try to make their resources and resolve last until the invaders run out of supplies, fall into disorder, succumb to disease, or are themselves attacked by a relief force. Harald triumphed over so many cities by simply refusing to participate in this construct. For Harald Hardrada, the siege was almost always just a cover for what he really had in mind.

For example, he would make a show of assaulting walls by day only to distract the defenders from his commando forces tunneling in at night. He was not using sappers to do the engineering-intensive work of undermining walls that larger armies might take a great deal of time doing – Harald only needed a few good men on to get inside to open the gates.

On one occasion, Harald found a Sicilian town to be especially well-fortified with trenches as well as walls. Instead of risking even a preliminary attack, he set up his army just out of bowshot and made a grand show of morale and confidence. The defenders reciprocated with cheers, jeers, and taunts. Every day for the next few weeks, Harald's men left behind their armor, shields, and the big Dane axes they were known for and gathered around the walls, just out of range. There they played games, ran races, and sang songs. Every day, the defenders taunted them, until gradually the people of the city lost interest. When Harald noticed that there were few people on the walls, he gave the order to attack immediately. His men were unarmored and only armed with weapons they could conceal (swords, hand axes, and seax knives), but Harald unfurled Land Waster and rushed the gates. The Sicilian defenders were complacent but not idiots; they reached their stations quickly and started dealing out death to the charging Vikings. But the momentary gap in their attention had been all Harald needed. By nightfall, he had taken the city and everything in it.

Harald Hardrada was happy to use other people's ideas as well as his own. When waiting outside of one well-fortified Arab town, he noticed the birds flying from the rooftops to forage in the surrounding fields. Perhaps he remembered his time with Yaroslav of the Rus, and stories told over mead horns about Yaroslav's great-grandmother, Saint Olga. Harald had his men catch birds and tie flammable material to their legs. All at once the tinder was set alight, and the birds were released. As with Saint Olga's destruction of the Drevlians a hundred years before, Harald's birds went straight back to their nests and burned the whole town down. The citizens grabbed their valuables and ran for safety – but found Harald's Varangians waiting for them. Once more, he gave quarter to those who surrendered.

That was not the only time Harald used his people's history to achieve his objective. Upon catching ill while besieging an ancient and well-built city, Harald remembered Bjorn Ironside and Hastein's stratagem at Luna, long ago. Harald faked his own death and then had his men appeal for a place to bury their leader. Though the city was in rebellion to Byzantium, it had a sizeable Christian population. The churches in the city began to compete with each other for Harald's body, knowing that they would receive a substantial donative for interring a royal corpse. But just as Bjorn had done, Harald leaped from the coffin the moment he was brought into the city and joined his attendants in slaughter as others ran to open the gates. The city fell just as Luna had.

With an unmatched success rate not only at taking cities and territories but in taking them quickly, Harald was becoming very, very rich. He could not carry that much treasure, though, nor expect it to stay safe as he moved ahead, so he periodically sent it north through trustworthy followers to Yaroslav's court where the Rus ruler agreed to keep it safe for him.

After a while though, Harald Hardrada began to think of going home. Perhaps it was the zero-sum gain of Maniakes's campaign that made him believe he had stayed south long enough. Maybe it was the increasingly chaotic nature of the Byzantine court itself – for the throne had its third emperor in just the few years Harald had been there. Perhaps it was just that Harald thought that his effort could be better spent winning back his own country and restoring his half-brother's strong, unified, and independent Norway. But for whatever reasons, Harald Hardrada decided to close the book on his successful career with the Varangian Guard and leave Byzantium.

His announcement of resignation to the Byzantine court did not go over well.

Escape from Constantinople

At the time, the Byzantine Empire was ruled by a string of weak, flawed, afflicted, wicked, or otherwise unsuccessful emperors who were all connected in some way to the real Empress. This Empress, Zoe, was the niece of Basil the Bulgar-Slayer. Zoe had little of her uncle's ability, but a great deal of his iron temper, at least according to the *Heimskringla*. Though she was married to the Emperor, she was enamored by Harald and lusted after the rugged, young Norse hero. So, when Harald announced that he was leaving, and added a request that he be allowed to marry Zoe's beautiful young niece, Maria, based on the merits of his royal pedigree, loyal service, and considerable wealth, it all hit a nerve with the tempestuous Empress.

So, instead of her gratitude and blessing, Zoe accused Harald of embezzling Byzantine funds (all that treasure sent to the Rus should have been Byzantine property, she said – which is one of the most insulting things that one can tell a Medieval warrior, that their plunder was unearned). At the behest of the scorned Zoe, the Emperor had Harald removed from command and thrown into a tower that only could be accessed from an opening high in the air. The Varangians were then dispersed so they could not help their leader.

Things looked bleak. But that first night Harald had a dream where his sainted half-brother, Olaf came to him. Olaf's shade told Harald not to worry because he would see that he got out. Harald awoke as a sturdy rope landed next to him. He looked up to see a woman and her two servants backlit by the moon. As Harald Hardrada climbed the great height, the woman whispered down to him that she had received a healing miracle from the spirit of Saint Olaf years before, and so she knew that it was her duty to save his brother. Harald thanked her for her bravery and then raced down the steps on the outside of the tower to find his men. They had to leave Constantinople that night, or they could expect no mercy from the treacherous Byzantines.

Harald Hardrada's Vikings were nearby, knowing that a Byzantine dungeon could not keep in what all the wiles of the east could not keep out. They gathered to his call. But the Varangians were not the only ones who expected Harald to escape. The Emperor himself caught them in the streets, accompanied by his new bodyguards. A fierce battle broke out, but Harald's axe-wielding Varangians cut their way through the imperial forces. They caught the faithless Emperor, and right then and there Harald put out his eyes.

This last detail may seem like some over-the-top cruelty, and it is, but at the time blinding was a standard way of removing someone from power – particularly in the Byzantine world. An earlier Eastern Roman tradition was just to cut the deposed leader's nose off because no one could follow someone who was disfigured, but when a nose-less Justinian II somehow came back from this end and immediately destroyed all of his enemies, the stakes were upped to blinding. Sometimes the nose was still cut off for good measure. By Harald's time, it is likely that no one entered Byzantine politics without realizing there was a fair possibility of being blinded, stabbed, or poisoned.

Victorious once more, Harald and his Varangians sped through Constantinople towards the harbor. But they were not ready to go yet. Harald broke into the palace and kidnapped Maria, making his intended bride his hostage. Only then did he and his men fight their way to their dragon ships and leave the great city behind.

There was only one more problem – the waters of the Bosphorus just past the walls of Constantinople were blocked by a massive iron chain that could only be lowered by coordinated efforts of Byzantine gatehouses. This feature kept Constantinople safe from attack and in control of commerce between east and west.

But Harald had a plan. As the dragon ships approached the stout chain, he had his rowers double their efforts. At the moment the racing vessels were about to hit the chain he shouted to everyone to run to the back of the ship. With the shifting weight, the ships tilted back, their dragon heads rising out of the water. The chain scraped the keels. Then, just as the chain was reaching near the center mass of the dragon ships and was about to cast them over, Harald shouted in his booming voice for the men to run up the deck to the front of the ship. The Vikings (carrying their war gear and treasures) did, and their weight tipped the prows down, and the ships shifted forward on the fulcrum of the chain. They cleared the barrier between the Golden Horn and the sea – all except one vessel that burst asunder from the force. The others circled back to pull their brothers from the water, but many of the Vikings from that one ship drowned.

Harald and the rest of his men were free. Their pursuers fell back, afraid to follow. Constantinople disappeared like a great pearl behind them. But Harald had one last thing to do. He ordered his dragon ship to pull up on the shore. He left Maria there, unmolested, with her captured ladies in waiting and a suitable escort of his most trusted men to take her back to the city and deliver a message to Zoe. Harald's letter to the Empress said something to the effect of, "See, I could have taken her if I had wanted to, and you could not have stopped me."

This was not a very gentlemanly thing to say, perhaps, but the complete release of Maria by one such as Harald probably did not happen lightly. Many years later, Harald would name his first daughter Maria.

From there, Harald and his followers escaped north back to the lands of the Kievan Rus.

A Little Historical Cross-examination

That at least is the story as it is told in the *Heimskringla*. Snorri Sturluson, the "Homer of the North" who committed to parchment this and many other sagas, myths, and poems in the 13th century actually takes the time to assure his reader that he has verified everything and that there were a great many other stories about Harald that he could have told if he had allowed a lower standard of authenticity. Nonetheless, there are a few problems with the tale when we compare it to Byzantine sources, and also a few things we should take a closer look at.

Empress Zoe appears in the *Heimskringla* in the role of a scarlet woman seeking vengeance. She was no stranger to this role in her own lifetime, but some of this is unfair. Zoe was the daughter of Emperor Constantine VIII, and though she was betrothed at an appropriate, marriageable age, the marriage fell through. Her father seemed to forget all about her marriage after that until he was on his deathbed and realized he had only her and her sister as heirs. Constantine hastily arranged a marriage for Zoe – who was then in her late 40s – to an older nobleman.

Zoe and her husband, Romanus III, then tried to have children for a time, but of course were not successful and grew apart. Soon both were reported to be unfaithful. Romanus became dissipated in general, and given his age and lifestyle, it might not have been strange that he was found dead in his bath one day. But when that very same day Zoe married Michael, a man half her age who was already said to be her lover, it was widely assumed that Zoe had either poisoned her hated husband or had assassins drown him in his bath.

Of course, her hasty marriage could have also been for the sake of preserving her power in that precarious political environment, and there is no proof she was an assassin – and yet, the veracity of the accusation has largely been taken for granted even to this day.

Her second husband, Michael IV, was a decent emperor, who – perhaps in large part to Harald Hardrada's help – secured a peace treaty with the Fatimid Caliphate. But Michael was epileptic and had other serious health problems (perhaps including heart and/or kidney failure, judging by the available descriptions) and so he, too died.

Michael IV was replaced as Emperor by his nephew (also named Michael) whom at his behest Zoe – now 64 years old – had adopted as a son. This new Michael dismissed the Varangian Guard and replaced them with "Scythians" (a deliberately archaic term Greco-Romans used for steppe peoples) and eunuchs. Michael V also released George

Maniakes from prison and sent him on his notorious campaign into southern Italy, as previously described.

Michael V did not want even the modest restraint on his power that his aging Empress imposed, and so he quickly had Zoe and her allies removed from power and put on house arrest.

But Michael misgauged the feelings of the Byzantine people, both to himself and to Zoe. Thousands of armed citizens rioted, overwhelming Michael's regime, dragging him out from sanctuary, and blinding him in the streets. It is possible that the recently unemployed Varangians, including Harald, could have been amongst them. Psellus mentions men with axes, specifically, though whether these were the signature Dane axes of the Varangians or just peasants with the farming implement he does not say. Harald could have taken part in the blinding of Michael V without breaking any oaths because the uprising was loyal to the real Empress and Michael had refused vows from the Varangians.

The *Heimskringla* specifies that Harald blinded Constantine IX Monomachos. Monomachos was Zoe's third husband (whom she married in her late 60s, but which somehow added to her profligate reputation). It would be understandable for Snorri to make this mistake because Monomachus stood out in the 13th-century imagination as the emperor associated with the Great Schism between the Catholic and Orthodox churches. But the blinding as the *Heimskringla* describes it would have broken oaths, which for Vikings was very serious. No

Varangian betrayed a sitting Emperor in the entire history of the Guard. Also, Harald was almost certainly back in Norway by the time Monomachos took the throne. In any case, Constantine IX Monomachos died of illness, in office, with his sight intact January 11, 1055 – when Harald was far away.

Thus, Harald Hardrada participating in the uprising against Michael V is plausible (though if the 64-year-old Zoe were indeed his enemy for spurned sexual advances, he probably left a few months before then). But Harald and his closest followers were likely heading home by 1042 and not involved in either side of his enemy George Maniakes's infamous actions that year or the reign of Constantine IX Monomachos afterward.

Harald Hardrada, King of Norway

Harald and his men returned to the court of Yaroslav of the Kievan Rus. He stayed there long enough to catch his breath, reclaim the treasure Yaroslav had been holding for him, and to further cement their friendship by marrying Yaroslav's daughter, Elizabeth (Ellisif in Old Norse).

The next season, Harald headed back to Norway. It was a bold move. Olaf's son, Magnus, had risen to the throne, and around the time Harald was with the Rus, Magnus gained dominion over much of Denmark, too. Swein Ulfson (also called Swein Estridson to emphasize his mother's strong ties to the late Cnut the Great) still held some control, particularly in Ragnar's old home of Zealand, Denmark.

When Harald finally arrived in Scandinavia, he first came to Denmark where he and Swein Ulfsson became fast friends (Harald always seemed to have a knack for this), and they agreed to join forces.

Norway did not seem likely to accommodate another king, but Harald Hardrada was done with being anything else. Harald had spent time with his nephew Magnus, who had also been an exile in Yaroslav's court back in 1031. Now he planned to set himself up in opposition to him.

Traveling the river routes of Europe, Viking traders had been bringing back tales of Harald's amazing exploits for years. So, when King Magnus the Good (who had so earned his moniker by showing mercy to his father's enemies) heard his uncle was coming back with a few hundred extremely battle-hardened Varangians, he knew that it would be prudent to welcome them rather than resist them. Magnus divided his domain in two, and then let his uncle Harald "pick a hand" to see which one he got. The exiled prince, Harald Hardrada, finally become a King of Norway around 1046.

The arrangement worked well enough, and the two had joint rule until Magnus the Good died about five years later. Magnus had been planning to invade England and re-establish the North Sea Empire of Cnut the Great, despite England's reversion to a Saxon king after the death of Cnut's Danish heir. But while preparing his forces, Magnus had an accident or illness (sources differ) and later died. Allegedly, on his deathbed, he bequeathed Norway to Harald and Denmark to Swein.

This last will and testament of Magnus the Good was meant to bring peace to Scandinavia, for the Danes under Swein had already been trying to cast off Norwegian rule, and Magnus had been using Harald to maintain control there.

Harald and Swein took their crowns and agreed to live in peace. This blessed respite from war and envy lasted for the length of one winter. In the summer, Harald Hardrada, now sole King of Norway, decided that he should be King of Denmark, too.

King Harald Hardrada forgot his friendship with Swein and unleashed a brutal war on Denmark. Perhaps Harald was addicted to battle. In his early life, he had been content to serve others, but now even the whole of Norway could not satisfy him. He was enough of a Christian to have once made a pilgrimage to Jerusalem and made large gifts of money there. He had even been baptized in the Jordan River. But now, in his late 30s he took a second wife as if he were a rule unto himself. His new bride, Thora, was apparently held in equal status to the living Elizabeth, and he acknowledged children from both.

This autocracy did not just apply to his personal choices. Harald became increasingly tyrannical, even sacking his own towns when he felt they had been light on their taxes. As the *Heimskringla* records,

King Haraldr was an imperious person. And this became more marked as he strengthened his hold on the land, and it reached the point that it was no good for most people to cross him in speech or to bring forward any matter other than what he wished to have done.

But Harald Hardrada could not best Swein Ulfsson – not in his own country and with his brave Danes fiercely resisting Norwegian rule. The Norwegian Vikings raided and invaded Denmark summer after summer and fought epic battles on land and sea. But autumn after autumn they returned with plunder and slaves but no real victory.

Appropriately, this war between two great Viking peoples culminated in a massive naval engagement, the Battle of Niz (or Nisa) in 1062. There, hundreds of ships were lashed together on the roiling seas to create islands of dragons on which the Vikings killed each other. Harald won, but Swein escaped.

Though both the winning and losing sides took great glory in the epic Battle of Niz, afterward the war lost its luster for the Norwegians, and even Harald seemed a bit depressed. Both kings began to listen to pressure from their exhausted people and finally agreed to meet for talks. A treaty of unconditional peace without recompense or reprisals was achieved in 1064. Fifteen years and two months after Magnus the Good had decreed that Harald should rule Norway and Swein should rule Denmark, all of Scandinavia agreed it could be no other way.

Harald was 49 years old when he settled into this awkward peace. Though even he had grown discouraged towards the end of the great war with Denmark, he immediately showed signs of restlessness and turned his violent impulses towards perceived rebels in his own kingdom. There was little enough of this to be had – only a fool would cross the Hard Ruler. Aging though he was, Harald had never known more than a few month's peace. He had no idea what to do with it.

But where could a Viking go? Raiding the coasts for trinkets as his ancestors had done was beneath him – he needed more. But by the 11th century, Ireland, France, the Holy Roman Empire, Spain, or Italy all had built up an immunity to Vikings. We can imagine Harald like a caged tiger, pacing his mead hall at night, bored, frustrated, and wondering what to do next.

Then, in June 1066, opportunity walked through his doors.

Tostig was the eldest son of the King of England's highest councilor, Godwin. But now, childless King Edward the Confessor was dead, and the Anglo-Saxon and Danish lords of England had made Tostig's talented brother, Harold Godwinson, king.

Tostig was convinced that the throne should be his – so convinced that he turned down generous offers of titles and lands from Swein and numerous other rulers who had empathized with him but declined his invitation to join his desperate plan to claim the English throne. Harald was at first not inclined to listen to the delusional Tostig either, but Tostig knew just what to say. Why should the greatest warrior alive sit idly when England could be his? With Tostig's connections and support, the North Sea Empire could again rise, with Harald Hardrada at its helm. All Harald needed to do was invade England.

Harald Hardrada did not need much more convincing.

Harald Hardrada's Invasion of England, and the End of the Viking Age

In August 1066, about 200 dragon ships (carrying an estimated 12,000 to 20,000 men) left the bays of Norway bound for England.

Many historians have wondered at – even doubted – that Harald Hardrada could assemble such a massive invasion force so quickly. But this is looking at the problem out of context. The Vikings of Norway had been invading Denmark every year for 15 years. The end of that war had left many of them exhausted – but two years was plenty of time for a Viking to get his wind back. Unlike the rest of Europe, Harald did not need to spend time raising support, and unlike his counterpart – William the Bastard, Duke of Normandy – he did not need to worry about the Pope's blessing or legitimacy. England had been part of a Scandinavian North Sea Empire up until recently, and between Tostig and Harald's pedigrees, they could undoubtedly garner more legitimacy than Harold Godwinson (whose claim to the throne was already the talk of Europe, in a negative way). All Harald had to do to raise a fleet of thousands of

Vikings was to put out the call. Who wanted to invade England? Everybody. They were Vikings.

The strategy was also simple: land in the north and secure Jorvik (York). From there gather strength while repelling counter-attack from a secure position and then penetrate south. The Great Heathen Army had done almost the same 201 years before, and every other Viking invasion had also prioritized Jorvik. This time, though, there was no Alfred the Great or Aethelstan to resist them. There was only a neophyte king with dubious support.

The army would only need a few weeks-worth of supplies because they were planning on taking everything else they required from the people of England when they got there. In the pre-industrial world, August was always the most precarious month because it was just before the harvest, but the stores from last year were nearing depletion. Thus, the arrival of several thousand Vikings "living off the land" would be especially dangerous to the English, and thus another part of Harald's strategy.

So, it was enthusiasm, experience, and practice that sped the Vikings in their preparations. Harald Hardrada, who never lost and was considered the wisest of kings, would lead the way under his magic banner, Land Waster. He would be accompanied by the survivors of his old, core group of Varangians, who had conquered more cities than they could remember. But these leaders would be backed up by an entire generation of Vikings who had grown up fighting other Vikings in Denmark. It was hard to see how they could possibly lose.

The vast fleet of dragon ships rolled over the waves of the North Atlantic, the white spray bursting over their prows. Harald Hardrada led the way aboard his double-sized royal longship. He was his old self again, his laugh booming as he extemporized poetry. The English traitor, Tostig, was beside him, barely able to control his anxiety at the whole situation and perhaps beginning to realize who was working for who. But the Saxon's thinly-disguised guile and gravity could do nothing to hamper Harald's mood. He had not gained Denmark after 15 years of fighting, but if he secured England for himself, anything would be possible. There had been a bright, bright light in the night sky in May of that year (Haley's Comet). Everyone in the world knew that it was a fell omen, but no one knew what it meant. Now, perhaps, Harald felt that it was a promise of victories to come. But Harald Hardrada needed no lights in the sky – his self-confidence and love of war were boundless, and these gifts were energized now as they had not been in a long time.

Not everyone shared his confidence though, for the *Heimskringla* tells us that many men in the fleet had bad dreams of wolves glutting on blood and troll-wives (inhuman witches) speaking dark riddles. Others saw evil omens as they sailed towards England.

When Harald Hardrada reached the coast and then traveled up the Humber and Ous Rivers, these dreams must have seemed baseless. The

Vikings grabbed some easy plunder from the coastal communities and burned the town of Scarborough for the fun of it.

The defending earls of northern England gathered their forces and attacked Harald near York. The Vikings swiftly moved into battle formation and eagerly advanced behind Land Waster. As the raven banner fluttered in the late summer wind, the Vikings routed the English and killed so many of them that they could cross the streams and waterways without getting their feet wet.

A few more battles followed, each violent, brief, and disastrous for the native forces. York surrendered. Harald Hardrada was unstoppable.

England was falling, and it was falling easily. Soon, English nobles were rushing to submit to Harald and Tostig. A meeting place was arranged to receive the surrender of most of the regional lords (along with 500 high-ranking hostages for reassurance) – Stamford Bridge, just outside of York, for Monday, September the 25th, 1066.

The Battle of Stamford Bridge

Harald Hardrada and Tostig set out for Stamford Bridge Monday morning. Two-thirds of the Viking Army accompanied them, but the remainder was left to guard the ships. Summer had just ended, but the day was hot, and the men were confident from their victories. All bad dreams had faded, and evil omens were forgotten, chocked-up to pre-battle jitters. So, Harald and most of his men brought their weapons with them, of course, but they left their heavy mail and padded jackets behind. They walked or rode the three hours or so from their ships to the bridge, talking animatedly, telling stories, composing poems of the last few days' glories, and probably enjoying a few drinks. They arrived at the bridge before the Saxons, and most of the Vikings plopped down on the flower-dotted meadow to wait in repose.

When they saw the cloud of dust in the distance, they assumed it was the expected lords and their 500 hostages bringing a large entourage of supplicants. They still were not afraid. It was only when the host came into view that they realized it was not the Saxons coming to surrender.

Can a man be called great when he only ruled for less than one year? It depends on the challenges he met. Harold Godwinson was a politician's son of noble but not royal blood. His father, Godwin, was intelligent and crafty enough to control a weak-willed and phlegmatic King Edward the Confessor. Harold's brother was the contemptible Tostig. But Harold was different. He was usually mellow and conciliatory, the man that his father had used to arbitrate disputes and garner peace deals. His temperament was probably why the earls and jarls of England's *witan* (Saxon democratic meeting of lords) had chosen him to be king. He had military experience and had fought alongside Duke William of Normandy against the Celtic Bretons in France, but was not hitherto known as an exceptional warrior. But Harold had a will of iron and a love of England that would drive him to one of the greatest feats in military history.

King Harold Godwinson had assembled and outfitted an army in anticipation of his former friend, William the Bastard of Normandy, invading England. William had made no secret of his intentions to take the country but had run into nothing but trouble in his own preparations to garner support, build a fleet, and time a channel crossing in the midst of bad weather. Now the campaigning season was almost over, and it looked like William was not going to show. Harold had been waiting in the south, where the Normans were likely to land, mindful that he would not be able to hold the *fyrd* (non-professional citizen components that made up most of the armies of the day) much longer.

Then, on Wednesday, September 20th, Harold received an urgent dispatch from the North. His brother Tostig had betrayed him, and Harald Hardrada had landed with a massive Viking fleet and burned the town of Scarborough.

Harold Godwinson immediately ordered his army north. It was about 190 miles to York (and another 10 to Stamford Bridge, though Harold figured that out later). The best Roman armies expected to go 20 miles a day, but the English army under Harold Godwinson made the 200-mile trip to meet the Vikings in just four days.

Archeologists have found hundreds of 11th-century horseshoes along the path they took, as both horses and men pushed themselves to the breaking point to defend their homeland. As the army sped towards the already-fallen city, their forces grew. Englishmen – the descendants of Britons, Angles, Saxons, and Danes – rallied to their King's banner. The Vikings would not take England unopposed. No one would.

Harold and his weary but inspired army reached York Sunday night and were greeted as saviors. Morale in the city was immediately restored, and the nobles who were to surrender and sign their children over to the Vikings instead found the will to fight again. Harold ordered guards posted all around York, to kill any spies who might tip off the enemy of his presence. He knew the reputation of Harald Hardrada not only as a fierce warrior but as an excellent tactician. The battle that would take place on the morrow must be a complete surprise.

***

The moment Harald Hardrada realized that the host approaching was no less than the strength of England, he ordered three riders to race to the ships and summon the rest of his force. Tostig advised him to retreat, but Harald laughed and said he would rather fight. The unarmored Vikings made a circular shield wall (to defend against cavalry, though the Saxons only had a small number of them) on the near side of the bridge and arrayed additional warriors to secure the bridge itself. Harald and his personal guard were in the middle so that they could reinforce the lines wherever the fiercest fighting might be. In the commotion, though, Harald himself fell off his horse.

"Who is the big man in the blue silk and fancy helmet?" Harold Godwinson asked his attendant, according to the *Heimskringla.* "For I sense I see a man who is at the end of his luck."

Harold Godwinson and some of his personal *housecarls* (professional warriors serving as the personal retinue of the King, who – like the Varangian Guard – were famous for fighting with two-handed Dane axes) road out to parley with the Vikings. Tostig and his entourage came out to meet him.

Perhaps at this moment, seeing all England behind his brother and arrayed against him, Tostig both found his courage and embraced his doom.

"The King," Harold himself began, speaking in the third person to hide his identity from the Vikings who might take advantage of his exposure, "would offer you, his brother, all of Northumbria if you will agree to peace."

It was a reversal of Harold's previous policy towards Tostig, but the King was now ready to give up for the sake of peace what the northern earls had been about to give up out of fear.

"If I had such an offer last year," Tostig replied, "a great many men that are now dead would be alive, and England would be a better place. And what would the King give my friend?"

"The King will give your friend six feet of English earth … or perhaps seven, as he is such a tall man," Harold answered.

"Tell the King to prepare for battle, then," said Tostig. "For I will not have it said among the Norsemen that Earl Tostig abandoned them when it came to a fight. We will stick together and die with honor or win England by victory."

With that, he returned to Harald's side.

"Who was that man?" Hardrada said. "He spoke well."

"That was King Harold."

"You should have told me! For he never would have escaped. Quite a small man, but he stood well in his stirrups."

But Harald Hardrada was only speaking his mind to Tostig and his rebuke lacked force. He was looking at his own life and death as dispassionately as any Viking ever did. Life and death were all a great game. It was all in the hands of fate. Harald then toyed with a few lines of verse, and not finding any he liked, he ordered the battle begun.

The Saxons that arrived on horseback set their steeds to the back and arrayed themselves in a shield wall. They attacked the Vikings, taking losses from archers as they went. When the Vikings felt the weakness of these timid attacks, though, they broke forth and charged the Saxons furiously. But this was Harold Godwinson's trap, and with a trumpet blast, his men pounced on the now-disorderly Vikings. There was a great slaughter, and again the stream became choked with bodies as warriors from both sides met their deaths. Harold Godwinson and his *housecarls* were in the thick of battle, swinging their Dane axes in limb-shearing force, or bashing and grappling with the long-hafted weapons when the fighting drew close.

But as the combat intensified, Harald Hardrada became taken as if by the berserker's rage of old. He burst forth, swinging his axe in one hand and his sword in the other, and "*not a helmet or mail coat could stand against him.*" Land Waster flapped in the hot breath of midday as Saxon and Viking bodies began to pile up on each other. Soon it was hard to find footing.

We do not know how many men Harold Godwinson had, but the *Heimskringla* calls it an "invincible army" for its size. Now, after what was probably two hours of battle, these superior numbers began to push the Vikings back to the bridge. At that moment a lone Viking stood in the center of the bridge, unarmored and possessed by the berserker spirit. He slew over 40 English warriors with his axe while his comrades retreated to the far bank of the stream. No man could move him. It was only when an English warrior – perhaps a member of the local *fyrd* –

slipped under the bridge in a watering trough (or small boat) and speared the berserker up through the floorboards that Godwinson's men were able to surge across.

But by then the Vikings had regrouped on the other side and had reformed their shield wall. The English had to come through the bottleneck of the bridge. The battle was already one of the bloodiest in English history. It was about to get worse. Even at that critical moment, as Harald Hardrada was slaying men with both hands, the Viking King of Norway was pierced through the neck with an arrow. He fought on for a few moments until the blood in his lungs exceeded the air and the mighty Harald Hard-Ruler fell dead in the reddened mud of England.

At that same moment, Land Waster fell – but Tostig caught the banner and held it aloft. Both Vikings and English had frozen in their fight as Harald dropped dead. Harold Godwinson took advantage of the sudden silence to offer Tostig and the Vikings one more chance at peace. But Tostig – a man who thought he should be King but who now was without a country – refused one final time. The Vikings all shouted defiance at the English, saying that they would not stop fighting until they all lay dead atop each other.

Scandinavia had been Christian for a few decades, and Magnus the Good may have killed and scattered the last of the Jomsviking heathens, but the Vikings at Stamford Bridge threw their lives to fate as earnestly and vigorously as their ancestors had sought Valhalla.

As if in response to the Vikings' defiance, their reinforcements began to arrive. The third of the army that Harald had left to guard the ships had run 10-13 miles to answer their King's summons. Some had dropped their costly mail coats along the side of the road to run faster. A number of them died of exertion or collapsed from exhaustion even as they arrived – but most forgot their weariness at the site of their hard-pressed army and fallen King. These Vikings, too, were immediately taken by the spirit of battle and leaped into the fray.

But for the Vikings, that day's fate was beyond the skill of valiant men to change. The English were too many, and they fought bravely for their homes, their families, and the future of their nation. One by one, the leaders of the Vikings were slain until most of the great jarls of Norway would not see the next morning. At some point, Tostig was cut down, the details of his death unrecorded.

Finally, as night deepened over the land and the corpse-choked stream, Land Waster fell for the last time. Only the setting sun stemmed the slaughter, and what few Vikings whose threads remained uncut by the Norns escaped into the darkness.

The next day, Harald Hardrada's son, Olaf, came and surrendered to Harold Godwinson. The King of England showed some of the magnanimity he was known for. He ordered Olaf and his survivors to swear never to come back to England, and then he let them all go. But only 24 ships were left to backtrack along the Ouise and Humber towards the sea. From this, we can estimate that only about 12 percent of those Vikings that came to England with Harald Hardrada were hale enough to go tell Norway and Orkney of his death. The other 88 percent lie dead or dying in a field and waterway that would remain littered with white bones for more than a hundred years to come. Stamford Bridge itself would fall into disuse and ruin, as people gave a wide berth to the graveyard of an age.

Harold Godwinson stayed in York for about a week, overseeing the internment of the English dead and re-establishing peace amongst lords who a few days before had been ready to surrender to foreign invaders. As had always been his way, he arbitrated disputes, including one that arose over the dispositions of spoils and Harald's abandoned fleet. It was not until a week later that anyone felt ready to have a victory feast, but finally it was arranged, and the war-sated English gathered to drink ale horns to their valor and to reflect on what they had achieved.

It is said that this feast had only just begun when dust-covered messengers burst in and knelt before the King.

William the Bastard, Duke of Normandy, had just landed in the south with a massive army of Normans, Franks, and Bretons.

Harold Godwinson and his *housecarls* left that night to repeat the march that had saved England. This time, the outcome would be different.

Like Ragnar Lothbrok's raven banner that the Ui Imar dynasty flew in battle until it fell at Clontarf in 1014, Land Waster appears to have been both assurance of victory but also promise of doom. It is tempting to think that Land Waster was, in fact, Ragnar's raven and that it was brought to Norway by Vikings retreating from Clontarf and passed on to Harald through Olaf 20 or so years after the Ui Imar fell. This is pure speculation – and perhaps it is more in keeping with the spirit of Norse lore to think that when Ragnar's Raven fell at Clontarf, the Norns had cut the thread guiding it and that its magic was finally discharged.

But if Harald's Land Waster were the same banner that the Ui Imar carried, then it would have symbolically flown from the beginning to the end of the Viking Age. For the Battle of Stamford Bridge was the end of the Viking Age, not only because of the epic proportions of that battle but because things were different from that point on. Viking values and ways of life continued, especially in the forgotten fringes of Europe, but Viking raiders would never hold the world in peril the same way again.

When the age had started, Vikings appeared out of nowhere and took what they wanted, smashing opposition as they went. Now, these raiders had become armies, but these armies were finding the native powers of Europe ready for them. Perhaps the response of Harold Godwinson at Stamford Bridge was the response that was always required, and that such a response would have prevented the Viking Age had it just happened 273 years earlier. But 273 years earlier, it could not have happened. The Vikings themselves brought about the changes that made the world an inhospitable environment for men like themselves. So, it is to the questions of *'what happened to the Vikings?'* and *'what legacy did the Vikings leave behind?'* that our last few chapters will turn.

Chapter XX: Robert Guiscard, William the Conqueror, and the Viking Evolution in Normandy

When Charles the Simple ceded the lush lands of Normandy to the Viking, Rollo the Walker (in the early 900's) he thought that he had solved many of his national security problems. Not only would Rollo stop attacking, but he would also defend the coasts and riverways from other Vikings better than Frankish forces had been able to. The Viking-led armies of Normandy would also serve as an effective deterrent to the ambitions of any political enemies that Charles had, such as the rebellious provinces of Brittany or Burgundy. Normandy would also be a source of troops and a buffer against any future aggression from the British Isles or Muslim Spain. All these benefits were worth Charles making humiliating terms with the northern savages, even to the point of giving his daughter in marriage to the newly-baptized Rollo.

But Charles probably never thought that Rollo's Vikings would go on to do as well as they would. He probably thought – as most others thought at the time – that the wild Vikings were incapable of order and good government, that they would not know what to do with the gift of fertile lands and defensible borders. Charles probably thought that his strategy was buying him and his heirs a few decades of relative peace in which to rebuild Francia and partially refill their coffers from the constant depletion of *danegelds*. He did not realize that the Dukes of Normandy would go on to vie with the kings of Francia for supremacy, and would even shape the history of Europe, the Middle East, and – through their political advancements – even the history of all democratic nations.

From Norsemen to Normans

While it may have been war-ravaged, the territory Charles the Simple gave Rollo was anything but empty. Even with new settlers arriving from Scandinavia behind Rollo's own army, the Vikings in Normandy would never be more than a minority amongst the mixed descendants of Franks, Goths, and Gauls that already lived there. This indigenous population was horrified by Charles's action, and resentful of the Norse that – in some cases – literally took their lands out from under them.

But, except for Rollo's infamous hundred-man sacrifice and a few other political catch-twenty-twos that plagued the early dukes of Normandy, the transplanted rulers took great pains to distance themselves from their Viking cousins and to live up to the new image they conceived for themselves. This meant an effective and inclusive administration of law and order. It also meant conspicuous patronage of the Church, and eager adoption of the language and shared culture of Francia. Naturally or by design, the Norse married local women. So – much as was the case with the Rus – within a few generations the genetic deck in Normandy was thoroughly shuffled. For the next hundred years, priggish nobles in the king's court turned up their noses at the Johnnycome-lately Norman aristocrats and whispered about their inherent heathenism and second-class manners; but the Normans saw themselves as something new. The Dukes of Normandy – who almost all were named William, Robert, or Roger – were neither Viking nor French, but were a new creature for a new age.

The Normans differed from their Viking forefathers politically. Back when Charles the Fat's envoys reached the Viking camp during the second siege of Paris in 885, they reported that whenever they asked who was in charge, the Vikings laughed and said that they were all equals (which seemed like more ungodly insanity to the Franks). Eventually, the envoys found Rollo and Siegfried, who were the "first among equals" in this band. From what we know of the Vikings, this curious episode may have been the envoys misunderstanding that the Viking army was a large conglomeration of followers of many different, independent jarls. These jarls and their ship crews could come and go as they pleased, and would have formed a democratic structure as seen in the *Thing*, the *Althing*, and throughout Germanic tribal politics. It is also possible that this democratic structure was even more pronounced at that time in reaction to the opposite (i.e., increasingly-centralist and tyrannical by Viking standards) changes that were happening in Scandinavia with Harald Fairhair and other nation builders.

In any case, the Vikings who settled Normandy were as democratically-minded and fiercely independent as their Icelandic cousins. However, in administrating a large area and diverse population, all while trying to appease benefactors and defy political opponents, Rollo and the early Norman dukes moved away from democracy toward feudalism. The Norse society of jarl, karl, and thrall gave way to a society of noble and serf, much to the detriment of freedom for the lower class. Soon democracy on an individual level was gone. Men and women were tied to the land and their duty to their lord was nigh unbreakable.

The independent spirit of their ancestors was far from gone, however, and it manifested itself in the Norman lust for adventure, as well as in the constant rebellions and civil wars of Norman barons. It also gave rise to two of the most significant political inventions that would eventually lead to the modern rediscovery of democracy – but we will talk about this later.

In the things that mattered most, the Normans still fought like Vikings. That is, they had an indomitable spirit, and though Heaven had replaced Valhalla, Medieval history is replete with tales of Norman valor. They also kept (and even refined) the Viking love of cunning and strategy. They continued to use the dragon ship (though the dragon head eventually disappeared) and all manner of naval and marine warfare. Like their Viking ancestors, they launched bigger and bigger foreign expeditions, including some of the largest overseas invasions before modern times.

On land, though, their method of warfare exhibited a few critical changes. Unlike the 9th century Vikings, the Normans finally had access to more standardized resources. The Bayeux Tapestry shows largely-uniform warriors, wearing heavy hauberks of steel armor – scales and mail – and simple but standardized metal cap helmets with nose guards. The center-gripped circular shield was replaced by a larger, strapped shield that was shaped like an inverted raindrop. This change in shield reflected the biggest difference in the Norman war machine – reliance on heavy cavalry.

Hitherto, the Vikings had not been cavalrymen. After the embarrassment of the first siege of Paris, Charles the Bald reinvigorated heavy cavalry as a means of catching and killing Viking warbands. The Normans now embraced mounted warfare and became some of Europe's best knights. Aristocracy based on owning and using horses in war goes back to Roman, Germanic, and Eastern peoples, but it was now reborn. The Medieval knight, with his high-stepping charger, shining armor, long lance, and code of chivalry is perhaps the most enduring image of the Middle Ages, and the Normans threw themselves into this role, defining it for centuries to come.

Another significant change in the Norman mode of warfare and dominion can still be seen throughout Europe and the Middle East today – castles. The Normans did not invent castles, and their Viking ancestors certainly understood the importance of fortifications, but the Normans would use castles extensively to systematically secure and control the many lands they conquered. The Normans built more castles during their time on the world stage than anyone else. For the subjugated peoples from Ireland to Syria, the Norman castle became both a hated symbol of their overlords and an effective deterrent to rebellion.

Even aside from language, culture, genetics, warfare, and religion, the land of Normandy itself affected change on the Vikings that came to live there. In Scandinavia, with its long winters and grudging soil, the Norse diet had depended on milk, cheese, and yogurt, supplemented with some meat and fish and accompanied by carbohydrates in the form of seedy, coarse bread and barley-based ale. Now in the rolling green of Normandy – at the sunny dawn of the Medieval Warming Period – there was so much more of all these things, plus orchards, vineyards, fat beef cows, vegetables, and easy trade with the abundance of the south. This period saw a population explosion throughout Europe, but in Normandy, this exponential growth of manpower was to have some important, long-acting consequences.

One of these consequences was what we will call the "second son effect." If a landowner had more than one son, and he left his land to be divided equally amongst them after his death, then the estate (and therefore the importance of the family) would shrink. Even if each generation has just two sons, 100 acres becomes 50, then 25, 12.5, and so on. To abate this diminishment of wealth, many Medieval landowners left most of their land to the oldest surviving male heir (a practice known as primogeniture). Other children were left to either make do with much less, join the Church, or go seek their fortune.

So, for the Normans of the 10th, 11th, and 12th centuries, the combination of population growth and Viking spirit became weaponized. For example, one minor knight by the name of Tancred d'Hauteville had 12 sons. His first son got his estates, so eight of his other children went out and did what seemed natural to them – they conquered Southern Italy and much of the Mediterranean.

Robert the Crafty

Like their Viking forefathers, the Normans had an eye for opportunity. While passing through Southern Italy on a return leg of a pilgrimage, sometime in the early 1000's, 30 Norman knights were approached by an old man begging them to help the Lombards (who were once masters of Italy) against the Byzantines (who were then masters of Southern Italy). The knights returned home, spreading the word of the fertile lands, the perfectly situated trading posts, and the vulnerable political situation.

Norman mercenaries began to stream into the region, taking up contracts with weak but wealthy Lombard lords. As word of their enrichment and the ample possibilities they were yet to exploit traveled back to Normandy, more and more Normans went to join them. The "second son effect" was on full display, for Normandy was churning out more knights than it could afford, and these young men were as capable as they were desperate.

Throughout the early 11th century, while the Viking Age was waning, Norman mercenaries were fighting in the Mediterranean. First, they fought for the Lombards – but then they began to also fight for the Byzantines. As they began to take their payment in land instead of money, and their numbers began to reach critical mass, they started fighting for themselves.

The tipping point occurred in 1053 when the Pope himself led an army against the Normans to stop their meddling and curb the mayhem they were causing throughout Italy. It was a disaster. The Pope was captured. He was treated with exaggerated deference and courtesy, but the austere man knew the precarious position he was in. The Normans returned him to his papal seat in Rome, but only after extracting from him terms that were very much in their favor.

After that, the Italian strategy turned from trying to crush the Norman power-usurpers to trying to contain them. In 1059, Robert Guiscard – or Robert the Crafty, one of the 12 sons of Tancred d'Hauteville – was granted the hitherto-nonexistent dukedom of Apulia, Calabria, and Sicily. This gave the Normans the southernmost extremity of Italy – which for the most part they already controlled – and the island of Sicily, which was a powerbase for northward-looking Arab Saracens.

The Pope was probably employing the old Roman strategy of using his enemies to fight his enemies. He thought that the Normans would exhaust their strength in an endless war against the entrenched Muslim forces that had been threatening Italy. This just shows that he did not yet really know Robert the Crafty.

Perhaps one of the reasons for the enduring popularity of early medieval studies is the sense that during such a time a man of strength, daring, and ability could accomplish almost anything. Robert had left Normandy with only five horsemen and 30 infantrymen only 13 years before his elevation. His older brother, Drogo, was already the head of a substantial Norman contingent in Italy. But instead of giving a hand-up, Drogo resisted Robert, knowing how much trouble the younger d'Hauteville was. Robert turned to brigandage to pay the bills and was successful enough to draw more followers despite the life of crime he offered. Drogo was later assassinated, though, and his successor (also one of Robert's brothers) offered Guiscard a chance to step out of the shadows on to the bigger stage.

Anna Comnena, daughter of the man who was to become Robert's arch-nemesis, offers this description of him:

This Robert was a Norman by birth, of obscure origin,
with an overbearing character and thoroughly villainous
mind; he was a brave fighter, very cunning in his assaults
on the power and wealth of great men; in achieving his

aims absolutely inexorable, diverting criticism by
incontrovertible argument. He was a man of immense
stature, surpassing even the biggest men; he had a ruddy
complexion, blonde hair, broad shoulders, eyes that all
but shot out sparks of fire...Homer remarked of Achilles
that when he shouted his hearers had the impression of a
multitude in uproar, but Robert's bellow, so they say, put
tens of thousands to flight. [44]

And so it was that as Robert was given military opportunities, he took them and he won. As he met political opposition, he overcame it. He combined cunning strategy with the Devil's luck, and he climbed meteorically. Within 13 years of landing in Italy, he had been given the suicide mission of dukedom of Sicily by the Pope. But with the help of his younger brother, the patient and wise Roger, Robert conquered Sicily and mopped up the remainder of Byzantine control in Italy in just over a decade.

Robert's keen military skill and cunning combined with Roger's policies of tolerance and ability to win over the Muslim and Greek populations of his domain enabled the Normans to not only take dominion of the island but to take it over as a whole and still productive property. There were no reigns of terror or costly rebuilding periods. In fact, Robert always had more trouble dealing with the independent spirit of his rebellious Norman barons than he did from his subjugated populations. Robert's Sicily was almost-immediately a source of trade wealth and allied forces for him and would go on to be one of the most successful European kingdoms for several hundred years.

William the Conqueror

Around the time Robert Guiscard and his brother Roger were conquering Sicily, there was another Norman conquest going on. William the Bastard – so called because he was the love child of Robert I, Duke of Normandy, and a tanner's daughter – had survived his childhood as an orphan dodging assassination attempts. He ascended to the throne of Normandy with a serious axe to grind with everybody. He was a decade younger than Robert Guiscard but showed similar characteristics in ambition and ability.

Across the channel in England, the Saxon line of kings had been failing. In January 1066, word reached Normandy that the English king, Edward the Confessor, had died without an heir. The son of the Edward's high councilor, Godwin, had been coronated as king.

William had some reason to believe that he had a stronger claim to the throne than this Harold Godwinson. His reasoning was more valid than it might seem, but is too complicated to go into here. It may be, though, that William was just feigning indignation (as many of his contemporaries thought) while he seized an opportunity. After all, England had recently been in the hands of Cnute the Great of Denmark, and William was more-or-less related to him. So, why couldn't

Normandy rule England instead of an elected regent with no royal blood to speak of?

The fact that William was not English, and that neither he nor some of his descendants could even speak English never seemed to factor into his reasoning. This is an early example of one of the tragic flaws in English history – many kings saw Britain as just one of their properties to exploit. Throughout Europe, too many kings had an underdeveloped sense that they were there for the people but instead thought that the people were there for them.

William was not just a warrior; he was also a political tactician. Before he set sail with his army of Normans, Franks, and Bretons, he secured the blessing of the Pope, which included an excommunication of Harold Godwinson. With excommunication came the release of all feudal obligations (in theory) to the excommunicate. We do not see much evidence of the people of England following through on this (though it is true that many stayed home during the Battle of Hastings) but it is likely that this removal of God's blessing was a severe blow to the English king.

The rest is history. Harold and the English fought furiously at Hastings, after marching 200 miles in just a few days – after defeating Harald Hardrada's Vikings at Stamford Bridge, which had also followed a 200-mile march. Harold was one of the shortest-serving kings of England, but he was undoubtedly one of their most heroic. He died at

Hastings, though, and just a few weeks after historians ended the Viking Age (with the Battle of Stamford Bridge) William the Bastard was coronated William I of England. Duke William the Bastard had become King William the Conqueror.

William the Conqueror would spend the next five years securing England, but in that short time, the Normans succeeded in doing more than the Vikings had been able to do in the previous 250 years. In the next century, the Normans would follow this success in Wales, Ireland, and across the Scottish border. It was not necessarily a matter of greater virtue or valor, though. Times had simply changed.

Robert Guiscard versus the World

The years after Hastings were far sunnier down in Sicily and Southern Italy. Maybe Robert Guiscard noticed the stream of Danish and Anglo-Saxon refugees and fallen nobility traveling through his ports on their way to seek service with the Varangian Guard in Constantinople, and maybe he did not. There was far more to keep him busy than wondering how his countrymen were faring in the British Isles. He had consolidated his holdings, and aside from putting down some Norman baronial rebellions here and there, he was doing well.

He was doing so well, in fact, that he attracted the attention of his former foes, the Byzantines. In 1081, they approached Robert Guiscard about marrying one of his daughters (the most attractive one, they specified) to their juvenile prince, Michael.

The Byzantines had been having a hard time. Ten years before, in 1071, their very worthy, capable Emperor Romanus IV had gone out with a large army to face the Seljuk Turks. Accompanied by Norman mercenaries and part of his Varangian Guard, Romanus had caught the Seljuk leader Alp Arslan in an exposed position with a smaller force. It should have been a slam-dunk for Romanus, but the resulting Battle of Manzikert was a disaster that marked the turning point of Byzantine history. Whether through communication problems or (more likely) through the avarice of Romanus's political enemies, most of Byzantium's army fled the field and the Emperor himself was captured by the Seljuks.

In the corrupt world of Byzantine politics, though, Alp Arslan was the only other gentleman Romanus could find that day. The Sultan let Romanus go, but the same Byzantine politicos who had fled the field at Manzikert had rushed back to Constantinople and deposed the Emperor in his absence, and then when they caught him they blinded him so viciously that the noble Romanus died of infection, with maggots crawling out of his eye sockets.

Byzantium had nothing but problems since, with unstable emperors and runaway inflation. But it was still the most opulent empire of the Middle Ages, and so Robert Guiscard jumped at the chance to have his daughter marry in and to see his progeny (possibly) rise to the Throne of the Caesars.

Byzantium moved too fast, though. Robert's daughter had just arrived there when the reigning emperor was replaced by a blood-thirsty psychopath. Michael was locked in a monastery and Robert's daughter was thrust into a nunnery.

While this would be horrifying to any other parent, it was the best news Robert Guiscard had in his life. It was the excuse he was waiting for to launch a great Norman campaign to conquer the opulent east.

The crafty king of Sicily immediately began raising a massive army and building a vast fleet of warships. He even went so far as to find a wondering young monk, who he claimed to be the escaped deposed-emperor Michael. We are told the young man was not a very good actor, but Robert had enough to go on for the time being. As the year sped on, he made ready to avenge his family's honor by invading Byzantium.

Again, Byzantium moved too quickly. The deranged usurper was easy to depose and fell within a few months. Instead of replacing him with the real Michael, though, another high-status Byzantine noble, Alexius, was crowned Emperor. Byzantium was very lucky that he was, for Alexius was one of the worthiest rulers of his age, and his long reign would buy that failing empire several more centuries. But first, they had a Norman invasion to worry about.

The deft Alexius immediately sent word to Robert. His daughter had been released, unharmed. Michael, too, was released (though given only a lesser status) and the two could go on with the wedding if they liked. With the real Michael in hand, there was no reason to go on pretending with Robert's imposter. There was really no reason why Norman Sicily and Byzantium could not be friends.

Robert was furious. He had spent a fortune raising an army and navy in the hope of snatching the legacy of the Roman Empire for himself. Now his chances were slipping away. Robert could not accept that, and so he invaded anyway.

The war that followed was strange and complicated. It was a war that pitched one of the greatest warriors of the day against one of the greatest politicians. Time and time again, Robert swept away Alexius's army, but time and time again Alexius outmaneuvered him. With Byzantine forces a shadow of what they were before Manzikert, Alexius's tactics included paying Robert's enemies at home to rebel against him in his absence.

The tactics worked, and Robert frequently had to leave his Byzantine campaigns in the capable hands of his bastard son, Bohemund (who would go on to be one of the most famous players of the First Crusade) and go home to restore order.

Luckily for Byzantium, something happened in Italy that Robert could not ignore, and that demanded all the military power he could swiftly generate. For years there had been discord in the Church over several matters of reform. While Robert had been fighting, a reformist pope had been elected. But the mighty Emperor Henry IV of the Holy Roman Empire (an empire of German principalities, founded by Charlemagne) had just backed an anti-pope, and the Germans had invaded Italy, chasing the elected Pope into his stronghold of Castel Saint'Angelo. The Pope immediately sent a desperate letter to the one man he could think of who was able and willing to take on the greatest power in Northern Europe to help him.

Whether out of piety, the desire to appear pious, or more likely the unwillingness to lose this vital ally and then have Europe's mighty northern empire at his back door, Robert Guiscard came running to the Pope's aid. His army of 36,000 Normans and other allies barely slowed at the walls of Rome. They put the German army to flight and liberated the Pope.

What happened next was truly horrible, though. After pushing themselves to the breaking point in the journey north and risking their lives in the battles that followed, the Norman soldiery sought to compensate themselves while punishing the Roman citizens for their support of the Germans and the anti-pope. A brutal sack of the city commenced, where no one was safe, and nothing was spared. When the Normans exceeded the boundaries that the medieval mind allowed for conquering armies, the Roman mob took to the streets to defend their city.

So furious was this counter-attack, that the Normans were pushed back to the walls of the Castel Saint'Angelo. There they rallied and unleashed hell on the people of Rome. The Eternal City was set on fire, and thousands of people were slaughtered or dragged off into slavery. The Norman sack of Rome under Robert Guiscard in the name of the Pope was more destructive and lethal than those of Alaric the Visigoth, Gaiseric the Vandal, or any other before or since.

It was on this black note that the illustrious life of Robert the Crafty ends. He and his blood-slated army marched away from a smoldering Rome, perhaps thinking of resuming Byzantine campaigns or maybe just exhausted. In his absence, Bohemund had lost much of the Norman gains in Byzantium, and so the next season Robert again launched a fleet. This time, though, a virulent plague struck, killing 500 knights and untold numbers of soldiers. Robert was among them. The ever-grasping warrior king was 70 years old when he died of septic shock in a war zone far from home.

The life of Robert Guiscard was exceptional in its scale but its themes were typical of the times. A lesser son of a lesser lord, he set out to carve out a domain for himself using just his wits, bravery, and force of will. He was a baptized Christian born in France, but like the other Normans of his day, he represented the Viking evolution. The Vikings were not disappearing. They were assimilating, learning, and changing, but they were also changing everything around them. Like the Rus, the Normans were Viking adaptations for a changing world.

The Normans were not very popular in their own lifetime. They were coveted allies but known to be capricious friends most interested in their own gain. During the few hundred years that they were independent political entities (before becoming absorbed by the broader national pictures of England, France, or the Italian States of the later Middle Ages) they were enemies of the Irish, Welsh, Cornish, Anglo-Saxons, Scotts, Franks, Germans of the Holy Roman Empire, Italians, Lombards, Rus, Berbers, Moors, Arabs, Jews, Syrians, Saracens, Turks, Kurds, Greeks and Byzantines, Papists, Anti-Papists, Bulgars, and anyone else they came in contact with. They were also usually at war with themselves during numerous baronial uprisings and struggles for control. Even other Vikings didn't like them. The Normans firmly seized an England and Ireland that other Vikings considered to be their birthright, and *Ragnar Saga Lodbrok* tellingly and symbolically includes an epilogue where William the Conqueror disinters and burns the corpse of Ivar the Boneless.

Despite the enmity of the Medieval world, there were moments when the Normans created some of the most promising scenes of the era. The court of Norman Sicily, for example, was at times the most modern and humanistic places in an age plagued by darkness and widespread war. During certain reigns, the Sicilian court was trade-rich and militarily-secure, and a place where Muslim scholars, Jewish physicians, Greek and Latin churchmen, French troubadours, Venetian businessmen, and merchants from all over the world enjoyed the sunny bounty of a well-governed land under beneficent rulers. A few princesses even married for love. Every traveler that entered a Sicilian port was brought to court and questioned about the wonders he had seen in his travels. These accounts were compiled into a massive encyclopedia so that the Normans would have access to the world's learning. The maps made from these accounts were in use until the Age of Exploration. Such things seldom last, but for all their faults, some Normans found a piece of enlightenment at a time when many other European powers did not even think to look.

But even these glimpses of the idyllic world were not the most significant contribution of the Normans. Two things happened (around the same time) that the Normans gave us as a gift from their Viking ancestors. But we will save these for a later chapter.

Chapter XXI: Where Did the Vikings Go?

Humans in general (and scholars in particular) love order and will impose it wherever we can. So, historians looking back at the story of the Vikings have set the end of the Viking Age with the Battle of Stamford Bridge in 1066. This was chosen not only because of the death of Harald Hardrada – perhaps the most quintessential Viking since Ragnar Lothbrok himself – but because it was the last major Viking offensive in European history.

But we would not expect the men and women who woke up on New Year's Day, 1067, to necessarily know that their world was different. Change in real time is far more gradual. Many of the factors that led to the end of the Vikings' starring role on the world stage had already been in motion for decades. Other factors would take decades more to mature.

In any case, the years that followed 1066 saw fewer and fewer Viking raids until it could be said that there were none. This was for a variety of reasons. We will offer some (in no particular order) of the significant differences between the 9th century and the 12th that made the latter an inhospitable environment for Vikings.

First, the political fabric of Europe changed. In the 9th century, there was largely-decentralized rule by numerous smaller kings, whereas by the 12th century both Scandinavia and the rest of Europe had become a continent of nations. Centralized authority with national goals meant that a jarl could no longer gather a few ships and go make war until he forced a petty ruler into favorable terms. After 1066, would-be warlords had the stark choice of serving the established national elite or resorting to small-scale brigandage and piracy. Thus, Vikings lost the independence that made them Vikings and simply melded into the political landscape as Norwegians, Swedes, Danes, Irish, English, Russians, etcetera.

Feudalism was an important political/socio-economic development of the era. People were no longer free to go off and do as they dared. They were connected to the land and had obligations to their lords that they could not step in and out of. To fail these obligations might mean outlawry and this came with severe consequences that most serfs wanted no part of. The change in the social structure was accompanied by changes in expectation and culture that meant the serf of the High Middle Ages was in no way qualified to take on the Viking lifestyle of an Early Medieval karl, even if he had wanted to. Many serfs did want to break free, and a few would, but they were forced to wait for the right opportunities to come by, now that the personal freedom of earlier ages was gone.

With centralized authority and feudalism, along with population growth from the Medieval Warming Period, would-be Vikings had less vacant land to grab. We can see this limiting phenomenon in Viking activity in Germany and the Low Countries during the late 9th century.

At that time, Vikings took advantage of any lapses of the Holy Roman Empire's attention (such as in 881, when Charles III foolishly left his lands almost-undefended while he went to Rome for his coronation), but they could never set up long-term bases there. Without these land bases, like the ones they had in Ireland, Britain, etcetera, large-scale Viking activity was unsustainable.

Christianity was another significant change – but perhaps not in the way that one might immediately think. Despite Christ's teachings of peace and love, Christians in the Middle Ages were very warlike. Most Vikings that converted to Christianity remained warlike. However, inclusion in the Church meant exposure of the would-be Viking to Church sanctions. A Christian could not expect to attack Church property and get away with it. The Church also used excommunication – something that most (not all) Medieval people took very seriously, as it released all others from their legal obligations to the excommunicated subject as well as potentially damned his soul to Hell until he made amends. Though plenty of Medieval wars happened despite – or even because of – the Church, overall the Church served as an adhesive to the kingdoms of Europe, aligning goals and arbitrating disagreements. This was one of the reasons kings like Alfred the Great insisted on the baptism of Vikings who surrendered. As with Viking rulers like Guthrum and Rollo, Christianity led to investiture in the broader European community that the Vikings had previously ignored.

The Church itself was less vulnerable to attack than it had been in the Early Middle Ages. Monasteries were not the banks full of easily-transferable goods they used to be. They had learned to protect their valuables. For years, monks had been building ingenious, anti-Viking watchtowers of stone, like the ones still standing at Glendalough, Cashel, or Clonmacnoise. If Vikings or other marauders were spotted from these heights, the treasure-laden monks could climb a ladder to the doors (elevated well above the ground level) and then pull the ladders up after them. Even by the middle of the 9th century, many monks were prepared to fight to protect their books, bones, and altar pieces. Later, more valuable Church treasures and relics naturally ended up in the new feature of the High Middle Ages – the cathedral. Cathedrals were usually associated with cities, where they could be protected by walls and garrisons.

The Church was not the only institution that had developed effective anti-Viking tactics, the secular powers had, too. Many of the nobles of Europe were descended from Vikings or from Viking fighters, and so they knew how the Vikings operated. King Alfred's strategy of fortified burghs throughout the land discouraged would-be Vikings while it shored up local and national power. Later rulers would take this a step further with the proliferation of castles. While armies still depended on levying troops from the land, professional soldiers and mobile cavalry were more plentiful. The dragon ship was no longer a cutting-edge innovation that only the Vikings had – Europe began to have effective navies. For the Vikings (as well as for the Moors of Spain), Europe was no longer a soft target.

Old Doors Close, New Doors Open

So, a young adventurer waking up on New Year's Day, 1067 may have considered his options and found that there were too many obstacles to go Viking. His lord would not let him leave his farm, and another lord would be waiting to kill him wherever his ship might go. Even if he took these chances, riches and land were not the low-hanging fruit they had been.

Other options were opening up though. The powers of Europe, suddenly self-aware and beginning to see their own potential, would go on to be almost perpetually at war with each other. There would still be places for brave men, though the rewards and freedoms were indeed nowhere near as high as they had been for the luckiest of the Vikings.

There was another option as the 11th century gave way to the 12th – our young adventurer could take the cross and go on Crusade.

For many modern people, the Crusades – wars fought in the name of Christ that helped doom the very thing they were meant to save (i.e., the Christian East) and were replete with well-documented atrocities against civilians of all faiths – are an unappealing topic. For the sake of understanding history, though, it is essential to consider these wars holistically. The Crusades (which began around 1095 and lasted on-and-off through 1492) were marketed as religious wars at the time they were waged, just as Muslims sometimes declare *jihad*. Doubtlessly some knights and soldiers joined in because they felt their faith demanded it. But others entered the Crusades because they were an opportunity for worldly gain, regardless of the lip service they may have paid to the religious cause. Crusader armies fought many battles against other Christians on their way to the Middle East and once they were there, so the notion of a faith-based war was a fluid one. While at times the religious fervor of the Crusaders was undeniable (such as an incident where a starving Crusader army, armed with a priest's vision and a holy lance, stormed out of Antioch and crushed a far-superior force). But naturally-enough, religious fervor seemed to be variable and circumstantial. Bohemund and other Crusader celebrities were more eager to out-compete each other for a larger slice of the spoils than they were to liberate Christian territory.

The Islamic world and the Byzantine Empire had both enjoyed a Golden Age, but this was now starting to show signs of weakness that the powers of Europe were eager to exploit. The "second son effect" was on full display as practically-landless knights from throughout Europe rushed to carve out Crusader states for themselves in the affluent east. Many of the same types of forces that had been at work in the Viking Age merely transferred to where new opportunities could be found.

The Viking Age was over, but men who were not content to merely take what was assigned to them and toil for the benefit of their lord could find a place in the ranks of the Crusaders or in the endless wars in Europe itself. Even these opportunities seemed reduced by the feudal system, though, with some lords becoming kings, but most of the men who risked their lives receiving little for their troubles. It is no wonder that works of literature like the *Volsunga Saga,* the *Nibelungenlied,* and the *Mabinogion* (to name a few) gained widespread popularity during this time. People thought back to the tales of their Viking grandfathers and thought of how much better things must have been.

There were many more rude awakenings to come as the High Middle Ages turned to the Late Middle Ages. Realities such as The Hundred Years' War, the Mongol Invasions, The Black Death, and the effects of the Little Ice Age all probably made tales of free men who sailed where they wanted and made realms for themselves seem like fairy tales. While we see the Early Middle Ages as the Dark Ages – a mysterious time of fire and sword – the people of the later middle ages might have seen it quite differently.

As people's expectations gradually adjusted to the changing world, it would carry over to their art and literature, too. To the learned, the sagas would seem less important than Dante, Boccaccio, or Chaucer. From our modern perspective, we see these changes in the arts to be

improvements, but they also suggest a sober shift in thinking. Slowly –
much more slowly than the glaciers advancing over the old Viking
homelands at the time – people were inching towards modernity.

But even during these centuries of change, when people like
Ragnar, Ivar the Boneless, or Harald Hardrada were transformed into
legend, there were a few living relics of Viking Age Europe still in
action. Such men were not Vikings, *per se*, but they were of Viking
descent and lived in a way that the Vikings would have instantly
recognized and identified with. These men were seen most often far
away from the courts of England, Germany, France, Russia, or even
Scandinavia in places where they were needed most. One of these places
was the wild periphery of Europe in regions known as "beyond the
Pale," and the other was in the very heart of one of the world's oldest
empires.

Chapter XXII: Varangians and Gallowglass, Vikings Relics in an Age of Change

Roman emperors had always valued Germanic mercenaries as bodyguards and personal troops. These warriors were big, intimidating, fierce in battle, and bound by deep cultural values to honor their oaths and never run from a fight. But as much as all these qualities, the Romans valued Germanic bodyguards because – as outsiders – they were far less likely to get into palace intrigues, coups, and all the other cloak and dagger dangers that were the daily reality of the imperial court. Though the Roman Empire dissolved in the west, it continued in the east for almost another thousand years. So, when these later Byzantine emperors first encountered the Vikings they immediately saw their potential.

Of course, these first encounters with Vikings were as enemies, as Swedish Varangians and the Norse-Slavic hybrid culture of the Kievan Rus attacked Byzantium in the 9th and 10th centuries. Even in-between attacks, though, the Byzantines put the Rus to work as mercenaries – perhaps employing the age-old Roman strategy of using enemies against each other. Eventually, the Vikings and their Rus cousins would learn that there was much more to gain by helping Byzantium than by attacking it.

In 988, Vladamir the Great – Saint Olga's grandson and the new brother-in-law of the Byzantine emperor, Basil II – sent 6000 Swedish

Vikings to Constantinople to help the Empire against its fierce Bulgarian enemies. These same 6000 Vikings had helped Vladamir regain his domain in what are now Ukraine, Belarus, and Russia. But once Vladamir had his throne, he found that 6000 bored Vikings were hard to contain, and more of a hindrance to the peace of his realm than a help to it. So, he sent them south to help his brother-in-law (or to transfer his troubles to him).

Luckily, Basil loved the gift. The Vikings swore oaths of loyalty to the throne of Constantinople (not necessarily to the person of the emperor himself, which would sometimes become an important distinction), and thus they confirmed the name Varangians ("sworn companions"). They proved very effective against Byzantium's enemies and helped earn the emperor the nickname, Basil the Bulgar-Slayer. From that time on, the Byzantine emperors would keep a troop of Nordic mercenaries as the Varangian Guard.

The number "6000" comes up often enough in our records of the Varangian Guard to believe that the force was intended to stay at that strength. This was a very large force by the standards of northwestern Europe, but Byzantium was part of the vast, prosperous east and had more than enough enemies to warrant such precautions. Around this time, the Empire had around 11 million people, with anywhere from 400,000 – 1,000,000 living in the city of Constantinople. Though its territory waxed and waned, at its height it stretched from the Middle East to the Balkans, with what are now Turkey, Greece, and the islands of the eastern Mediterranean as its core. Its enemies were also prosperous, sprawling, and highly-active, with Islamic caliphates, Turkic tribal confederations, a rival Bulgarian empire, and so-on. History would show that the Vikings of the Varangian Guard were joining the Byzantine Empire at a time when it needed them most.

The Varangian Guard was a bodyguard in the sense that the emperor always had them with him when he went into battle, and numerous sources mention various emperors being followed around by tall men with big axes. But the Varangian Guard was also what we would think of as special forces. They were used as shock troops, marching into battle shoulder to shoulder with the southern sun shining on their mail and glittering scales, filling the air with dread-inspiring battle cries.

Unlike the early Vikings, the Varangian Guard was well-equipped with armor, shields, helmets, swords, spears, and various armaments. The signature weapon if the Varangian Guard, and symbol of their identity and status, was the long-hafted, single-bitted "Dane axe." This weapon required strength and skill to use, but in competent hands, it was matchless in power, reach, and penetration. Primary sources describe the Varangians using these fearsome axes to take out Norman cavalry and cut through Pecheneg battle wagon formations. Modern cutting tests suggest that in trained hands it could hew a man in half.

Archeological findings show that these long-hafted (i.e., from the ground to the warrior's mid-sternum or so), large-bladed axes represent only a small percentage of axes from the Viking Age. Though the axe was a standard weapon, most Viking axes were two to three feet in length for speed and to facilitate their use in the shield wall. These findings further emphasize the high-status of the Varangian's ax and the exceptional abilities of the men who used it.

As Basil's 6000 needed replacements, new members volunteered from the Swedish Vikings and the Rus who sailed down the Volga and Dnieper Rivers on what some Norse sagas call "the road to Miklagard (their name for Constantinople). Over time, word of the splendors of Miklagard and the tremendous opportunities there spread all over the Viking world. Soon, the Varangian Guard also featured many western Vikings from Norway, Denmark, and elsewhere. These included many heroes and men from noble houses, including Harald Hardrada, who would go on to be king of Norway.

When William the Conqueror forced Norman rule on England after five years of brutal war, the Varangian Guard was inundated by dispossessed Anglo-Saxon and Danish warriors fleeing the collapse of the Viking Age and yearning for revenge. They would soon get their chance.

Some Varangian Guardsmen were the sons of other Varangian Guardsmen. There were enough northerners in Constantinople to warrant their own quarter, and travelers record in primary sources hearing English spoken on certain streets of the city. We are told that the Varangian quarter had its own churches, though we are left to wonder whether this religious separatism is related to the role Rome's excommunication of Harold Godwinson played in the demise of old England.

There does not seem to be a set time of service for Varangian Guardsmen (though we would expect that oaths would be taken to serve for a minimum of a campaign season or year). Harald Hardrada served for six years. Even after the Viking Age, in the newly unified nations of Sweden, Norway, Denmark, and the newly-dependent islands of Iceland, Orkney, etcetera, it became the family tradition for many noble houses to send their sons to serve in the Varangian Guard to start off their careers. It seems that this was not only so that the young scion could gain wealth and experience, but because the Scandinavian elite considered the status of the far-off Byzantine emperors to be higher than their national kings. As in our modern militaries, well-performing warriors could stay for as many terms of service as suited them.

For the Varangians, the pay and fringe-benefits were excellent, the chance for plunder exceptional, opportunities for advancement were good (they were sometimes used to lead other troops) and the job security far-better than what they could expect at home. For the northerners, life in the sprawling, glittering metropolis of Constantinople was easy, the food was plentiful, the women exotically beautiful, and the entertainment endless. These sons of Vikings took full advantage of it all, earning the derisive title from jealous courtiers, "the Emperor's winebags."

There was only one major drawback of being a member of the Varangian Guard – the danger. The Varangians were nearly wiped out defending Romanus IV at the Battle of Manzikert in 1071. They were again wiped out when their bravery (and thirst for vengeance) exceeded the courage of the rest of the army, and their frenzied attack on Robert Guiscard in 1081's Battle of Dyrrachium got cut-off from the main force. Almost 100 years later, the Varangians were again practically wiped out by Turks at the disastrous Byzantine defeat at Myriokephalon. Though 6000 strong as an organization, the Varangian Guardsmen were often divided into much smaller groups and sent to various trouble spots. This sometimes resulted in a few hundred Varangians defending unsupported outposts against the full strength of Byzantium's many enemies.

The Varangians were used to do what other men could not. Though this resulted in catastrophic defeats sometimes, it also led to glorious victories. A Varangian Guard charge finally crushed the dreaded Pechenegs around 1122. They defended Greece from the Normans and defeated them in Cyprus in 1156. They were instrumental in the victory over the Turks at Claudiopolis in 1179, just three years after being almost destroyed.

Not all Varangian Guard victories involved charges and axe-wielding. They had a subtle side, too. Numerous assassination attempts and coups were prevented by their alert intervention.

In victory and in defeat, the Varangian Guard proved that the Viking spirit was not dead just because the Viking Age was over. They ran into battle, heedless of their own safety. Like their ancestors, they sought only glory, whether that be found in life or in death.

But in 1203-1204, the ancient Byzantine Empire would have the most significant defeat in its history and reach a point of no return. This defeat did not come at the hands of the Turks, the Mongols, or any caliphate – it came from Crusaders. The Crusades had been going on with variable success since 1096, but what had started as an appeal for help against Muslim forces by the Christians of Byzantium had been bringing greedy, unprincipled, equally-aggressive western forces into the region. Thus, the wealth and the weaknesses of Byzantium were now well-known to the European powers. An opportunity was sensed, and so excuses were quickly found, and in 1203 the Fourth Crusade turned into a crusade against Constantinople.

The Varangian Guard defended Constantinople vigorously against a massive Crusader army and Venetian navy. As the crisis stretched over months, turmoil inside the capitol proved as disruptive as the enemy, and – to make a long story very short – the throne changed hands several times. The faithlessness and flight of these emperors would stand in contrast to the bravery and fortitude of Constantinople's final emperor, but in the Fourth Crusade, only the Varangian Guard held their ground.

The Varangians fought valiantly despite heavy losses, but the forces of Western Christendom finally broke through. Because the emperors had each taken flight, the Varangians had no one left to defend, and so they, too, surrendered.

The Crusaders unleashed three days of theft, destruction, rape, and murder on the people of Constantinople, but then held the city as their own.

Constantinople would be under "Latin" (western) emperors for almost 60 years. During that time, Varangians served Byzantine emperors in exile throughout the Greek and Anatolian lands. Meanwhile, the Latin emperors in Constantinople had Varangians of their own. Eventually, the Byzantines would win Constantinople back, though the next two centuries would be the twilight of that great empire.

The Varangians were still active, with their last headline-grabbing victory being in 1265, but, over time, they began to play more and more of a ceremonial role, and the size of their corps shrunk. The last mention of Varangians we have was in 1404. We do not know if there were any Varangians left when the powerful Turkish Sultan Mehmet II besieged an isolated and exhausted Constantinople in 1453, or whether the last, brave Roman Emperor (appropriately named

Constantine XI) was joined by a Varangian Guard or just by their descendants mingled within the ranks of his army. Emperor Constantine and many others died defending the city, and the long story of Rome ended on the same day that the Viking legacy in the south did – May 29, 1453.

The Gallowglass

The Viking Age ended in Ireland with Brian Boru's victory at the Battle of Clontarf. Though Vikings were fighting on both sides of that struggle, the devastating Viking losses in the bloodbath and the disproportionate representation of Irish-based Viking powers on the losing side effectively ended Norse power in Ireland. The Battle of Clontarf also led to a High King being on the throne of Ireland (which unfortunately was not Brian or his heirs, as they did not survive the battle and the aftermath). So, the cursory glance at history would reinforce the nationalist belief that Brian's Irish kicked the Vikings out, and they subsequently enjoyed a time of peace and prosperity until the English interfered about a century and a half later.

As usual, the truth is muddier. The Irish had never liked central authority much and soon fell back into their age-old ways of local rulers feuding amongst themselves. In 1166 (100 years after the Viking Age), the King of Leinster, Dermot MacMurrough, was deposed by a neighboring ruler. Dermot appealed to the Norman English for help. The Normans were happy to comply, and soon a steady stream of knights from England and Wales were pouring into Ireland. The "second son effect" was once again at work as trained warriors with a few followers and a modicum of financial backing took whatever they could grab.

As it had been during the Vikings' first raiding period, Ireland was again a place where a reasonably-competent warlord could carve out lands and earn titles for themselves and their posterity. This Anglo-Norman invasion came to fruition in 1171, when King Henry II of England (grandson of William the Conqueror) arrived and declared himself Lord of Ireland.

Calling oneself Lord of Ireland and being Lord of Ireland are two different things, though, and so a long struggle ensued between the Anglo-Normans and the native Irish. The Irish, by this time, had absorbed any Norse-Irish who had stayed after Clontarf. Within a generation, the Anglo-Normans could be called Hiberno-Normans (from *Hibernia*, the Roman name for Ireland). These Hiberno-Normans adopted much of Celtic culture and played a big role in Irish history – though that is far too much to go into here. For our purposes, we need only understand the next few hundred years of Irish history as a constant struggle between many domestic and foreign powers, with enmities, feuds, alliances, and all-out war continually forming and breaking down over time.

In these troubled years, the lords of Ireland needed help. They found that help on the islands and west coast of Scotland. The Hebrides, Orkney, and the hundreds of other islands had been bases of Viking activity since the 9th century and were still part of Norway until ceded to Scotland in 1266. To this day, Norse DNA is higher in this part of the world than anywhere else outside of Scandinavia and Iceland. In the 13th and 14th centuries, these people of western Scotland and the Isles still very much held on to this Norse Viking culture. In the Highlands of mainland Scotland, Viking culture combined with the indigenous culture of these proud, rugged descendants of Picts and Scots. So, it was to the men of these regions that the beleaguered Irish appealed.

Starting around 1250, Norse-Scot mercenaries began entering into the pay of Irish lords. These men were called *galloglaigh*, meaning "foreign warriors." In context, the "foreign" referred not so much to them being from Scotland or the Isles (for the Irish had many common ties with Scotland) but rather to their Norse heritage. By 1290, the term *galloglaigh* had morphed into *gallowglass*. These warriors would be known by that name – and dominate the battlefields of Ireland – for the next 300 years.

The Gallowglass were often mostly recruited from "loose men" such as "brigands, younger or bastard sons of noblemen, runaway servants ... kerns [soldiers] of broken lords, prizefighters, wild men ... renegades ... a ragtag pack of violent and desperate men."[46] However, there were many families of Gallowglass that found a home in Ireland. MacRorys, MacSweeneys, MacCabes, MacDonnells, and MacDowells were a few of the more conspicuous Scottish families that made their living on Irish war. The son of a Gallowglass was likely to become a Gallowglass, so wayward adventurers gave rise to family professions. Soon the name referred more to a type of warrior rather than an ethnicity, but still, the old Viking ethos found a roost in these later Scots-Irish warriors.

In Ireland, warfare was usually conducted with mounted nobles (knights, essentially) and lightly-armed, lightly-armored infantrymen (called kerns) levied from the land as needed. The Gallowglass added a third component to this arrangement. The Gallowglass were well-armed, fully-armored, heavy infantry. Like the Varangian Guard of Byzantium, they were both shock troops and the bodyguard for their lords. Like the Varangians, they fought with the long-hafted, single-bitted Dane axe. But where the Varangian was armored in shining scales or gleaming mail, the Gallowglass wore a heavy, calf-length, dull-colored iron riveted mail coat or a jacket of small iron plates sewn onto leather or cloth. They wore a mail coif, and either a bassinet-style helmet or full-faced "sugarloaf" helmets like Crusaders. They had swords, shields, spears and *seax* knives. The Gallowglass would keep this Dark Age appearance up to the beginning of the 17th century.

The Gallowglass were heavyweight fighters. At a time when the Irish peasants lived on grain products supplemented by dairy and a little inexpensive meat (potatoes had not yet been introduced from the New World), the diet of the Gallowglass was chiefly beef, pork, butter, milk, ale, and whiskey. As the soldiers of the Roman republic were paid in salt (hence our word "salary") and the Japanese samurai were paid in rice, the Gallowglass were paid in cattle. They would keep what they needed and trade the surplus for what they wanted, and in this time-honored model, every professional soldier was also a small businessman.

Gallowglass battles were furious, bloody, and brief. They fought in battalions numbering anywhere from 180 to 400, but of these numbers only one-third were Gallowglass. Each Gallowglass was accompanied by two attendants (some of whom may have been Gallowglass-in-training), and it was the job of these lightly-armed, unarmored warriors to harry the enemy with javelins, arrows, or stones in preparation for the fight. When it was gauged that the skirmishers had accomplished their goal, the Gallowglass themselves barreled into the fray, running shoulder to shoulder and smashing into the enemy with powerful sweeps of their big axes. Their body mass and weight of their armor increased the momentum of the attack, and their unyielding attitude meant that there was never any retreat. Eye-witness sources say, "*In every sharp and severe engagement, where they come to close fighting, they soon either kill or are killed,*" and, "*The greatest force of the battle consisteth in them, choosing to die rather than yield; so that when it cometh to hardy blows, they are quickly slain or win the field.*"[46]

The Gallowglass seemed to have no fear of death but unfortunately seemed to hold little respect for life either. They did not have the pretense of chivalry that the knight had, nor the ties to the local community of the Irish kern, so, in this might-makes-right age, the Gallowglass were often a law unto themselves. Their military discipline was severe – to disobey an order could result in hanging, and one account even tells of a Gallowglass being nailed to a post by his hand for a minor infraction. But this accountability did not carry over to their conduct outside of camp or off the battlefield. In terms of atrocities on campaign, they were perhaps no worse than the English or other freebooters in Ireland at the time, though they were no better. In between engagements, Gallowglass were guilty of a long list of crimes ranging from cattle-rustling to murder. One primary source remarks that the Gallowglass had an *"odium humanitas"* – a hatred of humanity – while historian Fergus Cannan (2010) describes them as "reveling in the chaos of war and repulsed by peace …a chimera of Scottish excessive violence and Irish anarchic nihilism."

The Gallowglass were an essential feature of an Ireland constantly at war. When Elizabeth I took the throne she was at first content to leave Ireland to its own devices, but quickly realized that she could neither afford the chaos in her own realm (as she saw it) nor the potential base for Catholic Spain and France to use against England. Elizabeth set in motion a long and brutal campaign in Ireland that ultimately culminated in the famous "Flight of the Earls," the exodus of many of the Irish and Hiberno-Norman nobles from the country. This, essentially, marked the end of the Gallowglass, too.

The "wild west" nature of Ireland was changing. Battlefields were changing, too, and a few decades later, the advent of the rifle would alter warfare forever. In the 1618 book, *The Glory of England*, Thomas Gainford stated, "*The name of Gallowglass is in a manner extinct.*" The last Gallowglass families remained in Ireland as minor landholders, but most of these were dispossessed and defeated by Cromwell's infamous 1649 invasion of Ireland. For many survivors, diaspora followed, and so many of these MacRorys, Sweeneys, MacCabes, and others can be met in America, Australia, Canada, and New Zealand today.

The sun set on the Viking Age in 1066, but the Viking spirit found many places where it was still needed throughout the Middle Ages and into the dawn of the modern age. Sometimes these manifestations were glorious victories or defeats. Sometimes these manifestations were only the wolf spirit of the Viking reveling in carnage. The Vikings were both noble and ignoble, as was their heritage through the rest of humankind's desperate story.

So, we have taken a look at how the Vikings changed with the times. In the next (and final) chapter we will see how the Vikings changed the times.

Chapter XXIII: How the Vikings Changed the World

The Vikings left their fingerprints all over the modern world. Everyday items, like snow skis, combs, and – of course – the boat keel were inventions they advanced and spread. They contributed words to our languages, place names in the lands we live, and personal names for our children. Four days of the week carry the memory of the Norse gods (Tuesday is Tyr's day, Wednesday is Odin's day, Thursday is Thor's day, and Friday belongs to Freya, Frey, Frigg or all three). Their myths, poetry, and sagas influenced literature ever since, and their symbols, patterns, and monuments contributed to the development of both fine and graphic art. The Vikings have not only affected the kinds of stories we tell but the way we tell them. When we use idioms like, "a little bird told me," when we decorate a Christmas tree, or when we count something by dozens, we are carrying on some of the cultural traits of our Viking ancestors. But there is much more to the Vikings' impacts than this random minutia of daily life.

The Vikings were innovative people who had a lot that their contemporaries did not, and – when the smoke settled – shaped the new places they lived into what they wanted them to be. They were also highly adaptable people who were formed in turn by these new environments. The Vikings in Ireland ended up very different from the Vikings in Russia, for example, because of this adaptability. It was this mutual exchange of ideas and this multifocal evolution that shaped the stories of changing peoples.

However, it is not only the things that these men and women made or did that impacted the world, but also what was made or done in response to them. First and foremost, the Vikings shaped the modern world by acting as catalysts to the larger, wealthier, older civilizations of Europe. In chemistry, a catalyst is something that makes change happen faster or makes change happen in a particular direction. In the 8th century, the various peoples of Europe were changing already and would have continued to evolve. Their civilizations probably would have eventually moved towards greater size, strength, and unity. But the outbreak of external oppositional activity in the Viking Age made these changes happen much faster, and in the specific direction that European history took. Once the Vikings were introduced into the equation, the kingdoms of Europe were forced to adapt or to fail.

Following are a few specific ways in which the Vikings shaped the world we live in.

Exploration

Human beings are explorers by nature and in the Stone Age spread all over the world without the benefit of technology or maps. Before the Viking Age was the Migration Era, where whole peoples picked up and walked into the unknown, looking to escape danger or find better ways to feed their families. Ships were continually crossing the Mediterranean, the Aegean, or the Irish Sea for centuries. But the invention of the keel and the other advances in ship design and the sailing prowess of the Vikings would exponentially change the boundaries of exploration. The Vikings did not just hop across the water to grab some loot, as others had before them. They sailed past the furthest edges of the world until they found a new one.

In the Viking Age, dragon ships could be found from the Euphrates River in Mesopotamia to the coasts of North America. As the Vikings assimilated, the technology of their ship craft and their broad-seeing outlook were spread to more and more peoples.

Over the centuries, ships would become larger and more sails would be added to carry bigger payloads of goods or soldiers. When the time was right, this expanded outlook and technology would be there to give birth to the Age of Discovery. For the explorers of the 15th -17th centuries, the world would simultaneously become much bigger and much smaller as ships circumnavigated the globe and reached every corner of the earth. This probably would not have happened had it not been for the groundwork laid by the Vikings.

Trade and Economics

The modern world enjoys the many fruits of globalization. On any given day a person living in the United States eats food from Mexico, wears clothes made cost-effectively in Indonesia, watches

Canadian television shows on a Japanese television, talks on a Chinese phone, and drives a car made in Korea using German engineering.

Life was much the same way in the Roman Empire, where a person might eat bread made from Egyptian grain with Tunisian olives and Spanish wine from Gallic glassware or British tin, wear cloth traded through Syria, and have jewelry made from Scandinavian amber set in African silver by Greek crafstmen. When the Roman Empire fell apart in the west, this trade sharply declined.

The Vikings did much to re-establish this trade. Indeed, some of the goods they traded were stolen (including stolen people), but much of their wares were exchanged legitimately. Caches of Arabic coins, along with clothes and other commodities have been found throughout Scandinavia, as have items from all over Europe. We have records of trade between Viking Ireland and Mauritania in West Africa, and evidence of trade between the Baltic and the Mediterranean.

When the Vikings went away, this trade did not. Wealth and expectations continued to grow steadily throughout the Middle Ages as new generations of merchants added onto the routes and networks the Vikings had built. These medieval merchants would form the basis for the reinvention of the middle class. There were again paths to advancement that did not require noble birth or large land holdings. Economists and historians agree that this exponential growth of international trade essentially created much of the world we know.

Law and Politics

As described in chapter two, the Norse were a people of laws. One feature of Norse law that is familiar to all of us is trial by jury. While juries were much larger and had different rules than they do now, the idea that a person should be tried by his peers instead of merely by the opinion, whim, or prejudice of a single judge is a gift to us from our Viking ancestors.

Modern democracies have a long history with many influences, but undeniably owe a great deal to ancient Germanic forms of government. Governing bodies like the *Thing*, the *Althing*, the *Witan,* and the *Folkmoot* would eventually give rise to parliaments and other features of rule by majority compromise rather than autocracy.

We do not want to overstate the Vikings' role in bringing these traditions to Europe. The Anglo-Saxons, Franks, and others had similar institutions at one time or another. It is also the doctrine of many political philosophers that human beings are wired for freedom and that democracy will eventually establish itself. Furthermore, some features of democracy were preserved from the Classical world and passed on through the Church, which itself exhibited these features in its own structure throughout the Middle Ages. But the Vikings did a lot to re-introduce and re-invigorate these ideas, applying their sense of good government, law, and individual rights in the places where they settled.

In fact, as autocracy extended in Scandinavia, the satellite Viking states like Iceland or the Norman baronies hardened their resolve to remain free, and later historians would remark of the enduing independent character of men from Yorkshire, Orkney, the Scottish Highlands, and other places where lots of Vikings settled.

Magna Carta

In the year 1215 – about 150 years after the close of the Viking Age – hundreds of barons and churchmen from all over England met on a broad meadow at Runnymede. They were there, along with their knights and their retainers, not in outright rebellion to the King of England, but to demand that he be brought to terms and to have limits set on his power and behavior. King John (of Robin Hood fame) was a deeply unpopular king, notorious for exploiting his people and for losing struggles abroad while picking fights at home. Yet, what these barons and bishops now demanded seemed anathema to the High Medieval mind. In feudalism, the serf served the lord, and the lord served the king. But for the men who risked their properties, families, and lives by standing up to the King at Runnymede, this was no longer acceptable. It was better to risk everything than to live in tyranny.

Instead of deposing this King and settling for whatever fortune would bring along next, the people of England wanted a way to ensure that their country was not at the mercy of despots or royal fools. They wanted to ensure the rule of law, the limitations of power, and the respect of individual freedoms.

That June day in 1215, King John had no choice but to respond to the peaceful but firm protest and he signed what would later be known as the *Magna Carta* (the Great Charter). It was only one stepping stone on the journey from absolutism to the democratic republics of the modern world, but it was a crucial one.

Unlike Jefferson's *Declaration of Independence* and other similar political milestones, the *Magna Carta* never launches into big statements about political philosophy or the rights of man. Instead, it was a practical list of checks and balances that would allow the King his necessary authority while curtailing abuse of that power. While it was fundamentally interested in protecting the baronial class, some of these protections trickled down to the common people and offered footholds for the improvements of later centuries. So, though the *Magna Carta* was never intended to be a rejection of Medieval Feudalism, indelibly imbued in its words is the idea that even the King is subject to the law. This simple idea continues to shape history.

King John signed the *Magna Carta* under duress, and he went on to try to overturn it and take revenge on the willful barons who acted against him. But the King died the following year. The *Magna Carta* survived the ascension of new kings and survived an official condemnation by the Pope. The 13th century was to become a time of parliamentary development and the people of England (and indeed, elsewhere) were moving slowly but inexorably towards liberty.

When the story of liberty is traced in history classes or discussions, the narrative usually begins with the ancient democracy of Athens and the Roman republic, then perhaps a nod to the Judeo-Christian ethic, and then straight on to the *Magna Carta* before accelerating into the Age of Enlightenment. It should not be overlooked, though, that the barons who brought the King to heel in 1215 did not come up with this idea out of thin air.

The English lords were the direct descendants of Normans, Anglo-Saxons, and Danes. Their anger at King John was in part related to his loss of Normandy to the French crown. This suggests that many of these barons still thought of themselves as Normans and were as full of the independent spirit the Normans demonstrated in Italy, Ireland, or the Crusader States. So, whether these English nobles were from Norman or older lines, many of their relatively-recent ancestors had carved out their families' wealth, prestige, and holdings as Vikings. Through their own family histories and legacies, they would have had some understanding of democratic principles and concepts of personal freedom. In fact, during this time the sagas of the Vikings were in circulation (and beginning to be set down in writing) and Iceland was still a commonwealth.

So, the barons who challenged King John were not struggling to achieve freedoms they did not know and only hoped they deserved, they were fighting to preserve rights that were an essential part of their deeply-ingrained cultural heritage. They did not need to look all the way back to Pericles of Athens, but instead to their great-great-grandfathers. Thus, the *Magna Carta* may not have been the sudden appearance of a beacon of freedom in a repressive age, but rather a reassertion of liberty by older political ideals over the heavy hand of feudalism.

So, it may be that even though the Vikings indirectly strengthened the centralization of authority and growth of the Medieval European powers, their values and traditions helped re-establish some of the more democratic directions in those powers, too.

The Growth of Nations

The Middle Ages began with a Europe cut into many small kingdoms but ended with many of the nations that we know today. The causes of this are varied and complex, but the Vikings provided external pressures as well as some of the military power required to speed these changes. We have focused on this topic throughout this book but will now recap ways the Vikings helped form some of Europe's most successful nations.

England, Scotland, Wales, and Ireland

In 865, the Great Heathen Army led by the sons of Ragnar invaded a Britain that was divided into numerous tribal kingdoms. The Vikings quickly submitted Northumbria, Bernicia, East Anglia, Kent, and Mercia, leaving Wessex as the only remaining Saxon kingdom. Simultaneously (more or less), Vikings destroyed Dal Riata and Strathclyde, driving the peoples of the north together into the multi-tribal political union that is now Scotland.

The political situation in Britain was then greatly simplified, and through the rest of the Viking Age, these territories would further coalesce into just three nations – England, Scotland, and Wales. The Vikings and their descendants in the Danish territories of Britain were not mere antagonists or subjects to be conquered but were active participants in the many events that forged these former competitors into new peoples with distinct national identities. England, Scotland, Wales, and Ireland, in turn, would sometimes be unified into the United Kingdom and would go on to exert tremendous influence on world history and the development of our age.

France

From the last days of Charlemagne, Viking raiders began exposing the weaknesses and limitations of his empire. While the Holy Roman Empire would learn from these mistakes and soon become impervious to meaningful Viking incursions, the kingdoms in what is now France would struggle greatly from ever-increasing raids and wildly-growing *danegelds*. The Frankish kings would learn to use the Vikings, though, and would put men like Rollo, Siegfried, and others to work against rebellious Bretons and Burgundians. Viking manpower was not only used to consolidate the various peoples into what would become France, it was used to protect the coasts from other Vikings. Meanwhile, measures against the Vikings, like mounted heavy cavalry and better fortifications would lead to the proliferation of knights and castles the Middle Ages are known for. These military advances combined with Viking daring and shipbuilding would find full expression with the Normans, and would also help protect France from Islamic invasion from Spain and the Mediterranean.

Italy and the Mediterranean

Norman knights – removed from their Viking ancestors by only a few generations – freed Italy from Byzantine control and protected it from Islamic expansion from the Fatimid Caliphate. Normans then created one of the most prosperous kingdoms of the age – Sicily. Meanwhile, Varangians from Sweden, Rus, and all over the Viking world would protect and preserve Byzantium for hundreds of years.

Norway, Sweden, Denmark, and Iceland

It is safe to say that the consolidation of various Norse principalities into the nations of Scandinavia happened in large part because of the Viking activities of the peoples of those nations. Vikings brought back wealth, well-honed military skills, more manpower, and new ideas every time they returned from their raiding and trading. Norse kings like Harald Fairhair, Olaf Trygvassen, Magnus the Good, and Cnut the Great were inspired by political powers like the Holy Roman Empire and the Church, and they had the money and warriors to try to make something like that at home. Today, Norway, Sweden, and Denmark are prosperous nations that repeatedly score among the highest in standards of living and other indicators of optimization.

Russia, Ukraine, and Belarus

Vikings brought the Slavic, Finnic, and Baltic natives of Eastern Europe together as the Kievan Rus. The Rus (often reinforced by more Vikings from Scandinavia) pushed further and further south until they came into contact (and vigorous exchange) with the Byzantines. They also took over the empire of the Khazars. The blending of these many diverse cultures, the vast spread of territory under their command, the extensive development of trade routes throughout the center of the known world, and the military strength to control it led to the eventual formation of several strong, enduring nations of Europe and a world superpower.

Conclusion

The Vikings came out of nowhere and took history by storm. For 273 years they were an X-factor that few could predict or control. They dominated Europe and defined an age. Much of what they did was destructive but overall their influence was positive – so much so that it would be hard to imagine the world without it.

The image of Viking warriors and their ships is indelibly branded into the popular imagination. Inacurate as some notions about these men and women might be, the idea of someone who is fearless, full of action, and beholden only to their own rules is what the Vikings truly were and what gives this sense of awe that stands the test of time. This is the reason that their name is taken for sports teams, for military mascots, or even for space exploration vehicles. Though the Vikings were hard people living in a cruel age, there is much that is noble about them and much that we ourselves could emulate. Their ethos, daring, and complete faith in themselves is as pertinent now as it ever was. The unflinching way in which they faced the dangers, adversity, and uncertainties of life, reveling in joys and shrugging off sorrows, is a model for anyone. Perhaps that is why the Vikings still inspire, long after they themselves have found their fate.

Bibliography and Citations

Norse Primary Sources

1. Saxo Grammaticus. *The Danish History, Book Nine. Circa 12th Century.* Retrieved January 4, 2018, from http://www.gutenberg.org/files/1150/1150-h/1150-h.htm

2. *The Saga of Ragnar Lodbrok and His Sons (Ragnar Saga Lodbrok).* Waggoner, B. (translator). Troth. 2009

3. *The Lay of Harold (Hranfnsmol).* Hornklofi, T. (translator). Sacred Texts. https://www.sacred-texts.com/neu/onp/onp11.htm

4. *Saga Heidrecks Konungs Ins Vitra (The Saga of King Heidrek the Wise).* Tolkien, C. (translator). Thomas Nelson Ltd. London, 1960. Available http://vsnrweb-publications.org.uk/The%20Saga%20Of%20King%20Heidrek%20The%20Wise.pdf

5. *The Prose Edda of Snorri Sturlson.* Brodeur, A. G. (translator). Retrieved from http://www.redicecreations.com/files/The-Prose-Edda.pdf. Published 1916, Accessed November 3, 2017.

6. *Voluspo* from *The Poetic Edda.* Bellows, H.A. (translator). Retrieved from http://www.sacred-texts.com/neu/poe/poe03.htm. Published 1936. Accessed November 3, 2017.

7. *Vafthruthnisimol* from *The Poetic Edda.* Bellows, H. A. (translator). Retrieved from http://www.sacred-

texts.com/neu/poe/poe05.htm. Published 1936. Accessed November 3, 2017

8. *Grœnlendinga Saga - The Saga of the Greenlanders.* Accessed August 16, 2018, https://notendur.hi.is/haukurth/utgafa/greenlanders.html

9. *The Saga of Erik the Red.* Sephton, J. (translator). 1880. Accessed August 16, 2018. http://sagadb.org/eiriks_saga_rauda.en

10. *The Settlement of Iceland: Ari Frodi (Landnámabók).* Ellwood, T. (translator). Kendall. 1898. Accessed December 23, 2017. https://ia801406.us.archive.org/29/items/booksettlementi00ellwg oog/booksettlementi00ellwgoog.pdf

11. *The Heimskringla of Snorri Sturluson (Haralds saga ins hárfagra).* Finley, A. & Faulkes, A. (translators). Viking Society for Northern Research. London. 2011. Accessed December 23, 2017. http://vsnrweb-publications.org.uk/Heimskringla%20I.pdf

12. *The Book of the Icelanders (ÍSLENDINGABÓK).* Finley, A. & Faulkes, A. (translators). Viking Society for Northern Research. London, 2006. Accessed December 23, 2017. http://www.vsnrweb-publications.org.uk/Text%20Series/IslKr.pdf

13. *'Brennu-Njáls Saga': The Story of Burnt Njal.* Translated by DeSant, G. W. (1861). http://sagadb.org/brennu-njals_saga.en

14. *Havamal.* https://www.pitt.edu/~dash/havamal.html#runes

15. *Volsunga Saga (the Saga of the Volsungs)*. Crawford, J. (translator). Hackett Classics. 2017.

16. *The Poetic Edda*. Crawford, J. (translator). Hackett Classics. 2015.

17. *Egil's Saga (Egils saga Skallagimssonar)*. Scudder, B. (translator). In *The Sagas of the Icelanders* (editor, Thorson, O. & Scudder, B.) Penguin Books, New York, 2001.

18. *The Saga of Hrafnkel Frey's Godi*. Gunnel, T. (translator). In *The Sagas of the Icelanders* (editor, Thorson, O. & Scudder, B.) Penguin Books, New York, 2001.

19. *Gisli Sursson's Saga*. Regal, M. (translator). In *The Sagas of the Icelanders* (editor, Thorson, O. & Scudder, B.) Penguin Books, New York, 2001.

20. *The Saga of Gunnlaug Serpent-tongue*. Attwood, K. (translator). In *The Sagas of the Icelanders* (editor, Thorson, O. & Scudder, B.) Penguin Books, New York, 2001.

21. *The Saga of Ref the Sly*. Clark, G. (translator). In *The Sagas of the Icelanders* (editor, Thorson, O. & Scudder, B.) Penguin Books, New York, 2001.

22. *The Tale of Sarcastic Halli*. Clark, G. (translator). In *the Sagas of the Icelanders* (editor, Thorson, O. & Scudder, B.) Penguin Books, New York, 2001.

23. *Krákumál*. Percy, T. (translator). Retrieved from https://www.rc.umd.edu/editions/norse/HTML/Percy.html translated 1763.

24. *The Galdrabok: An Icelandic Grimoire*. Flowers, S. (translator) Baker Johnson, Inc. Ann Arbor, MI. 1989

25. *The Saga of Grettir the Strong.* Scudder, B. (translator). Penguin. London. 2005.

Non-Norse Primary Sources

26. Tacitus. *Annals, Book XIV*. Retrieved from http://penelope.uchicago.edu/Thayer/e/roman/texts/tacitus/annals/14b*.htmlPublished 1937. Accessed November 10, 2017

27. Conollen, O. (OCleary, M. editor). *Annals of Ireland by the Four Masters as translated into English*. Irish Roots Café Press. Ireland. 2003

28. *Cogadh Gaedhel re Gallaibh = The war of the Gaedhil with the Gaill, or, The invasions of Ireland by the Danes and other Norsemen* : the original Irish text, edited, with translation and introduction by Todd, James Henthorn, 1805-1869 https://archive.org/details/cogadhgaedhelreg00todd/page/44

29. *The Annals of Ulster.* Corpus of Electronic Texts. https://celt.ucc.ie/publishd.html

30. *The Annals of Tigernach.* Corpus of Electronic Texts. https://celt.ucc.ie/publishd.html

31. *The Annals of Inisfallen.* Corpus of Electronic Texts. https://celt.ucc.ie/publishd.html

32. *The Annals of Loch Ce.* Corpus of Electronic Texts. https://celt.ucc.ie/publishd.html

33. *Annals of Conacht.* Corpus of Electonic Texts. https://celt.ucc.ie/publishd.html

34. *Chronicon Scotorum.* Corpus of Electronic Texts. https://celt.ucc.ie/publishd.html

35. *Fragmentary Annals of Ireland.* Corpus of Electronic Texts. https://celt.ucc.ie/publishd.html

36. *The Anglo-Saxon Chronicle.* The Internet Archive. https://archive.org/stream/anglosaxonchroni00gile/anglosaxonchroni00gile_djvu.txt

37. *Asser's The Life of King Alfred.* The Internet Archive. https://archive.org/stream/asserslifeofking00asseiala/asserslifeofking00asseiala_djvu.txt

38. *The Russian Primary Chronicle by Nestor the Chronicler (1113).* The Internet Archive. https://archive.org/details/TheRussianPrimaryChronicle

39. *Ibn Fadlan and the Land of Darkness: Arab Travelers in the Far North.* (Translated by Lunde, P. & Stone, C.). Penguin. London. 2012.

Classic Secondary Sources

40. Churchill, W. S. *The History of the English Speaking Peoples: Volume 1, the Birth of Britain.* Barnes and Noble Books. 1956

41. Gregory, I. A., Yeats, W. B., and Boss, C., *A Treasury of Irish Myth, Legend & Folklore (Fairy and Folk Tales of the Irish Peasantry / Cuchulain of Muirthemne).* New York, Avenel Books. Published 1986. Originally published 1888.

42. Keating, G. *The History of Ireland, Books I & II.* https://celt.ucc.ie//published/T100054/index.html. Originally published 1634.

43. Gibbon, E. *The Decline and Fall of the Roman Empire.* https://www.gutenberg.org/files/25717/25717-h/25717-h.htm Originally published 1782.

Secondary Sources: Books

44. Norwich, J. J. Byzantium: The Apogee. Knopf. New York. 1992

45. Norwich, J. J. Byzantium: The Early Centuries. Knopf. New York. 1989.

46. D'Amato, R. *The Varangian Guard, 988-1453.* Men-at-Arms. Osprey, Long Island. 2010.

47. Gaiman, N. *Norse Mythology.* Norton. 2017.

48. Brownworth, L. *The Sea Wolves: A History of the Vikings.* Crux Publishing, Ltd. United Kingdom. 2014.

49. Brownworth, L. *The Normans: From Raiders to Kings.* Crux Publishing, Ltd. United Kingdom. 2014.

50. Brownworth, L. *In Distant Lands: A Short History of the Crusades.* Crux Publishing, Ltd. United Kingdom. 2017.

51. Brown, P. *Through the Eye of the Needle: Wealth, the Fall of Rome and the Making of Christianity in the West, 350-550 AD.* Princeton University Press, Princeton. 2012.

52. McCoy, D. *The Viking Spirit: An Introduction to Norse Mythology and Religion.* Columbia. 2016

53. Brown, N.M. *Songs of the Vikings: Snorri and the Making of the Norse Myths.* Palgrave MacMillan, New York. 2012

54. Brown, N. M. *Ivory Vikings: The Mystery of the Most Famous Chessmen in the World and the Woman Who Made Them.* St Martin's Press. New York, NY. 2015.

55. Dougherty, Martin J., *A Dark History: Vikings.* Metro Books, New York. 2013.

56. Cannan, F. *Galloglass 1250-1600, Gaelic Mercenary Warrior.* Warrior, 143. Osprey Books. 2010.

57. Howarth, D. *1066: The Year of the Conquest.* Penguin. 1978.

58. Kane, Njord. "Norse Armor and Weaponry." *The Vikings: The Story of a People.* 2nd ed. Yukon: Spangenhelm, 2015.

59. Frankopan, P. *The Silk Roads: A New History of the World.* Vintage Books, New York, 2015.

Secondary Sources: Lectures, Articles and Papers

60. Kane, N. Bjorn Ironside Ragnarson. *Spangenhelm: An Adventure in History*. November 22, 2016. Retrieved January 4, 2018, from http://spangenhelm.com/bjorn-ironside-ragnarsson/

61. Price, N., Hedenstierna-Jonson, C., Zachrisson, T., Kjellström, A., Storå, J., Krzewińska, M., . . . Götherström, A. (2019). *Viking warrior women? Reassessing Birka chamber grave* Bj.581. *Antiquity, 93*(367), 181-198. doi:10.15184/aqy.2018.258

62. Bjorn Ironside, Ragnar Lothbrok's Son. *Mythologian.* 2012. Retrieved January 4, 2018, from http://mythologian.net/bjorn-ironside-ragnar-lothbroks-son/

63. Bjorn Ironside: Famous Viking Who Captured Luna By Mistake Instead of Ancient Rome As Planned. *Ancient Pages*. June 2016. Retrieved January 4, 2018, from http://www.ancientpages.com/2016/06/11/bjorn-ironside-famous-viking-who-captured-luna-by-mistake-instead-of-ancient-rome-as-planned/

64. Greek Fire. *Encyclopedia Britannica*. Retrieved January 4, 2018, from https://www.britannica.com/technology/Greek-fire

65. Godson, E.F. Hastein Halfdan Ragnarsson, Jarl of Hastings - is this Hastein this Hastein? *Geni*. June 16, 2012. Retrieved January 4, 2018, from https://www.geni.com/discussions/110099?by_or_about=600000 0013308770957

66. Greshko, M. Famous Viking Warrior Was a Woman, DNA Reveals. *National Geographic.* Retrieved from https://news.nationalgeographic.com/2017/09/viking-warrior-woman-archaeology-spd/ Published September 12, 2017. Accessed November 10, 2017

67. Viking Dig Reports., *BBC History.* Retrieved from http://www.bbc.co.uk/history/ancient/vikings/dig_reports_0 1.shtmlPublished 2014. Accessed November 10, 2017

68. Trowbridge, B., Meeting Grace O'Malley, Ireland's Pirate Queen. *The National Archives.* Retrieved from http://blog.nationalarchives.gov.uk/blog/meeting-grace-omalley-irelands-pirate-queen/. Published June 16, 2016. Accessed November 10, 2017.

69. McCoy, D. Ragnarok. *Norse Mythology for Smart People.* Retrieved from https://norse-mythology.org/tales/ragnarok/. Published 2017. Accessed November 3, 2017.

70. Mandia, S. *Vikings During the Medieval Warm Period.* Accessed August 16, 2018, http://www2.sunysuffolk.edu/mandias/lia/vikings_during_mwp.h tml

71. Mandia, S. *The End of the Vikings in Greenland.* Accessed August 16, 2018, http://www2.sunysuffolk.edu/mandias/lia/end_of_vikings_greenl and.html

72. Mandia, S. *The Little Ice Age in Europe*. Accessed August 16, 2018,

http://www2.sunysuffolk.edu/mandias/lia/little_ice_age.html

73. Shoalts, A. Reverse Colonialism: How the Inuit Conquered the Vikings. *Canadian Geographic*. March 2011. Accessed August 16, 2018. https://www.canadiangeographic.ca/article/reverse-colonialism-how-inuit-conquered-vikings

74. Poppick, L. Forget GPS: Medieval Compass Guided Vikings After Sunset. *Live Science*, March 25, 2014. Accessed December 23, 2017. https://www.livescience.com/44366-vikings-sun-compass-after-sunset.html

75. McCoy, D. Odin. *Norse Mythology for Smart People*. Accessed December 23, 2017. https://norse-mythology.org/gods-and-creatures/the-aesir-gods-and-goddesses/odin/

76. Short, W. The Settlement of Iceland in the Viking Age. *Hurstwic*. Published 2014. Accessed December 23, 2017. http://www.hurstwic.org/history/articles/society/text/settlement_of_iceland.htm

77. Johnston, W. *Travel Through the Ireland Story: The Vikings*. N.D. Accessed December 23, 2017. http://www.wesleyjohnston.com/users/ireland/past/pre_norman_history/vikings.html

78. Fountain, H. Vikings Razed the Forests; Can Iceland Regrow Them? *The New York Times*. Published October 20, 2017.

Accessed December 23, 2017.
https://www.nytimes.com/interactive/2017/10/20/climate/iceland-trees-reforestation.html

79. Althing: Icelandic Government. *Encyclopedia Britannica.* Accessed December 23, 2017. https://www.britannica.com/topic/Althing

80. The Irish DNA Atlas: Revealing Fine-Scale Population Structure and History within Ireland Edmund Gilbert, Seamus O'Reilly, Michael Merrigan, Darren McGettigan, Anne M. Molloy, Lawrence C. Brody, Walter Bodmer, Katarzyna Hutnik, Sean Ennis, Daniel J. Lawson, James F. Wilson & Gianpiero L. Cavalleri, *Scientific Reports* **7**, Article number: 17199 (2017). Published December 8, 2017. Accessed December 20, 2017. https://www.nature.com/articles/s41598-017-17124-4

81. Mulligan, M. The Viking in the Room. *Ancestry DNA*. Published June 23, 2015. Accessed December 23, 2017. https://blogs.ancestry.com/ancestry/2015/06/23/ancestrydna-the-viking-in-the-room/

82. Why People in Iceland Look Just Like Us. *The Irish Times.* October 2, 2000. Accessed December 23, 2017. https://www.irishtimes.com/news/why-people-in-iceland-look-just-like-us-1.1104676

83. Public Library of Science. "Largest-to-date Genetic Snapshot of Iceland 1,000 Years Ago Completed." *ScienceDaily.*

ScienceDaily, 18 January 2009. Accessed December 20, 2017. www.sciencedaily.com/releases/2009/01/090116073205.htm

84. Johnston, W. *Travel Through the Ireland Story: The Vikings.* N.D. Accessed December 23, 2017. http://www.wesleyjohnston.com/users/ireland/past/pre_norman_h istory/vikings.html

85. Olaf Curan. *Library Ireland.* 2017. Accessed December 23, 2017. http://www.libraryireland.com/biography/OlafCuaran.php

86. Young, G. & Young-Tamel, J.W. *The Isle of Mann Under the Norse.* 2013. Accessed December 23, 2017. http://www.academia.edu/4386441/Isle_of_Man_under_the_Nors e

87. Prelude to the Battle of Clontarf, 1014. *Battle of Clontarf.* N.D. Accessed December 23, 2017. http://www.battleofclontarf.net/the-battle-of-clontarf-23rd-april-1014/prelude-to-the-battle-of-clontarf-1014/3435

88. The Battle of Clontarf, 23 April, 1014. *The Battle of Clontarf.* N.D. Accessed December 23, 2017. http://www.battleofclontarf.net/vacations-ireland/the-battle-of-clontarf-23rd-april-1014/3433

89. Hope, J. Life of the Week: Romulus Augustus. *History Extra.* Published September 2015. Accessed January 21, 2018. http://www.historyextra.com/article/international-history/life-profile-romulus-augustus

90. Mark, J., Odoacer. *Ancient History Encyclopedia.* Published September 20, 2014. Accessed January 21, 2018. https://www.ancient.eu/Odoacer/

91. Abernathy, S. (2015). The Siege of Paris 885-886. *The Freelance History Writer.* Retrieved from https://thefreelancehistorywriter.com/2015/04/17/the-siege-of-paris-of-885-886/

92. Atkins, X. (2015). The Viking Siege of Paris. *The Manchester Historian.* Retrieved from http://manchesterhistorian.com/2015/the-viking-siege-of-paris/

93. Dzahk, Y. (2016). The Viking Siege of Paris. *War History Online.* Retrieved from https://www.warhistoryonline.com/medieval/vikings-sieges-paris.html

94. Zolfagharifard, E. Hammer of Thor' unearthed: Runes on 1,000-year-old amulet solve mystery of why Viking charms were worn for protection. *Daily Mail.* Published July 1, 2014. Accessed January 9, 2018 http://www.dailymail.co.uk/sciencetech/article-2676386/Hammer-Thor-unearthed-Runes-1-000-year-old-amulet-solve-mystery-Viking-charms-worn-protection.html

95. Gunn, R. (2003). Scottish Origins to William Wallace, Chapter 3 – *The Viking Invasions and Scottish Nationality.* http://www.scottish-history.com/origins3.shtml

96. Kelly, J. (2011). How Scandinavian is Scotland? BBC News Magazine. December 8, 2011. http://www.bbc.com/news/magazine-16050269

97. Mitchell, N. (2011). The Vikings and Scotland, 10 Lesser-Known Facts. The Scotsman. October 20, 2011. https://www.scotsman.com/lifestyle/vikings-and-scotland-10-lesser-known-facts-1-1919750

98. Goodacre, S., Helgason, A., Nicholson, J., Southam, Fergusson, L., Hickey, L., Vega, E., Steffanson, K., Ward, R., & Syches, B. (2005) *Genetic evidence for a family-based Scandinavian settlement of Shetland and Orkney during the Viking periods.* Heredity 95 (129-135). https://www.nature.com/articles/6800661

99. Constantine II King of Alba. Scotland's History. BBC. 2014 http://www.bbc.co.uk/scotland/history/articles/constantine_ii/

100.   Ó CORRÁIN, D. (1998). The Vikings in Scotland and Ireland in the Ninth Century. Chronicon, UCC. https://www.ucc.ie/research/chronicon/ocor2fra.htm

101.   Kenneth MacAlpin (Cináed mac Ailpín) *Scotland's History.* BBC. 2014. http://www.bbc.co.uk/scotland/history/articles/kenneth_macalpin/

102.   Krzewińska, Maja et al. "Mitochondrial DNA Variation in the Viking Age Population of Norway." *Philosophical*

Transactions of the Royal Society B: Biological Sciences 370.1660 (2015): 20130384. PMC. Web. 10 Aug. 2018. https://www.ncbi.nlm.nih.gov/pmc/articles/PMC4275891/

103.   Redon, A. *Female Warriors of the Viking Age: Fact or Fiction?* University of Iceland School of Humaniteis: Archeology. 2017.

104.   Research: Vikings Did Not Hide Behind Shield Walls. *Thor News*. August 30, 2017. Retrieved from https://thornews.com/2017/08/30/research-vikings-did-not-hide-behind-shield-walls/

105.   Georgas, G. (2014). The Use of the Sword Behind the Shield Wall and Phalanx. Retrieved from http://hroarr.com/article/the-use-of-sword-behind-the-shield-wall-and-phalanx/

106.   Viking Age Arms and Armor: Viking Shields. *Hurstwic*. Retrieved from http://www.hurstwic.org/history/articles/manufacturing/text/viking_shields.htm

107.   Jakobson, H. Old Arabic Texts Describe Dirty Vikings. *Science Nordic*. July 17, 2013. http://sciencenordic.com/old-arabic-texts-describe-dirty-vikings

108.   Harl, K. *Vikings: The Great Courses*. The Teaching Company, Chantilly, VA. 2005

Visit SonsofVikings.com for the best in Viking information, updates, and merchandise.